Comparing Postcolonial Diasporas

Comparing Postcolonial Diasporas

Edited by

Michelle Keown, David Murphy
and
James Procter

First published 2009 by
PALGRAVE MACMILLAN

Palgrave Macmillan in the UK is an imprint of Macmillan Publishers Limited,
registered in England, company number 785998, of Houndmills, Basingstoke,
Hampshire RG21 6XS.

Palgrave Macmillan in the US is a division of St Martin's Press LLC,
175 Fifth Avenue, New York, NY 10010.

Palgrave Macmillan is the global academic imprint of the above companies
and has companies and representatives throughout the world.

Palgrave® and Macmillan® are registered trademarks in the United States,
the United Kingdom, Europe and other countries.

ISBN-13: 978-0-230-54708-7   hardback
ISBN-10: 0-230-54708-7   hardback

This book is printed on paper suitable for recycling and made from fully
managed and sustained forest sources. Logging, pulping and manufacturing
processes are expected to conform to the environmental regulations of the
country of origin.

A catalogue record for this book is available from the British Library.

Library of Congress Cataloging-in-Publication Data

Comparing postcolonial diasporas / edited by Michelle Keown, David
   Murphy, and James Procter.
      p. cm.
   Includes index.
   ISBN 978-0-230-54708-7
   1. Emigration and immigration. 2. Intercultural communication. 3.
   Transnationalism. 4. Group identity. 5. Postcolonialism. I.
   Keown, Michelle, 1972– II. Murphy, David, 1971– III. Procter,
   James.
   JV6035.C57 2009
   304.8—dc22   2008037611

10 9 8 7 6 5 4 3 2 1
18 17 16 15 14 13 12 11 10 09

Printed and bound in Great Britain by
CPI Antony Rowe, Chippenham and Eastbourne

This book is dedicated to the memory of
Vanessa Knights (1969–2007)

Contents

Plates and Figures

Tables

Acknowledgements

The origins of this volume lie in a symposium held at the University of Stirling in September 2004. The symposium was part of a two-year project, entitled 'Europe and Diaspora', which was generously funded by the Faculty of Arts Research Development Fund in Stirling. Since 2004, the project has spun off in various directions and two of the editors have moved on to new posts at other universities. However, we are delighted that most of the scholars who spoke at the original symposium have agreed to contribute to this book, supplemented by a number of newly commissioned pieces; we would like to extend a warm tribute to our contributors, whose innovative and scholarly work made it such a pleasure to prepare this volume. We also acknowledge the support of our friends and colleagues in Edinburgh, Stirling, Newcastle and elsewhere; we are also very grateful to Steven Hall, Paula Kennedy and Christabel Scaife at Palgrave Macmillan for their help in bringing this volume through to completion.

However, there is one person in particular to whom we would like to express our respect and gratitude: Vanessa Knights, who sadly passed away in 2007. Vanessa was a distinguished young Hispanic studies scholar from the University of Newcastle, who spoke at the original symposium in 2004 and provided one of the sample chapters on 'Puerto Rican boleros in New York and Nuyorican Poetry', which we submitted to Palgrave Macmillan along with our book proposal. Thus, it is fair to say that without her contribution, this book may never have been commissioned. In respect and admiration, we dedicate this volume to Vanessa.

Notes on Contributors

Elleke Boehmer is the Professor of World Literature in English at the University of Oxford. She is best known for her research on international writing and postcolonial theory and is the author of the world best-seller *Colonial and Postcolonial Literature: Migrant Metaphors* (1995, 2005); the monographs *Empire, the National and the Postcolonial, 1890–1920* (2002); *Stories of Women* (2005); and of the acclaimed edition of Robert Baden-Powell's *Scouting for Boys* (2004). Her study of Nelson Mandela appeared in 2008 – concurrently with the novella *Nile Baby* – to coincide with his 90th birthday in July. She has published three other novels and many short stories.

Celia Britton is Professor of French and Francophone Studies at University College London. She has published widely on French Caribbean literature and thought, in particular on Edouard Glissant. Her most recent books are *Edouard Glissant and Postcolonial Theory: Strategies of Language and Resistance* (University Press of Virginia, 1999); *Race and the Unconscious: Freudianism in French Caribbean Thought* (Legenda, 2002); and *The Sense of Community in French Caribbean Fiction* (Liverpool University Press, 2008).

Elizabeth Ezra is Professor in French at the University of Stirling. She is the author of *The Colonial Unconscious: Race and Culture in Interwar France* (Cornell, 2000); *Georges Méliès: The Birth of the Auteur* (Manchester University Press, 2000); and *Jean-Pierre Jeunet* (Illinois, 2008). She is the editor of *European Cinema* (Oxford University Press, 2004); co-editor (with Terry Rowden) of *Transnational Cinema: The Film Reader* (Routledge, 2006); and (with Sue Harris) of *France in Focus: Film and National Identity* (Berg, 2000).

Frances Gouda is Professor of History and Gender Studies in the Political Science Department of the University of Amsterdam. She is the author of *Poverty and Political Culture: the Rhetoric of Social Welfare in the Netherlands and France, 1815–1853* (1994); *Dutch Culture Overseas: Colonial Practice in the Netherlands Indies, 1900–1942* (1995; reissued in 2008 by Equinox Publishers in Jakarta, Indonesia); and *American Visions of the Netherlands East Indies/Indonesia: US Foreign Policy and Indonesian Nationalism, 1920–1949* (2002). She edited (with Julia Clancy-Smith)

Domesticating the Empire: Race, Gender and Family Life in French and Dutch Colonialism (1998). In recent years she has published articles on constructions of femininity and masculinity in colonial cultures as well as on the role of social science in European constructions of gender and racial differences in the Dutch East Indies from a comparative perspective.

Michelle Keown is Lecturer in English Literature at the University of Edinburgh. She has published widely on Maori, Pacific and Aotearoa/ New Zealand writing and is the author of *Postcolonial Pacific Writing: Representing the Body* (Routledge, 2005) and *Pacific Islands Writing: The Postcolonial Literatures of Aotearoa/New Zealand and Oceania* (Oxford University Press, 2007). She has edited (with Stuart Murray) a special issue of the *Journal of New Zealand Literature* (21, 2003) focusing on the diasporic connections between New Zealand and the UK. At present she is writing a book on the literatures of British settler diasporas in Australia, New Zealand and Canada.

John McLeod is Reader in Postcolonial and Diaspora Literatures at the School of English, University of Leeds, UK. He is the author of *Beginning Postcolonialism* (Manchester University Press, 2000); *Postcolonial London: Rewriting the Metropolis* (2004); and *J. G. Farrell* (Northcote House, 2007). He has edited *The Routledge Companion to Postcolonial Studies* (Routledge, 2007) and is the co-editor of *The Revision of Englishness* (Manchester University Press, 2004). He has published over twenty essays on postcolonial, Caribbean and black British literatures in a number of books and journals, including *The Journal of Commonwealth Literature*, *Wasafiri*, *Moving Worlds*, *Interventions*, *Critical Survey* and *Kunapipi*.

David Murphy is Professor of French at the University of Stirling. He has published widely on African literature and cinema, as well as on the relationship between Francophone studies and postcolonial theory. He is the author of *Sembene: Imagining Alternatives in Film and Fiction* (James Currey, 2000), and is co-author (with Patrick Williams) of *Postcolonial African Cinema: Ten Directors* (Manchester University Press, 2007). He is also co-editor of three volumes of essays: (with Aedín Ní Loingsigh) *Thresholds of Otherness* (Grant & Cutler, 2002); (with Charles Forsdick) *Francophone Postcolonial Studies: A Critical Introduction* (Arnold, 2003); and (also with Charles Forsdick) *Postcolonial Thought in the Francophone World* (Liverpool University Press, 2009).

Mohit Prasad teaches Pacific Literature, Diaspora and Postcolonial Studies at the University of the South Pacific (USP) in Fiji. He is Director of the Pacific Writing Forum and Divisional Head of Literature.

Among his publications are three volumes of poetry: *Eyes of the Mask* (1998), *Eating Mangoes* (2000) and *Kissing Rain* (2006). His latest collection, entitled *Jahajin's Songs*, was due to be published in late 2008. His research interests lie in postcolonial and diasporic studies, with a particular emphasis on popular culture.

James Procter is Reader in Modern English and Postcolonial Literature at Newcastle University. He is the editor of *Writing Black Britain 1948–1998: An Interdisciplinary Anthology* (Manchester University Press, 2000) as well as the author of *Dwelling Places: Postwar Black British Writing* (Manchester University Press, 2003) and *Stuart Hall* (Routledge, 2004). His most recent work has been on the 'Postcolonial Everyday' (see *New Formations*, 58) and 'Reading after empire'. He is currently Principal Investigator on a large AHRC-funded project (2007–10) examining the relationship between readers, location and diasporic literature: http://www.devolvingdiasporas.com/.

Siobhán Shilton is a lecturer in French Studies at the University of Bristol. She has written articles on travel, exile, colonialism and postcolonialism in Francophone literature and the visual arts; she is also co-author (with Charles Forsdick and Feroza Basu) of *New Approaches to Twentieth-Century Travel Literature in French: History, Genre, Theory* (Peter Lang, 2006). She is currently working on an AHRC-funded book project entitled 'Diasporic Encounters: Journeys between France and the Maghreb in Contemporary Art'.

Patria Román-Velázquez is a lecturer in the Sociology Department at City University, London. She is the author of *The Making of Latin London: Salsa Music, Place and Identity* (Ashgate, 1999) and of numerous journal articles. Her main research interests include theories of place and identity. She continues to do research on Latin Americans in London. She is also an Associate Fellow at the Institute for the Study of the Americas, University of London.

Terry Rowden teaches in the Department of English at The College of Staten Island/CUNY. He is the co-editor (with Elizabeth Ezra) of *Transnational Cinema: The Film Reader* (Routledge, 2006) and is the author of *Dancing in the Dark: African American Music and the Cultures of Blindness* (forthcoming from the University of Michigan Press).

Patrick Williams is Professor of Literary and Cultural Studies at Nottingham Trent University, where he teaches courses on postcolonial theory and culture, diaspora, and race and nation in twentieth-century

Britain. His publications include *Colonial Discourse and Post-Colonial Theory* (Columbia University Press, 1993); (with Peter Childs) *Introduction to Post-Colonial Theory* (Longman/Pearson, 1996); *Ngugi wa Thiong'o* (Manchester University Press, 1999); *Edward Said* (Sage, 2000); (with David Murphy) *Postcolonial African Cinema* (Manchester University Press, 2007); and (co-edited with Alison Donnell and John Noyes) *The Routledge Companion to Diaspora and Migration Studies* (forthcoming, 2010).

Janet Wilson is Professor of English and Postcolonial Studies at the University of Northampton. She is editor of the *Journal of Postcolonial Writing* and currently Chair of EACLALS. Her research interests include: white settler societies; New Zealand and Australian cinema; New Zealand diasporic writing; and the movements of scholars between New Zealand, Australian and northern hemisphere universities during the twentieth century. Recent publications include *Fleur Adcock* (2007); *The Gorse Blooms Pale: The Southland Stories of Dan Davin* (an edition published in 2007); and *Global Fissures: Postcolonial Fusions* (a 2006 essay collection co-edited with Clara A. B. Joseph).

Introduction: Theorizing Postcolonial Diasporas

Michelle Keown, David Murphy and James Procter

Diaspora has become an increasingly 'diasporic' concept within postcolonial studies during the past decade. The term once referred specifically to the dispersal of the Jews, but within contemporary cultural analysis the term is now more likely to evoke a plethora of global movements and migrations: Romanian, African, Asian, black, Sikh, Irish, Lebanese, Palestinian, 'Atlantic' and so on. A corresponding expansion of diaspora's conceptual horizons has also taken place in recent years, since it has evolved to operate as a travelling metaphor associated with tropes of mobility, displacement, borders and crossings (Procter 2003: 13). This edited collection reflects critically on the specific significance of what we have termed 'postcolonial diasporas', drawing together the parallel and equally contested fields of postcolonial studies and diaspora studies at a time when the horizons opened up by these research areas appear more stretched and hazy than ever before. Bringing together a group of leading and emerging intellectuals working across the disciplines of cultural studies, history, literary analysis, modern languages, sociology and visual studies, it examines both the contributions and limitations of the terms 'postcolonial' and 'diaspora', and the problems and possibilities they present for future work in the humanities.

It is notable that in exploring the legacy of empire, postcolonial research has tended to focus on individual nations rather than on investigating comparative links between empires. This edited collection will move beyond the predominantly Anglophone focus of postcolonial diaspora scholarship to date, and will instead investigate postcolonial diaspora culture within a much wider range of cultural and linguistic contexts: Anglophone, Francophone, Hispanic and Neerlandophone. Contributors to this collection offer complex and nuanced analyses of postcolonial diaspora culture by establishing links across various transnational axes,

1

thus eschewing reductive binaristic approaches to the analysis of Europe and its former colonies.

The essays in the collection are grouped into three main sections, each of which explores postcolonial diaspora culture within a particular methodological, geographical or thematic paradigm. Essays in section one ('Discovering Europe'), for example, offer carefully situated analyses of cultural production across Europe in order to raise fresh questions about the continent as an internally differentiated, diasporic location. Contributors to sections two ('Nostalgia and the Longing for Home') and three ('Comparative Diasporic Contexts') primarily explore a range of diasporic contexts beyond Europe, focusing not only upon the dialectic between the absent 'homeland' and the new diasporic community, but also upon relationships between different diasporic communities dispersed across multiple geographical locations. Individual essays and subsections are summarized in more detail below, but this introductory chapter also explores some of the crosscurrents running through the collection by situating the work of the various contributors within wider debates in postcolonial studies. The section immediately below, for example, discusses one of the most important methodological shifts currently taking place in postcolonial studies: the move beyond Anglophone studies and into more complex comparative linguistic and disciplinary paradigms – some of which are explored and advanced in this collection. The remaining two sections of the chapter refer more specifically to some of the main theoretical frameworks informing the tripartite structure of the book by offering a brief overview of the essays included in each individual category.

Beyond Anglophone postcolonial studies

Almost since its inception, postcolonial studies has been subjected to intense critical interrogation: both by hostile critics external to the field and by scholars working largely within its framework. Since the events of 9/11 and the subsequent US-led invasions of Afghanistan and Iraq, this (self-)questioning has reached a new pitch amidst growing fears that the field risks stagnation in a sterile process of anthologization, in which a heavily circumscribed range of critics and concepts are endlessly cross-referenced (see Huggan 2001). To cite just a couple of the more prominent recent publications: a special issue of *New Formations*, 'After Iraq: Reframing Postcolonial Studies' (Gopal and Lazarus 2006) and the somewhat apocalyptically titled dossier in *PMLA*, 'The End of Postcolonial Theory?' (Yaeger 2007), have portrayed a field in crisis – uncertain of its moral, political and intellectual moorings. However, to posit the demise of postcolonial studies would be premature, for these recent publications clearly indicate that, despite the field's ongoing anxiogenic tendencies, it is also being reinvigorated through engagement with academic partners beyond its heartland in English literature departments.[1]

This desire to move beyond postcolonial studies' primary focus on Anglophone literary texts and contexts forms one of the organizing principles of this collection. Postcolonial 'theoretical' texts may well wander across philosophy, political science and history (among other disciplines), but this theory has been largely put to use in order to provide critiques of English-language literary texts. In their analysis of *The Empire Writes Back* (1989) – often considered the foundational textbook of postcolonial studies – Celia Britton and Michael Syrotinski (2001) argue that the attempt by Ashcroft, Griffiths and Tiffin to define the boundaries of a new academic field within English Literature departments effectively led to the exclusion of non-English material from the postcolonial paradigm. On their opening page, the authors of *The Empire Writes Back* claim that '[t]his book is concerned with writing by those peoples formerly colonized by Britain, *though much of what it deals with is of interest and relevance to countries colonized by other European powers, such as France, Portugal and Spain*' (1989: 1; our emphasis). This brief sentence captures a major ambiguity that has marked the development of postcolonial studies: a transcolonial comparatism is posited as essential, but its realization is perpetually deferred.[2] Our purpose here is not to apportion 'blame' for real and perceived omissions in the creation of the postcolonial field, but rather to signal the fragmented fashion in which the analysis of different European colonial contexts has developed – largely due to the arbitrary nature of disciplinary boundaries.

The development of comparative postcolonial studies has already been promoted by many scholars, not least within the field of French/ Francophone Studies. From the early 1990s, there has been a rapid growth in critical reflection on the relationship between postcolonial and Francophone studies.[3] After a phase of intense critical inquiry and debate on the connections between what have widely been seen as interrelated but largely parallel fields, we are now witnessing self-conscious attempts at field-construction under the title 'Francophone postcolonial studies' (see Forsdick and Murphy 2003; 2009). The emergence of this new linguistic awareness within the postcolonial field must not, however, be reduced to an injunction to read in the original, which is at times portrayed as the source of a 'true', 'originary' meaning. For, as John McLeod has argued so convincingly, the act of 'translating' ideas

from one language/culture to another is in itself a process of creating new meanings (McLeod 2003a). Essentially, what we are arguing for here is the value of opening the field to new contexts – both linguistic and cultural. For example, within this collection, Elleke Boehmer and Frances Gouda's chapter on Dutch postcolonial studies as well as Patrick Williams's piece on Palestine both open up new lines of inquiry within the field; or to use John McLeod's terms, they '[render] visible the presence of other colonial and postcolonial trajectories which cannot be neatly bracketed or ignored' (McLeod 2003b: 58–9).

Some major recent publications have already begun to trace the contours of a comparative postcolonialism. Certain of these initiatives have been the product of scholars working on non-Anglophone contexts: for example, the editors of a new *Historical Companion to Postcolonial Literatures* (Poddar, Patke and Jensen 2008) deliberately shift the focus away from Britain to continental Europe and its empires (including Belgium, Denmark, France, Portugal, Spain and the Netherlands). Equally, the 2004 American Comparative Literature Association (ACLA) Report on the state of the discipline remarks upon the significance of a comparative postcolonial project that has emerged recently from activity in the Francophone postcolonial studies field (see, in particular, Apter 2006: 55–6). Equally, scholars of English-language material are also increasingly aware of the need to engage with other colonial trajectories: in the introduction to his *Companion to Postcolonial Literatures*, which examines the British, French, Spanish and Portuguese empires, John McLeod argues that '[t]he field's centre of gravity is shifting, so that postcolonial studies is now generally more alert to the *different European empires*, and their legacies' (2007: 11; emphasis in original).

This desire to promote a postcolonial comparatism must not lead to excessive generalization: scholars must constantly be aware of the differences both *between* and *within* colonial traditions. Consequently, the chapters in the thematically organized sections of this collection seek to tease out both the possibilities and the limitations of a comparative postcolonial approach that might serve to inform the work of scholars undertaking more in-depth comparisons in the future. The comparative dimension of this collection extends beyond the mere juxtaposition of different contexts in different chapters. The final section of the collection contains explicitly comparative analyses of different diasporic contexts, while each of the chapters in the first two sections clearly attempts to situate itself comparatively in relation to a wider body of research on diaspora/postcolonial studies. Indeed, the chapters by Boehmer/Gouda and Román-Velázquez seek to explore the very limits of our conception of 'postcolonial diasporas' through analysis of contexts in postcolonial Europe that involve migration from non-European locations that are *not* former colonies of the host countries. What characteristics do such contexts share with specifically postcolonial diasporas?

In its choice of essays, this collection also chooses to approach the question of diaspora from a range of disciplinary angles. Alongside the literary analysis that has been central to the development of postcolonial studies (in chapters by McLeod, Williams, Wilson and Britton) there are also chapters on cinema (Ezra/Rowden) and performance art (Shilton), as well as more general cultural studies or sociological approaches (Marshall, Prasad, Román-Velázquez, Boehmer/Gouda). This desire to bring together scholars working from a range of disciplinary standpoints should be seen in the context of Graham Huggan's ideas on what he terms the 'anti-disciplinary tendencies' that have marked postcolonial studies since its inception (Huggan 2002). Huggan argues that the field now needs to develop teamwork-based projects by involving academics from various disciplines while simultaneously addressing common sets of issues and problems if it genuinely wishes to expand beyond the analysis of 'Literature'. He distinguishes this interdisciplinary approach from an interdiscursive approach, which, he argues, involves the borrowing of language and ideas from different disciplines in a theoretical, 'synoptic' fashion. For Huggan, this latter approach has been dominant within postcolonial studies and has contributed to the oft-criticized theoretical pretensions of the field. An interdisciplinary, teamwork-based approach would provide much-needed empirical analyses with which to reassess certain theoretical paradigms. In his important article, 'Exiles on Main Stream' (2003), Chris Bongie draws on Huggan's ideas in order to highlight the irony of postcolonial studies' commitment to 'Literature' when so much of its focus has been on breaking down arbitrary cultural and political hierarchies, which one might have presumed would include the attribution of 'value' to certain types of text. Bongie writes of 'the need for a transformative dialogue with cultural studies' that might allow postcolonial studies to address the main concerns of its critics. Through its exploration of diaspora from a range of perspectives and within a range of postcolonial contexts – Europe, the Americas, the Caribbean, the Pacific and the Middle East – this collection acts as a contribution to this 'transformative dialogue'. In the following sections, then, we will explore some of the comparative and collaborative aspects of diaspora both in Europe and in the wider world respectively by addressing issues that inform the three main groupings of essays included in the collection.

Comparing diasporas in Europe

The gradual retreat of national frontiers across Europe has not only fostered a culture of inclusion, unchecked movement and borderless reunification, but also of resurgent nationalism, ethnic absolutism and racism. The Channel Tunnel draws Paris, London and other northern European capitals together at the same time as it generates gatherings of refugees and camps like Sangatte. A decade after the iconic images of the fall of the Berlin Wall we were presented with pictures of the so-called 'fences of death' designed to seal off North African migrant routes to Spain. It is estimated that thousands of migrants have died trying to breach the borders of 'Fortress Europe': drowning in the Mediterranean and the Atlantic, or dying of thirst crossing the Sahara.

Similar contradictions mark the field of postcolonial studies, which is typically celebrated for its interdisciplinarity and its transgressive disregard of borders, but which has traditionally tended to fence itself off from Europe. Europe tends to exist as either postcolonialism's *bête noire* (for example, as something to which we must 'write back'), as an abstraction figured metonymically in the form of key metropolitan centres (London, Paris) or as an undifferentiated landscape that forecloses comparative thinking. Not surprisingly Europe repeatedly features in postcolonial and diaspora studies as a site of departure rather than of arrival. Thus, Ashcroft, Griffiths and Tiffin have argued that '[c]olonialism itself was a radically diasporic movement, involving the temporary or permanent dispersion and settlement of millions of Europeans over the entire world' (1998: 69). More recently, Poddar and Johnson's otherwise rich volume, *A Historical Companion to Postcolonial Literatures in English* (2005), contains two entries on 'European Exploration and Settlement': one focusing on Australia, New Zealand and the Pacific; the other on Canada. 'European' here carries only its older imperial meaning, which Etienne Balibar has noted was dominant until the mid-twentieth century: Europeans as colonizers overseas (Balibar 1991). Discussion of Europe's *postcolonial* status is thus foreclosed, as is its diasporic significance as a site of voyages out *and in*. Within this context it is worth reminding ourselves that while 1492 has acquired a foundational significance in postcolonial studies as the year in which the Spanish explorer Christopher Columbus 'discovered' the Americas, it is often forgotten that 1492 was also the year in which the North African Moors, who had occupied Spain for some 700 years, were ousted from Granada. As Paul Gilroy argues, such prolonged *internal* presences need to be recovered and reiterated so that:

> The little-known historical facts of Europe's openness to the colonial worlds it helped to make, might then be employed to challenge fantasies of the newly embattled European region as a culturally bleached or politically fortified space, closed off to further immigration, barred to asylum-seeking, and wilfully deaf to any demand for hospitality made by refugees and other displaced people.
>
> (2004: xii)

Thankfully, recent postcolonial studies are being reinvigorated by fresh research into French, Spanish, Italian and Germanic cultures: see, for example, Forsdick and Murphy (2003); Ponzanesi and Merolla (2005); Srivastava and De Donno (2006). This work takes us beyond the comfort zone of Anglophone contexts and challenges the centrality of Britain to current theorizations of diaspora. We hope that future work within the field will build upon these nation-based studies to consider the comparative and continental implications of Europe to postcolonial and diaspora thought. For example, what might be gained by locating the national (English) narrative of the so-called Windrush generation within a wider European ambit? To what extent, for example, do George Lamming's French readership, Samuel Selvon's travels in Spain or Henry Swanzy's correspondence with *Présence Africaine* in the 1950s unsettle received understandings of this major diasporic moment? Or more recently, why might it be important to consider the riots in the suburbs of Paris in 2005 – and the Madrid and London bombings of 2004 and 2005 – as articulated events rather than national crises?

The essays in this section of the collection offer no easy solutions to the comparative conundrums raised by such questions. John McLeod's essay focuses on how black British writing's encounter with Europe might posit dynamic new directions for postcolonial and diaspora studies. At the same time he explores how black British writing has itself been complicit in the provincialization of postcolonial Englishness by precluding – even as it seems to foreground and foster – dialogues across European communities. Within this context, McLeod offers a sober, strategic and provisional 'negotiation' of postcolonial Europe that is both suggestive in terms of where future comparative research might go, and alert to the limits of any easy, premature or celebratory comparatism.

Similarly, Elleke Boehmer and Frances Gouda's exploration of postcolonial studies in the diasporic Netherlands exposes the various institutional, historical, political and linguistic boundaries that have served to detach and insulate Dutch multiculture from postcolonial Europe in particular, and from postcolonial studies in general. Cutting across these boundaries, Boehmer and Gouda insist:

> that it is in the Netherlands' heterogeneous diasporic writing – many-tongued, palimpsestic, only jaggedly connected to the former colonial project – that the deep belatedness of the Dutch postcolonial condition might prolifically and tumultuously generate new meanings.

This belatedness is perhaps most powerfully illustrated in Boehmer and Gouda's consideration of the heated public debate sparked by the choice of Salman Rushdie's *Fury* (which was, ironically, first published in Dutch as *Woede*) for Book Week in 2001.

Where McLeod, Boehmer and Gouda remain predominantly concerned with literary cultures, Siobhan Shilton's essay suggests the importance of other genres (notably here, visual and performance art) to the comparative study of postcolonial Europe. By focusing on the work of two Paris-based diasporic artists – Majida Khattari and Marjane Satrapi – Shilton considers transculturation as a gendered and distinctively *visual* process that allows for comparative reflection on cross-cultural encounters between European and non-European subjects. In so doing, this essay initiates a move beyond Europe that is explicitly foregrounded in the next section. Ultimately, Shilton's essay reveals how the transcultural serves to destabilize any easy demarcation between European insides and outsides.

Postcolonial diasporas beyond Europe

This final section of our Introduction moves largely beyond the European contexts outlined above and engages with a range of diasporic communities – particularly within the Americas, the Middle East and the Pacific – that are explored in sections two and three of this book (entitled 'Nostalgia and Longing for Home' and 'Comparative Diasporic Contexts'). The essays in these sections investigate the complex relationships between diasporic communities and those who have remained in the 'homeland', as well as analysing interchanges of people, capital and ideologies across multiple diasporic locations beyond Europe.

The Americas feature a long and complex history of migration and settlement: from the founding of various European 'New World' communities in the late fifteenth and early sixteenth centuries, through the transportation of West African slaves between the sixteenth and nineteenth centuries, to the influx of various ethnic groups (such as Italians and Jews) fleeing poverty and persecution in Europe during the early-to-mid-twentieth century. As historian Paul Spickard points out, within the United States in particular and until quite recently, dominant models of immigration commonly offered a utopian narrative of 'assimilation' in which non-native minorities were 'transplanted from their unattractive native country and deposited in more fertile soil in the United States', thus implying a 'one-way' flow of people who abandon their ancestral identities to assume 'an undifferentiated American identity' (2002: 9, 10).

The 1990s and beyond, however, have witnessed the emergence of new postcolonial diasporic paradigms that transcend some of these theoretical limitations. For example, rather than reproducing a unidirectional migratory model privileging the US as the final destination, more recent studies have recognized the transnational, multidirectional nature of migration, observing that immigrants from a single country of origin are often dispersed (and maintain links) across multiple locations, and that many migrants return – sometimes permanently – to their countries of ancestral origin, or form new diasporic communities in other parts of Europe (see Spickard 2002). A particularly notable study in this context is anthropologist Roger Rouse's 1991 study of the interlinked Mexican communities of Aguililla (Michoacán) and Redwood City (California), which eschews earlier unidirectional or core-periphery models of migration: instead he traces the ways in which developments in telecommunications and other technologies have created 'spatially extended relationships' between Mexicans throughout the Americas (1991: 13; quoted in Spickard 2002: 12). In our collection, Bill Marshall's essay, further stretches the boundaries of migration theory by underlining the importance of French diasporic communities in an Atlantic world commonly deemed to have been shaped by British and Spanish colonialism. Marshall's analysis thus moves beyond orthodox views of French diaspora culture as centred on the reception of immigrants into the metropolitan nation-state; instead he explores the complex circulation of cultural forms and representations within and across various French diasporic locations throughout the Americas. In so doing, Marshall's analysis of the traces of French diaspora in the Americas opens up a potential dialogue between former rival colonizers and the colonies themselves: for these French diasporas were in constant dialogue and/or conflict with the French and British populations around them.

Patria Román-Velázquez's contribution to the collection, on the other hand, traces a further step in the evolution of American diaspora cultures by exploring the ways in which migrants from various Latin American nations have settled in London, while maintaining a link with their homelands by transforming specific London locations into sites of 'Latinness'. This community represents a particularly complex 'postcolonial diaspora', not only because it comprises migrants from a number of different South American nations, but also because there is no direct colonizer-colonized relationship between Britain and Latin America. Post-imperial Britain, like France and the Netherlands, is increasingly attracting migrants from around the world, including peoples from the former territories of *other* colonial powers: such are the complex population flows that have marked the development of postcolonial diasporas in recent decades.

Celia Britton's essay, which opens the third section of our collection, explores a similarly complex transatlantic dialogue by investigating the ways in which the incarcerated Jew of the holocaust has been invoked as a model for the sense of 'imprisonment' experienced by French Caribbeans who migrated to France in the decades following the Second World War. As Britton notes, Old Testament narratives of the exile of the Jews, coupled with the horrors of the Holocaust, formed a 'natural' point of reference for diasporic Caribbeans suffering racial discrimination in post-war France. In discussing literary explorations of this dynamic, Britton focuses in particular on two Guadeloupean novels: Gisèle Pineau's *L'Exil selon Julia* (1996) and Simone and André Schwarz-Bart's *Un plat de porc aux bananes vertes* (1967).

Britton's references to the Middle East resonate with Patrick Williams's essay on the Palestinian diaspora, which appears in section two of this collection. As Williams points out, while the Israeli Law of Return allows Jews from anywhere in the world to settle in Israel, Israelis have consistently refused to allow exiled Palestinians to return to the land of their birth. In focusing in particular on the work of renowned Palestinian poet Mahmoud Darwish, Williams considers the efficacy of conventional formulations of diasporic identity – in which an eventual return to the homeland remains a perpetual possibility – in a context in which the right of return is denied.

Settler colonies, such as those in Australia, New Zealand, Canada and South Africa, present a further context in which particular ethnic groups have been displaced (and in some cases, exterminated) by others. While indigenous patterns of migration and exile within white settler colonies have been well-documented in postcolonial studies, much less attention has been devoted to the complex relationship between white settler diasporas and their metropolitan homeland(s). By the early 1990s, when postcolonial studies was firmly established as an academic discipline, antipodean scholars such as Stephen Slemon noted that in its focus upon the dialectical relationship between the 'first' and 'third' worlds, postcolonial studies had overlooked the importance of white settler diasporic literature, putatively:

> because it [was considered] not sufficiently pure in its anti-colonialism, because it [did] not offer up an experiential grounding in a common 'Third World' aesthetics, [and] because its modalities of *post*-coloniality [were considered] too ambivalent, too occasional and uncommon, for inclusion within the field.
>
> (Slemon 1996 [1990]: 77)

The first decade of the twenty-first century, however, has witnessed the emergence and consolidation of 'settlement studies' – the analysis of white settler societies – as a distinct field within postcolonial and cultural studies, particularly within the antipodes (see Calder and Turner 2002; Huggan 2007; Keown 2007; Pearson 2001; and Turner 1999, 2002). Janet Wilson's essay in this collection on the white settler societies of New Zealand and Australia extends the parameters of these recent debates by investigating the ways in which twentieth-century antipodean authors have refashioned idealized images of the British metropolitan homeland inherited from the early settlers. After providing an exhaustive analysis of the ways in which antipodean literary representations of the British 'homeland' have evolved since the colonial period, Wilson's essay concludes with a discussion of the ways in which the outdated binary opposition of 'empire and colony' is being further revised by contemporary diasporic antipodean writers. Like Román-Velázquez's Latin Londoners, many of these antipodean travellers have settled in European locations with which they have no colonial ties, thus demanding modes of analysis that move beyond the restrictions of much previous postcolonial diaspora theory.

Mohit Prasad's essay on the Indo-Fijian diaspora introduces a further layer of complexity to the discussion of Pacific diaspora culture. Moving beyond the white settler/indigene dialectic discussed in Janet Wilson's essay, Prasad explores the experiences of the descendants of indentured labourers transported from India to colonial (British) Fiji during the late nineteenth century. Indo-Fijians have undergone two major diasporic phases: the first between 1879 and 1916, when some

sixty thousand Indian labourers were transported to the sugar plantations of Fiji; and the second in the wake of the Fiji military coups of
1987 and 2000, after which thousands of Indo-Fijians left the country
to escape discriminatory legislation designed to prioritize the claims of
indigenous Fijians. By building upon the work of established scholars
of Indo-Fijian diaspora culture such as Vijay Mishra and Brij Lal,[4] Prasad
offers an innovative comparative analysis of Indo-Fijian diasporic communities within Fiji and Sydney (Australia), demonstrating the way
in which the 'work ethic' embraced and idealized by Indo-Fijians has
been transported and transmuted within (and beyond) these multiple
diasporic locations.

As was mentioned above, Bill Marshall's essay, which concludes the
third section of the collection, also provides new perspectives on settler cultures in the Americas, stressing not only the importance of
the neglected French diasporic presence in the Atlantic world, but also the
complex interrelationships between French populations and their Spanish
and British counterparts. It is precisely this type of comparative diasporic
approach that our collection is seeking to promote, and that we hope will
be developed further in future studies in the postcolonial field.

The third section of this collection is followed by a postscript in
which Elizabeth Ezra and Terry Rowden undertake a comparative
analysis of contemporary cinematic images of diaspora. This final piece
extends and moves beyond the diasporic debates of the earlier chapters
by examining the transnational formations now emerging within postcolonial discourse, and by suggesting ways in which the boundaries of
postcolonial diaspora theory are being redefined in some of the most
experimental zones of contemporary cultural production. In this sense,
the postscript encapsulates the objectives of this entire collection,
which seeks to delineate, develop and anticipate future directions in
postcolonial diaspora studies in the new millennium, as well as advancing new transcolonial and transdisciplinary approaches that promise to
shape future developments in the field.

Notes

1. For a more sustained version of the ideas developed in this section, see
   Murphy (2006).
2. This new comparatism re-engages with the project of Edward Said in his
   seminal 'postcolonial' texts, *Orientalism* (1978) and *Culture and Imperialism*
   (1993), which are both the work of a comparatist heavily influenced by
   French-language material. One of the first explicit efforts to offer a comparative postcolonialism results more in the juxtaposition of intellectual

traditions rather than their interpenetration (see Bery and Murray 1999). Ironically, it is in the field of history – often so hostile to postcolonial theory – where extremely interesting research has endeavoured to compare colonial practices and traditions (see Cooper and Stoler 1997; Clancy-Smith and Gouda 1998).

3. In particular, there have been many special issues of prominent journals dedicated to this topic over the past few years. To cite just two of the most important examples within the past decade, see Britton and Syrotinski (2001); Laroussi and Miller (2003).

4. See, for example, Mishra's essays (1977; 1992) and Lal's autobiography *Mr Tulsi's Store* (2001) as well as his edited collection *Bittersweet* (2004).

Bibliography

Apter, E. (2006) '"Je ne crois pas beaucoup à la littérature comparée": universal poetics and postcolonial comparatism' in H. Saussy (ed.) *Comparative Literature in an Age of Globalization* (Baltimore, MD: Johns Hopkins University Press), pp. 54–62.

Ashcroft, B., Griffiths, G. and Tiffin, H. (1989) *The Empire Writes Back: Theory and Practice in Post-colonial Literatures* (London and New York: Routledge).

Ashcroft, B., Griffiths, G. and Tiffin, H. (1998) *Key Concepts in Post-Colonial Studies* (London: Routledge).

Balibar, E. (1991) 'Es Gibt Keinen Staat in Europa: Racism and Politics in Europe Today', *New Left Review*, 1.186, 5–19.

Bery, A. and Murray, P. (eds) (1999) *Comparing Postcolonial Literatures: Dislocations* (Basingstoke: Macmillan).

Bongie, C. (2003) 'Exiles on Mainstream: Valuing the popularity of postcolonial literature', *Postmodern Culture*, 14.1: 64 paragraphs; www.iath.virginia.edu/pmc/; accessed 1 May 2008.

Britton, C. and Syrotinski, M. (2001) 'Introduction' in Britton and Syrotinski (eds) *Paragraph*, 24.3, 1–11. Special issue: 'Francophone Texts and Postcolonial Theory'.

Calder, A. and Turner, S. (eds) (2002) *Journal of New Zealand Literature*, 20. Special issue: 'Settlement Studies'.

Clancy-Smith, J. and Gouda, F. (eds) (1998) *Domesticating the Empire: Gender and Family Life in French and Dutch Colonialism* (Charlottesville and London: University Press of Virginia).

Cooper, F. and Stoler, A. (eds) (1997) *Tensions of Empire: Colonial Cultures in a Bourgeois World* (Los Angeles and London: University of California Press).

Forsdick, C. and Murphy, D. (eds) (2003) *Francophone Postcolonial Studies: A Critical Introduction* (London: Arnold).

Forsdick, C. and Murphy, D. (eds) (2009) *Postcolonial Thought in the Francophone World* (Liverpool: Liverpool University Press).

Gilroy, P. (2004) 'Foreword: Migrancy, Culture and a New Map of Europe' in H. Raphael-Hernandez (ed.) *Blackening Europe: the African American Presence* (London: Routledge), pp. xi–xxi.

Gopal, P. and Lazarus, N. (eds) (2006) *New Formations*, 59. Special issue: 'After Iraq: Reframing Postcolonial Studies'.

Huggan, G. (2001) *The Postcolonial Exotic: Marketing the Margins* (London and New York: Routledge).

Huggan, G. (2002) 'Postcolonial Studies and the Anxiety of Interdisciplinarity', *Postcolonial Studies*, 5.3, 245–75.

Huggan, G. (2007) *Australian Literature: Postcolonialism, Racism, Transnationalism* (Oxford: Oxford University Press).

Keown, M. (2007) *Pacific Islands Writing: The Postcolonial Literatures of Aotearoa/ New Zealand and Oceania* (Oxford: Oxford University Press).

Lal, B. (2001) *Mr Tulsi's Store: A Fijian Journey* (Canberra: Pandanus Books).

Lal, B. (ed.) (2004) *Bittersweet: the Indo-Fijian Experience* (Canberra: Pandanus Books).

Laroussi, F. and Miller, C. L. (eds) (2003) *Yale French Studies*, 103. Special issue: 'French and Francophone: The Challenge of Expanding Horizons'.

Lazarus, N. (1999) *Nationalism and Cultural Practice in the Postcolonial World* (Cambridge: Cambridge University Press).

McLeod, J. (2003a) 'Contesting contexts: Francophone thought and Anglophone postcolonialism' in Forsdick and Murphy (eds) *Francophone Postcolonial Studies*, pp. 192–201.

McLeod, J. (2003b) 'Reading the Archipelago', *Francophone Postcolonial Studies*, 1.1, 55–9.

McLeod, J. (ed.) (2007) *The Routledge Companion to Postcolonial Studies* (London and New York: Routledge).

Mishra, V. (1977) 'Indo-Fijian Fiction: Towards an Interpretation', *World Literature Written in English*, 16.2, 395–409.

Mishra, V. (1992) 'The Girmit Ideology Revisited: Fiji Indian Literature' in Emmanuel Nelson (ed.) *Reworlding: The Literature of the Indian Diaspora* (New York: Greenwood), pp. 1–12.

Murphy, D. (2006) 'Beyond Anglophone Imperialism?', *New Formations*, 59, 132–43.

Pearson, D. (2001) *The Politics of Ethnicity in Settler Societies: States of Unease* (Basingstoke and New York: Palgrave Macmillan).

Poddar, P. and Johnson, D. (eds) (2005) *A Historical Companion to Postcolonial Literatures in English* (Edinburgh: Edinburgh University Press).

Poddar, P., Patke, R. and Jensen, L. (eds) (2008) *A Historical Companion to Postcolonial Literatures: Continental Europe and its Empires* (Edinburgh: Edinburgh University Press).

Ponzanesi, S. and Merolla, D. (eds) (2005) *Migrant Cartographies: New Cultural and Literary Spaces in Post-Colonial Europe* (Lanham, MD: Lexington).

Procter, J. (2003) *Dwelling Places: Postwar Black British Writing* (Manchester: Manchester University Press).

Rouse, R. (1991) 'Mexican Migration and the Social Space of Postmodernism', *Diaspora*, 1.1, 8–23.

Said, Edward W. (1978) *Orientalism: Western Conceptions of the Orient* (London: Routledge and Kegan Paul).

Said, Edward W. (1993) *Culture and Imperialism* (London: Vintage).

Slemon, S. (1996 [1990]) 'Unsettling the Empire: Resistance Theory for the Second World' in P. Mongia (ed.) *Contemporary Postcolonial Theory: A Reader* (London: Arnold), pp. 72–83.

Spickard, P. (2002) 'Introduction: Pacific Diaspora?' in P. Spickard, J. L. Rondilla and D. H. Wright (eds) *Pacific Diasporas: Island Peoples in the United States and Across the Pacific* (Honolulu: University of Hawai'i Press), pp. 1–27.

Srivastava, N. and De Donno, F. (eds) (2006) *Interventions*, 8.3. Special issue: 'Colonial and Postcolonial Italy'.

Turner, S. (1999) 'Settlement as Forgetting' in K. Neumann, N. Thomas and H. Ericksen (eds) *Quicksands: Foundational Histories in Australia and Aotearoa New Zealand* (Sydney: University of New South Wales Press), pp. 20–38.

Turner. S. (2002) 'Being Colonial/Colonial Being', *Journal of New Zealand Literature*, 20, 39–66.

Yaeger, P. (2007) 'Editor's Column: The End of Postcolonial Theory? A Roundtable with Sunil Agnani, Fernando Coronil, Gaurav Desai, Mamadou Diouf, Simon Gikandi, Susie Tharu and Jennifer Wenzel', *PMLA*, 122.3, 633–51.

Section 1 Discovering Europe

1
European Tribes: Transcultural Diasporic Encounters

John McLeod

Eighteen years ago, at the beginning of the 1990s, the Guyanese-born, London-raised writer David Dabydeen cast a weary eye over Europe's near future. Deeply affected by a recent experience of racial harassment at Frankfurt airport, his muted vision of a stumblingly multicultural Europe anticipated yet more opportunities in the future for the indulgence of cultural exoticism and the continued presence of racism against the black peoples of Europe. Yet, as he put it in a wearily indecisive concluding passage, there still was perhaps a glimmer of hope for the Europe of tomorrow:

> We'll all be eating more pizzas, downing more lager, spraying more French perfumes, driving more German cars and exchanging more footballers. My limited and symbolic experience of immigration controls makes me fear that British blacks, the original New World folk, will be largely excluded from the New World jamboree. [...] Perhaps West Indians will eventually slip their cultural moorings and get lost in the swamps of New World Europe. Or perhaps we will be able to adapt, modify and enrich our culture in the new environments. Perhaps new excitements will arise when we encounter the Dutch blacks, the French blacks, the German blacks, and discover what we share that transcends colonial boundaries.
>
> (Dabydeen 1991: 105–6)

Dabydeen's swiftly stated vision of a diasporic community of discovery enabled by encounters between divergently located black Europeans perhaps recalls an earlier, distinctly hopeful and creative moment in the history of black peoples in Europe, when European cities such as Manchester, London and Paris became sites of creative encounter in

19

the early and mid-twentieth century for anticolonial intellectuals from Caribbean and African countries – both Anglophone and Francophone. It was in Gray's Inn Road in London, not in Trinidad, that C. L. R. James discovered that George Padmore was his boyhood friend George Nurse, while 1930s Paris brokered the encounter between the Senegalese radical Léopold Senghor, the Martiniquian writer Aimé Césaire and the French Guianese poet Léon-Gontran Damas that would lead to the revolutionary formulation of Négritude. And as James declares, it was in Dalmatia, on the coast of the Adriatic Sea, where Césaire began to write *Cahier d'un Retour au Pays Natal* (1939), after having been taken there by some friends he had made in Paris (James 1984). In recalling these previous European-based, cross-cultural encounters – perhaps unwittingly – Dabydeen's language hints at the creative possibilities, both political and cultural, which historically have emerged from the chance encounters of Europe's black peoples keen to share the excitements of a common cause, and which might emerge again in a new world order. The chance for (once-)colonized peoples from different cultures, colonial histories and language traditions to adapt, enrich and modify cultural imperatives in Europe has a significant history, one which might indeed resource the provision of a critical and resistant encounter with the impending jamboree of 'New World Europe'.

But in the wake of terrorist attacks in New York and Washington in 2001, and the bombing of trains and buses in Madrid (2004) and London (2005), the 'new environments' of black peoples across Europe today have turned out to be far from enriching – and it appears that Dabydeen's predominantly sober vista of the immediate future which he voiced in 1991 has established itself in even darker ways than he could ever have anticipated. The gloomy fate that perhaps connects the disparate experiences of Moroccan migrants in Spain, British Asian Muslims, young black French men and women as well as others in the 'New World Europe' has been one of increased discrimination, hostility, inequity and – above all – racism. The small but significant support for Far Right political movements across Europe testifies to a renewed racism which today is encroaching dangerously upon mainstream politics in Austria, Holland and Britain. In New World Europe, perhaps much worse than the one Dabydeen soberly envisaged, 'the life-threatening jeopardy provoked by being racialised as different is undiminished and may even have increased now that "race" and its certainties can claim to heal or at least calm the anxieties over identity, which have been precipitated by the insecurities and inequalities of globalization' (Gilroy 2004: 60). As Paul Gilroy here suggests, in a progressively unstable and frightening world – increasingly globalized and terrorized from contrary sides by suicide bombers or state-sponsored scaremongering over the 'axis of evil' – the old hierarchies of race seem all the more attractive as the means to stabilize, codify and judge fellow Europeans as different. In a Europe injured by the global conflicts of the twenty-first century, it might seem hard to see opportunities for, and evidence of, the 'new excitements' that Dabydeen tentatively mooted.

So how can it be that – if cultural critiques of multiculturalism are to be believed – the last eighteen years have been notable for the amount of transcultural innovation that, in Britain at least, has come almost to typify mainstream cultural life? In the rarefied world of literary publishing, important British novels since 2000 have emerged from or explored that country's postcolonial descendants, while several have taken as their theme the productive, fertile yet often abrasive interaction between white and black Britons: Monica Ali's *Brick Lane* (2003), Caryl Phillips's *A Distant Shore* (2003), Andrea Levy's *Small Island* (2004) and Gautam Malkani's *Londonstani* (2006). Phillips and Levy received major literary awards for their work; Malkani's advance payment for his remarkable portrayal of British Asian youth in West London in his first novel is reported to be in the region of €450,000. The continued success of these writers of course might be due to the prevalence of what Graham Huggan has called the 'postcolonial exotic': namely, the fetishization and marketing of difference which does little to engender genuine multicultural fusion and exchange (Huggan 2001). Yet this explanation does not always sufficiently take into account the ways in which cultural consumers may use cultural outputs for their own ends and in their own innovative, subaltern ways; it falls into the rather tiresome trap of mistaking popularity as both inevitably conformist and politically vulgar. As Michel de Certeau reminds us, ordinary folk – as both producers and consumers – may rescript the intentions and impositions of officious modes of social and cultural agency 'by reintroducing into them the plural mobility of goals and desires' (de Certeau 1984: xxii). The unpredictable meanings and agency of cultural products are not finally or firmly defined by the markets in which they are circulated or by the media in which they are primarily promoted. Certainly Paul Gilroy's recent critique of the hopeful conviviality of cultural encounters in his book *After Empire: Melancholia or Convivial Culture?* (2004) retains a faith, which may be traced to his earliest work, in the subversive street-level, streetwise vernaculars of a resolutely cosmopolitan popular milieu that can appropriate lucrative cultural capital for the purpose of productive, subversive revaluation. Mike Skinner, Nitin Sawhney,

Corinne Bailey Rae, Andrea Levy and Caryl Phillips – such creative Britons in their own special ways look to a diverse array of cultural modes when beckoning cultural newness into the world (to misquote Salman Rushdie's famous phrase). Whether intended or not, their new cultural vernaculars may in fact point the way to rendering outmoded and irrelevant the nomenclature of race and nation in both their production *and* their consumption.

Gilroy's determined utopianism has long influenced my own thinking about the cheerful agency and empowering propensity of cosmopolitan, diasporic cultural innovation that might ultimately open up new routes of social and cultural habitus for us all – even if his unsubtle analyses of vernacular cultures seem to belong more to the dilettante. In the current terrorized climate, a postcolonial politics of optimism seems to me all the more urgent and necessary, although Huggan's work should nonetheless counsel us that the alleged agency of subaltern innovation – of making new by 'making do' – must not be automatically assumed or breathlessly celebrated as engendering concrete change (as, perhaps, is the case in de Certeau's otherwise inspiring, rich thinking). Gilroy's cheerful support of 'that diminishing and valuable commodity: hope' (2004: 58) importantly underwrites his faith in the diasporic engagements that have little truck with officious discourses of difference. But if we bear in mind Dabydeen's remark and the long history of transcultural encounters in Europe, it appears that hopeful vistas of vernacular multiculturalism nearly always take their examples from a singular postcolonial context. More often than not, those transfigurative forms of innovative cultural borrowing from seemingly remote sites that are offered as examples of enduring untameable *transcultural* cosmopolitanism have tended to be bounded by either a shared language or a colonial legacy. One thinks of British-based Caribbean diaspora subjects scratching with Jamaican records; or London's British Asian youth cross-pollinating English with diverse terms of reference drawn from Urdu, Gujarati or Hindi and in so doing confecting a shared trans-Asian vernacular British Asian argot accessible to *all* the children of Sikhs, Muslims, Hindus and beyond. The legacies, locations and language of the British Empire have contributed to a distinct diasporic context that detains the rhizomic manoeuvres of such endeavours within a singular – if internally manifold – circumscribed milieu.

So something is missing. Dabydeen's anticipation of a series of international encounters between black people in Europe is voiced at the end of a long century characterized by the demise of colonialism and the emergence of European diaspora communities in a number of former colonial centres: the Netherlands, France and Germany. Even as late as 1991 it appears that these divergent diaspora communities across Europe are not speaking to each other. How multicultural is British multiculturalism when set within a European, rather than a strictly Anglophone or British colonial frame? Have any significant itinerant exchanges emerged which have allowed 'new excitements' to be nurtured by distinctly trans-European axes of cross-diasporic cultural – and specifically multilingual – engagements? Multiculturalism in Europe remains locked inside linguistic borders, perhaps: postcolonial London and postcolonial Paris seem very far away from each other, give or take the occasional (and important) Linton Kwesi Johnson concert. In what ways have British writers – often lauded as cosmopolitan and receptive to cross-cultural fusion – endeavoured to inaugurate the kinds of pan-European encounters that Dabydeen projected in 1991?

In pursuing some of these questions I wish to focus on three textual examples from different moments during the past twenty years. I shall turn first to Caryl Phillips's early, angry account of a year spent travelling through Europe and (briefly) Morocco, *The European Tribe* (1987) – published just before Dabydeen's essay – in which Phillips addresses his 'anxieties of knowing that I was a member of the larger European tribe, a member who felt uncomfortable at being such, but who had no alternative' (Phillips 1987: x). Secondly, I shall consider Mike Phillips's recent musings on Europe and race in his eclectic, predominantly nonfictional book *London Crossings* (2001). Finally, I shall explore briefly Bernardine Evaristo's playfully serious novel *Soul Tourists* (2005), which returns us to Europe in 1987, but from the vantage of a twenty-first century cosmopolitan sensibility deeply aware of the silences regarding black people which may be found in Europe's many and varied histories. As I shall argue, these examples of black writing in Britain instructively demonstrate some of the possibilities and problems of striking up engagements between and across Europe's black people. In particular, the challenges faced by black British writers of Europe index some of the difficulties in brokering intra-European innovation and engagement from a (by no means homogeneous) British perspective.

Caryl Phillips's first non-fiction book *The European Tribe* (1987) concerned a year he spent travelling in such diverse locations as Morocco, Spain, Holland, Northern Ireland, Germany, Poland, Norway and Russia. Published before the fall of the Berlin Wall and the end of Communism in Eastern Europe, his travelogue reveals a stubbornly racist continent characterized by tourism and vapid Americanisation, struggling to cope with the various legacies of British, French, Spanish and Dutch colonialism – especially the large African and Caribbean diaspora populations to be found in metropolitan sites such as Amsterdam and Paris. The conclusion he reaches at the end of his tour is both eloquent and irate – it is perhaps the angriest moment to be found throughout his usually composed and solemn prose, and in this early book it is clear that he has yet to discover the beautifully still prose style of his later writing in which the passions of personality are deliberately anonymized. Warming to his theme, Phillips accuses white Europeans of knowing little about Europe's exploitative past of colonialism and slavery as well as its bleakly racist present. 'You justify your Empire', he writes, presumably to white Europeans, 'your actions, your thought with your "civilisation", forgetting that in this century, in the Congo, Belgians chopped off black hands and feet as legal punishment for under-production ... Your eyesight is defective. Europe is blinded by her past, and does not understand the high price of her churches, art galleries, and architecture' (Phillips 1987: 128). Phillips freely admits that his book is not a sensitive work of historical and sociological analysis and makes its points through short polemic and vignette. Note how the thrust of the polemic is distinctly postcolonial: a British descendant of a once-colonized country (St Kitts, Phillips's birthplace) writes back to the former colonial power to contest the continuing divisive legacies which have survived, and are prospering anew in the wake of the end of Empire. Yet, while *The European Tribe* often succeeds in engendering a postcolonial critique of the present, it struggles to facilitate the kinds of multicultural conversations across diasporas which Dabydeen was still waiting for a couple of years later.

A multilingual, multicultural Europe seems some way off in *The European Tribe*. In his chapter 'Autumn in Paris', Phillips begins by describing his dislike for France because it reminds him too much of Britain, both in its weather – in the rain Paris looks 'suspiciously like London' (1987: 56) – and due to the racist graffiti he sees from the window of his train. It is a humdrum yet revealing beginning that describes the limited optic that Phillips perhaps cannot help but adopt. On more than one occasion he finds it difficult to look critically at several of the places he visits outside of the purview of British experience, no matter how hard he tries. 'I could not possibly live in Paris', he decides. 'All that would happen was I would learn a new language to tackle old problems' (57). The problems might look familiar to a writer who grew up in 1960s and 1970s Britain amidst the worst kinds of racism and prejudice, but is it enough to assume that they are necessarily the same? After his encounter with a French Government spokesman on

North African affairs, and having visited the Belleville district and La Goutte d'Or, Phillips concludes that racism in France is pretty much like it is in Britain and wonders (presciently, as it turned out) if the future establishment of a second-generation Parisian diaspora community may force France 'to experience the problems of inner city rioting that Britain has already had to come to terms with' (65). Phillips is sensitive to some of the particular racial issues of Paris and makes mention of the different attitudes among the French to North African and Caribbean diasporic peoples; yet his ability to discern the specificities of Parisian diasporic life leads him more often than not to frame the situation of non-Anglophone black diasporas always in terms of the British example. Phillips is intellectually and politically sympathetic to the black French, whose plight he soberly outlines, yet the shape of his communication is unidirectional: there seems little opportunity for some of the particularities of Paris – historical, cultural, social or linguistic – to inform, reframe or inflect black British experiences.

On the Métro platform in La Goutte d'Or, Phillips encounters a young black man with whom a few words are exchanged: '"I am a black man", he said. This was all the English he knew. "I am a black man." And then he added *"Je suis un petit bois"* as an afterthought' (Phillips 1987: 63). The unnamed man makes reference, perhaps, to the Senegalese writer Sembene Ousmane's third novel *Les bouts de bois de Dieu* (1960), which was translated into English in 1962. It is a moment of potential multicultural exchange, as brief contact is brokered through a shared allusion to an important postcolonial work. Yet the encounter seems fleeting and unable to nurture an important relationship; it is over as quickly as it appears, and a familiar frame reasserts itself. Phillips begins the next paragraph with the phrase 'France, like Britain, combines racialism with an admiration for semi-chic black fashions in music' (63). The possibility for prolonged dialogic transcultural exchange seems unavailable: France is quickly framed within a British context as the alleged resemblance between each nation is asserted. At moments such as this one in Paris, there emerges a temporary alliance of race, based on similarity and partial recognition of solidarity across different language groups, which perhaps falls short of the new discoveries that Dabydeen hoped for in the encounters between New World black peoples. Phillips sees a great deal in Paris and rightly contests the inequities that are to him depressingly familiar. Yet he discovers little that is new to himself, partly because of the difficulties that he faces in trying to move outside of a predominantly Anglophone frame of reference. The pan-European black voice which Phillips adopts at the close of his book – speaking for

European blacks against the ignorance of white European 'liberalism' – is a necessary and important one, and part of a much needed attempt to link up racialized diasporas to form a new community of resistance. As Phillips shows – considering the relatively small numbers of black Europeans in the Arctic Circle or Eastern Europe – the creation of a communal sense of black identity across the continent may assist those who do not live in diaspora communities in forging a sense of identity alternative to national and/or racially subordinating models. Yet in 1987 this is still some way away from the establishment of reciprocal, mutually informing diasporic encounters, in which it is hoped that there is more to share than parallel experiences of racism.

In reading Phillips's book in this way, I am not at all dismissing the integrity of his attempt to look at non-Anglophone European diasporas. *The European Tribe* is an important book that opens an important vista on postcolonial and diasporic Europe. But I am suggesting that there are also significant problems with such attempts at pan-European vision, and I am using his inspiring work as an example of the kinds of problems which scholars might need to consider when looking to diasporic contexts across Europe – chiefly the temptation and tendency to read the history of black British politics and culture as either anticipatory of or talismanic for black European diasporas in general. Phillips's reluctance to learn a new language to describe old problems is understandable, but perhaps not necessarily the best decision: the problems of Paris's diaspora peoples may well have something in common with, say, London's, but there may be specific problems which are unique to Paris and not easily rendered with recourse to the British example. Similarly, the 'new language' may afford novel ways of thinking about British problems as well as opening access to fresh forms of resistance that can be transculturally appropriated. Is the moth-eaten modality of race firm enough to knit together such diasporic alliances, or might prolonged forms of transcultural, multilingual engagement begin to forge a productively diasporic consciousness where the logic of 'Europe and its tribes' gives way to new modes of pan-diasporic engagement?

Looking ahead to Phillips's later and mature writing of Europe – such as his novel *A Distant Shore* (2003) – it still seems difficult to find an affirmative answer. In this novel, an African refugee, Gabriel, flees across Europe in fear of his life and manages to find his way to a refugee camp in France (which recalls the controversial Sangatte refugee camp that was functional between 1999 and 2002). At serious risk to himself, Gabriel makes it to England with the assistance of a people trafficker and extortionist (whom his travelling companion, Amma, pays), first by jumping dangerously onto a passing French train and then by clinging perilously to the side of a ship as it crosses the English Channel. The friendships he makes with other refugees on his difficult journey are fleeting and temporary, while few words are ever exchanged between them. The 'fatigued group' of migrants that make it to France break up quickly at the camp – a scene of 'lethargic misery' (Phillips 2003: 121, 123) – and no lasting relationships are established. Gabriel's attempt to help Amma and her child secure passage to England backfires; instead he makes his journey across the Channel with two Chinese migrants. One of these figures, who is unnamed, dies in the crossing; the second, called Bright, stays briefly with Gabriel in England, but soon disappears when Gabriel is arrested on a (mistaken) charge of sexual misconduct. While *A Distant Shore* is at one level an understated and moving depiction of the many ways in which the everyday kindness of strangers stubbornly refuses the effects of racism and prejudice on migrants, its predominant vision of refugeeism in contemporary Europe gloomily suggests that there is a very long way to go indeed as regards the creation of a convivial and multicultural Europe where reciprocity is the *sine qua non* of vernacular life, and where the human rights of all its peoples are duly appreciated.

Although such conclusions make for unhappy contemplation, it must be said that black writers in Britain have remained keen to explore links with other European countries and cultures with an inquisitiveness and consciousness that contrasts with the depressingly familiar Europhobia that has marred much of contemporary British debate about the mainland. Mike Phillips (no relation to Caryl Phillips) has also recorded his engagements with post-Communist Europe in his book *London Crossings* (2001) – a Europe very different politically to that in *The European Tribe* – although once again the tendency to enfold black Europeans' problems within a British framework is prevalent. Mike Phillips is a less subtle and skilled writer than Caryl Phillips, and *London Crossings* is notable at times for its remarkably unthinking approach to life outside London – at times one struggles to find evidence of a series of intellectual crossings that might match the physical crossings in and out of London which the book occasionally catalogues. In a chapter called 'European Tribesmen', Mike Phillips recounts a recent visit to Prague in 2000. As a Londoner used to seeing black people regularly in day-to-day life, he finds the visit unnerving. Although he feels close to home in Prague, his sense of isolation as the only black person for miles around is acute, even though he knows that this is probably not the case. When searching for the language to describe a new place and his reactions to it,

Phillips can only voice his feelings in relation to the old problems of migrant London life. Another chance for discovery is missed:

> [Prague] had the same sense [as 1950s London] of reflecting something old yet incomplete, the same sense of drabness and nostalgia, the same indifference to my presence. English friends who knew these places tend to come up with the same question over and over again: 'How do they treat you? What about racism?' The answer is that for anyone who lived in England during the 1950s and 1960s, there is nothing remarkable about most forms of racist abuse or harassment. Short of physical attack, any form of racism I encountered in the region seemed more or less routine.
>
> (Phillips 2001: 197)

'The same sense...the same indifference...the same question.' As in Paris, so in Prague: the fifteen or so years between Caryl Phillips's and Mike Phillips's accounts of their European journeys seem to have effected little change in approaches to the mainland by British writers. Indeed, Mike Phillips's account seems to lack even the impulse for or attempt at exchange that Caryl Phillips's writing displayed. A privileging of black British experience and knowledge is to the fore in the above quotation, despite Mike Phillips's worthy attempt to account for the differences between, in this instance, Western and Eastern Europe.

Like Caryl Phillips, Mike Phillips notes the lack of a black presence in received European history, remarking that 'it would be next to impossible to find a reference to anyone of African descent in any history of Europe, and, ironically, even where a "black" person is unmissable, the commentaries avoid or skate over any discussion of the fact' (Phillips 2001: 198). Yet in moving to explain some of the particularities of racial politics in the Czech Republic, he tends to view the country's contemporary problems in a way that highlights the successes of British diasporic agency while suggesting that other European nations have yet to gain British levels of sophistication. 'My claim to Britishness was practically incomprehensible to many people I met in Central Europe', he writes. '[People] didn't understand the notion of a national identity which overrode ethnicity' (199). Later he quotes, with more than a hint of satisfaction, a Guyanese migrant to Poland who tells him that 'you boys in London are showing the way' (202). This leads Phillips to reflect on the subaltern transformative energies of London, where he argues it is thankfully neither possible these days to pursue a racially exclusive notion of British identity nor a segregated Garvey-esque nor

Pan-African black politics of resistance. The conclusion to his chapter is unequivocal in its advocacy of London's enabling cosmopolitanism:

> London, a place whose habit was to make and remake itself with each new generation, was the arena of our transformation, and in its turn became a hybrid of styles and cultures. Within Britain its influence is irresistible, and its heterogeneous population has come to redefine the nature and content of Britishness. In the present day, the ferment which marks the centre of London makes it possible to imagine identities which are mobile and adaptable, formed by a variety of circumstances in which ethnicity is only one of a list of priorities. Right now, if there's hope for a continent struggling to come to terms with the clash between modernity and tradition, it may rest in London's diversity and adaptability; and if this is a dream, it's also a necessary vision, but London is a city made for dreamers.
>
> (203–4)

This is an admittedly romantic vision of London, however necessary, which does not sit easily alongside recent representations of its heterogeneous population in films such as *Dirty Pretty Things* (2002) or Nirpal Singh Dhaliwal's cynical novel of metropolitan multicultural mélange, *Tourism* (2006). Phillips's vision's hopefulness is perhaps characteristic of – as I have argued elsewhere – the millennial optimism one finds in recent representations of postcolonial London (McLeod 2004); yet the view that the problems of Central Europe can be solved if mainland cities like Prague become more like London perhaps signals Phillips's failure to engage dialogically with other diaspora peoples as well as a familiar appraisal of non-Anglophone contexts via a firmly British framework. Be more like us, Mike Phillips seems to say to other black Europeans, because we'll show you how it's done: our present is your future. Although his conclusion is an important celebration of the agency of diaspora peoples in Britain and makes a vital commitment to the continued struggle against racism across Europe, a mutually informative encounter between oppressed peoples fails to materialize on Mike Phillips's narrated journey. Once again, much is seen but little is discovered. Any such conversations between New World black folks – multilingual, multicultural – remain muted and distinctly monological.

Perhaps a more productive example of fertile engagement between black British and European diasporic experiences can be found in Bernardine Evaristo's recent novel *Soul Tourists* (2005), which depicts the 1987 journey across mainland Europe of two young black Britons,

Stanley Williams and Jessie O'Donnell, who are attempting madly to drive to Australia. Using a literary technique that is formally innovative and freely mixes poetic and prose styles, the central conceit of the novel concerns Stanley's peculiar ability to encounter ghostly presences as he travels across the continent in Jessie's battered jeep. The spectres he meets embody the hidden histories of Europe's black people, and collectively suggest that the presence of black Europeans is central to – rather than a marginal part of – the continent's fortunes. Evaristo's use of the rhetoric of ghosts in her novel of Europe is particularly choice, and its significance can be uncovered by noticing how the postcolonial critique of modernity is figured in terms of the spectral. As Simon Gikandi argues, the fortunes of European modernity secrete the phantoms of Europe's colonial ambitions which in many ways provided modernity with its logics of territorialization and economic expansion, as well as its vocabulary of the self: 'the great categories that came to define the modern age – race and citizenship, civility and authority, for example – were haunted from the start by the colonial question' (Gikandi 1996: 3). Hence, modernity is haunted by 'the hitherto invisible spectre whose presence we have felt around us, whose effectivity we have encountered in the texts of our identity, but whose logic we could not name until now' (3). The 'ghosting of colonialism' (3), as Gikandi terms it, is being exposed at modernity's twilight when the inseparability of metropolis and colony is being laid bare, very much against the wishes of nationalists in Europe. Evaristo's appropriation of the ghostly in her postcolonial European odyssey projects fantastically a shared history of colonial hauntings that transcend singular colonial or national frames. The ghosts which glide through her narrative include Lucy, an African prostitute in Shakespearean London; Nabo, a black dwarf resident at the Palace of Versailles in Revolutionary France; Zaryab, a Mesopotamian Moor exiled to Spain in 821 whose love of music, cuisine and culture helped transform the region; Alessandro de' Medici, the son of an African slave girl and ruler of Florence until his murder at the age of 26; and Mary Seacole, veteran of the Crimean War. The novel begins with a quotation from G. K. Chesterton: 'They say travel broadens the mind, but you must have the mind to travel' (Evaristo 2005: n.p.). Like the previous examples I have looked at, *Soul Tourists* attempts to journey creatively through a continent defined by colonial conquest and yet to come to terms with its legacies of racism and prejudice. However, in a new departure, Evaristo's book requires an intellectual travail and invites its readers to think across and beyond comfortable frames of reference – we must journey in our minds if we wish to engage with a broad vista of experience.

Rather than reaching for an Anglophone frame to make sensible the different experiences of European black folks, *Soul Tourists* seeks to displace British experiences from a position of primacy. And although the novel and its Anglophone characters speak nearly always in English, there is an important cross-pollination between different European legacies which points to a kind of historical multilingualism – one which looks forward to the more radical kinds of exchange, literally multilingual and mutually instructive, that could make possible a distinctly European cosmopolitanism. Evaristo's previous work, especially *Lara* (1997) and *The Emperor's Babe* (2001), explores closely the long history of a black British presence, influenced by Peter Fryer's classic work of history *Staying Power: The History of Black People in Britain* (1984). *Soul Tourists* continues Evaristo's playful and inventive fictional exploration and excavation of hidden histories, but in so doing challenges Britons to discover more than the unarticulated stories of their nation. It is significant that one of her central characters to whom the spectres appear is a black British man, Stanley, who is made to confront the evidence of black people in Europe about whom he clearly knows nothing. Evaristo's fictional strategy enables her to avoid the all-knowing imperious narrative position of Mike Phillips, for example, and also invites her readers to question if a knowledge of black British history is adequate to address the problems of Europe's past and present.

It is also significant that the novel does not end with a return to Britain after enfolding the European mainland within a departure from and return to London – as my earlier examples suggested, some black British writers never really leave a London of the mind even when they travel and look overseas. The 1987 narrative thread of *Soul Tourists* ends with Stanley standing on the shore of the Kuwaiti desert looking towards the Gulf, only months before the Iraqi invasion of Kuwait and the beginnings of Operation Desert Storm mounted by the United States, Britain and other European armed forces. The location of this scene suggests a continuity between the colonial endeavours of the past by European nations and the imperial, global wars of the present that are indebted to the Old World order. Significantly, Stanley refuses to consider a return to Britain. Drawn by the temptations of another life born out of his geographically and historically itinerant experiences, he experiences an epiphany of adventurousness which rejects the provincialism of (black) Britain and faces towards the global problems of the present:

Behind are the oil refineries of Iraq, the endless fields of Turkey and, further back, the vacillating topography of Europe: the A-roads,

autoroutes, autostrada, the freeway that has led me here to this rasp-
ing beach, these waves littered with casually flung diamonds, the
blow torch on my back, turning me a madder red and all else blazing
glitter.

I cannot return home. Perhaps not ever. The mammoth ocean-
going junks are anchored way off. They are waiting for me. Weighed
down with the desert's siphoned blood supply. They know how to
steer down the side of the world without falling off it.

(Evaristo 2005: 280)

At this moment, Stanley is faced with a beatific vision of the possibilities of the world that is at the same time aware of its bloody legacies and
conflicts (more of which will soon erupt in the desert at Stanley's back).
The tone of this passage may well be evidence of the kind of hopeful,
utopian cosmopolitanism upon which I remarked at the beginning of
this essay; the passage points to how new forms of cultural creativity
may well promise, or at least incubate, alternative responses to the New
World order which refuse the imperious logic of First World power and
foreign policy, of which the war in Iraq is perhaps the latest and most
spectacular example. It is also significant that Evaristo seems to regard
an attention to the multifaceted history of Europe's black people as
making possible a form of consciousness which ultimately takes one
beyond Europe, just as her work on black British history has taken her
intellectually and creatively beyond a strictly British frame. In so doing
she perhaps participates in the provincialising of Europe (to borrow
Dipesh Chakrabarty's phrase), although one danger here is that the
untold stories of Europe's black people remain only fleetingly visible as
the novel journeys rapidly along its spectral historical freeways. Yet the
ultimate location of Stanley – looking out to sea with Europe behind
him – suggests a radically different position to that taken by Mike
Phillips, and perhaps shares something in common with the complex
multicultural consciousness which Caryl Phillips has engendered in his
work since *The European Tribe*. On the shore's edge of Kuwait, before the
Gulf, Stanley refuses the comforts of home and opens himself to the
unpredictability of the future: 'I cannot return home. [...] I will be ready
for anything' (Evaristo 2005: 280). His travels have led to important
new discoveries that break beyond a boundary.

Soul Tourists does not end here with Stanley's epiphanic vision of the
Gulf, but concludes back in England in the novel's final ghostly scenario
at the court of King George III, during whose reign the British slave trade
was abolished. The scene features a witty conversation between George

III and his wife, Charlotte of Mecklinburg-Strelitz, Germany, and they reflect upon the fortunes of Britain and its monarchy over the last two hundred years. The scene neatly exposes the many intermarriages between the aristocratic families of Europe which makes a nonsense of geneticist notions of 'pure' English or German blood epitomized by the nobility – of course, 'royal blood' is perhaps the most 'impure' to be found in Europe and the least likely to qualify as guarantor of the presence of a genetic national character, were such things to exist in the first place. Evaristo goes a stage further, however, in also raising the issue of Charlotte's facial appearance that suggests her black ancestry. 'Surely', Charlotte muses, 'it was not my descent from the Moorish line of the Portuguese royal house in the fifteenth century, as some are hypothesising these days? [...] Did not the reason lie closer to home? *Mutti? Papi?* Infidelities and embarrassments swept under the carpet, as usual?' (Evaristo 2005: 285). As well as the suggestion that the British royal family also shares black ancestry with many other Britons, past and present, the novel's concluding scene also has consequences for British forays into Europe. Rather than journeying to the mainland to confirm the primacy of black British experience, Europe might afford Britons the opportunity to make new discoveries that alter their own sense of past history and present concerns. Europe can teach Britain much about itself; the conversation must be dialogic and mutually enabling. There is much that those of us in many European locations can discover about each other and our selves through productive, equitable conversation. The new excitements – intellectual, cultural and political – to be made may well help beckon the kind of adventurous, non-parochial cosmopolitanism that Dabydeen wondered about in 1991.

Of course, the writers whose works I have explored collectively represent only one element or axis in the quest of the non-parochial cosmopolitanism that Evaristo's novel in particular demands. In exploring the ways in which British writers have voyaged into mainland Europe, I have inevitably and quite deliberately focused upon this axis of engagement perhaps at the expense of those textual passages which may move in the other direction, from Frankfurt, or Amsterdam, or Paris to London and Britain. This is partly due to the fact that my research engages primarily with British diasporic writing – and so I choose to make my intervention specifically by exploring such non-parochial models of cosmopolitanism from within an Anglophone postcolonial vantage. In calling my approach specifically a 'negotiation', I have in mind Gayatri Chakravorty Spivak's sense of the term: 'all I mean by negotiation here is that one tries to change something from that one is obliged to inhabit, since one is not working from the outside' (Spivak 1990: 72). In exploring the problematic optics of such writers strategically from *within* the horizon of their visions, this essay has deliberately worked to resource and change, rather than perpetuate, their dynamics.

Beyond the immediate limits of my strategic negotiation, of course, there remains a great deal of work to be done when evaluating how European diasporas have encountered and remarked upon each other in recent years. For example, Mike Phillips's confidence in the multicultural chic of millennial London may be harder to sustain in the light of this remark from Maryse Condé's novel *Histoire de la femme cannibale* (2003):

> quelle ville est plus racist que Londres? Sa reputation de paradis multiculturel est une invention des intellectuals comme Salman Rushdie qui a d'ailleurs émigré aux Etats-Unis [is there a city that is more racist than London? Its reputation as a multicultural paradise is an invention of intellectuals such as Salman Rushdie who, moreover, has emigrated to the United States].
>
> (Condé 2005: 244; translation mine)

Even after taking on board such a cautionary point of view, the task of re-evaluating European diasporas will involve the labour of writers, translators and scholars – in equal measure, perhaps. As we have seen, the kinds of engagements made by diasporic writers from Britain have not always been usefully open to the lessons and languages of other Europeans. While this has been, at times, a challenging matter of translation, the relative lack of translated diasporic accounts of Britain from non-Anglophone sources means that many monolingual English speaking readers and writers may remain oblivious to the visions of others. (This cuts in more than one direction, of course: of all Caryl Phillips's books published to date, *The European Tribe* is the only one which has not been translated into another European language.) Meanwhile, while contemporary postcolonial and diasporic scholarship is becoming increasingly concerned with thinking about Europe as a single, internally various unit, there remains the tendency to compare *national* migrant trajectories with each other, rather than think more solidly across migrant and diasporic visions. For example, the essays in Sandra Ponzanesi and Daniella Merolla's excellent edited collection *Migrant Cartographies: New Cultural and Literary Spaces in Post-Colonial Europe* (2005) maintain a focus on migrant voyages into Europe – Turkish-German, Caribbean-British and African-Dutch – rather than opening up these different trajectories to a more comparative, mutually-informing approach. This essay has attempted to uncover and negotiate some of the problems of remaining too securely within the former, while also acknowledging the significance of such recent initiatives in reading the texts of 'postcolonial Europe'.

There is a lesson to be learned particularly when venturing beyond our predominant languages and cultural contexts. As I have shown, scholars can learn from those black British writers who have attempted to write about Europe and non-Anglophone diasporas, that we must attend with great sensitivity to the diasporic differentials – language, culture, history or resistance – of contemporary Europe. In doing so one avoids using certain conceptual models of diaspora, as well as the knowledge of black British history and culture, as definitive and originary. Remembering Dabydeen's words, as well as the historical examples of Aimé Césaire, C. L. R. James and others, it is perhaps through dialogic encounters (such as the present volume of essays) that we might look ahead more purposefully and learn creatively from the 'new excitements' that are being opened up across Anglophone, Francophone and further versions of postcolonial and diasporic studies.

Bibliography

Ali, M. (2003) *Brick Lane* (London: Doubleday).

Condé, M. (2005 [2003]) *Histoire de la femme cannibale* (Paris: Mercure de France).

Dabydeen, D. (1991) 'On Cultural Diversity' in M. Fisher and U. Owen (eds) *Whose Cities?* (London: Penguin), pp. 97–106.

de Certeau, M. (1984) *The Practice of Everyday Life*, trans. Steven Rendall (Berkeley, CA: University of California Press).

Dhaliwal, N. (2006) *Tourism* (London: Vintage).

Evaristo, B. (2005) *Soul Tourists* (London: Hamish Hamilton).

Gikandi, S. (1996) *Maps of Englishness: Writing Identity in the Culture of Colonialism* (New York: Columbia University Press).

Gilroy, P. (2004) *After Empire: Melancholia or Convivial Culture?* (London: Routledge).

Huggan, G. (2001) *The Postcolonial Exotic: Marketing the Margins* (London: Routledge).

James, C. L. R. (1984) *At the Rendezvous of Victory: Selected Writings* (London: Allison and Busby).

Levy, A. (2004) *Small Island* (London: Headline).

McLeod, J. (2004) *Postcolonial London: Rewriting the Metropolis* (London: Routledge).

Malkani, G. (2006) *Londonstani* (London: Fourth Estate).

Ousmane, S. (1960) *Les bouts de bois de Dieu* (Paris: Le Livre Contemporain).

Phillips, C. (1987) *The European Tribe* (London: Picador).

Phillips, C. (2003) *A Distant Shore* (London: Secker and Warburg).

Phillips, M. (2001) *London Crossings: A Biography of Black Britain* (London and New York: Continuum).

Ponzanesi, S. and Merolla, D. (eds) (2005) *Migrant Cartographies: New Cultural and Literary Spaces in Post-Colonial Europe* (Lanham, MD: Lexington).

Spivak, G. (1990) *The Post-Colonial Critic: Interviews, Strategies, Dialogues* (New York and London: Routledge).

2
Postcolonial Studies in the Context of the 'Diasporic' Netherlands

Elleke Boehmer and Frances Gouda

Introduction

In his recent and much-discussed bestseller *Het land van aankomst* [the country of arrival], the sociologist Paul Scheffer insists that in contemporary public discussions about the 'multicultural drama' generated by the integration of new immigrants, the history of Dutch colonial governance in South East Asia and the Caribbean should play a constitutive role. He writes: 'If we don't reconsider our image of the past and if we don't grant our colonial history a definite space in our collective memory, we violate the truth and distort the historical record' (Scheffer 2007: 183).[1] The long-anticipated publication of *Het land van aankomst* generated an outpouring of critical review and debate in the printed media and television. However, none of the commentators seriously engaged with the irony of Scheffer's title, which alludes to a modernist classic in Dutch literature published in 1935, written by the Indo-Dutch Eduard du Perron, entitled *Het land van herkomst* [the country of origin]. As this suggests, the publication of Scheffer's book potentially might have – yet in the event did not – generated an exploration of the ways in which the Netherlands' history of colonization in South East Asia and the Caribbean is intertwined with the present day.

Scheffer's analysis of the Dutch situation in comparison to the treatment of and attitudes towards foreign immigrants in other European countries and the United States or Australia, touches throughout on the significance of the continuities between the colonial past and the postcolonial present (Van Doorn 1995; Gouda 2007). In a context where such intertwinings are frequently avoided or denied, he formulates a subtle postcolonial and transnational perspective. No matter how remote the colonial period may now appear, he admonishes, Netherlanders should approach hotly contested political issues concerning ethnically 'other' migrants in their society with a critical backwards look towards their past, as well as an ongoing attention to colonial history. The Netherlands, he suggests, should not fail to acknowledge the etiolated yet indelible imprint of its colonial legacies: its history of participating in the trans-Atlantic slave trade; the astronomical profits earned in Java, which financed the infrastructural socio-economic modernity the country enjoyed during the second half of the nineteenth century and beyond; as well as its nineteenth- and early twentieth-century colonial dealings with Islam.

In this essay, we want to address to what extent and how postcolonial perspectives inform contemporary political and academic discussion in the markedly 'diasporic' Netherlands (van Dis 2006; Kopijn 2007). Our primary focus is on the academic analysis and pedagogy of literature. Therefore we want to emphasize from the outset our view that postcolonial practice in this context should be concerned to construct colonial histories not merely as a subsidiary national and transnational backdrop to the study of literary texts. Rather, we suggest, a postcolonial perspective would see colonial history as formative in the making of imaginative literature, and pay particular attention to the construction of critical readings of that literature. Western cultural hegemonies over Asian or African worlds were woven into the very fabric of Europe's literary canons or, as Frantz Fanon powerfully put it, 'the sweat and dead bodies of Negroes, Arabs, Indians and the yellow races have fuelled the [literary] opulence of Europe' (Fanon 1986: 76–81). It is true of course that even in the face of this stark reality, interpretations of the postcolonial – whether as coming after the colonial period or as a critical response present in the first act of colonization – are notoriously divergent. Here we settle for the working definition that in a context of cultural and physical oppression, as described by Fanon, the postcolonial is that which interrogates the colonial master-servant (white/other) relationship – often in the language of the colonizer. The postcolonial embraces critical responses both insidiously oblique and starkly oppositional to the colonial experience.

In the British Isles – as is now widely accepted – the cultural lineages and community memory of the contemporary immigrant population are deeply imbricated in the history of the British Empire (see Nasta 2002; McLeod 2004; and Procter 2000: to cite only three examples). A different – possibly less obviously postcolonial – situation obtains in the Netherlands. Communities designated as 'problematic' in contemporary Netherlands multicultural society – whether Turkish, Moroccan, Croatian or Somali – have few to no cultural traditions or colonial antecedents that provide them with historical points of connection, neither do they have constructed memories of and insights into Dutch culture (as we will show). The result is that the practice of postcolonial criticism, whether in the Netherlands political arena or in academic discourse, does not possess the relatively firm historical base it can in many ways draw upon in either Britain or France. Accordingly, as we will investigate, the critical stance implied in postcolonial literary analysis elsewhere reverberates differently or less loudly in Dutch academic writing and teaching. The lack of fit in terms of history between colonialism then and multicultural society now is taken to explain – and more importantly to justify – a hermeneutic disconnect between concepts drawn from (predominantly Anglophone) colonial discourse theory and the analysis of contemporary diaspora cultures. At the same time, the hegemony of Anglo-American postcolonial and poststructuralist theory, which is sometimes cited as a factor contributing to the lack of fit between diaspora discourse and diaspora-in-practice, is allowed to go unchallenged. So the status of the Netherlands as an ex-colonial power remains unproblematized, and consequently the manner in which the history of colonialism might link up with the formation of contemporary national and migrant identities is left insufficiently examined. Debates – about race, racism and identity in university forums, for example – are not seen to link up in a direct way with conditions in the country at large. Concomitantly, the Netherlands is widely said to lack a home-grown postcolonial critical discourse with which properly to address the experiences of its diasporic populations.

Written jointly by a postcolonial literary critic (Boehmer) and a historian of Dutch empire (Gouda), this essay explores the postcolonial pedagogic landscape at the tertiary level in the 'diasporic' Netherlands through a discussion of Netherlands' colonial legacies and the interpretation of the postcolonial in the Dutch present-day context. We draw on long-standing teaching and research experience in these different – at times overlapping – areas, on our critical perspectives on colonial and migrant discourses, and also on individual observations offered in a questionnaire format by academic colleagues involved in 'postcolonial studies' in the Netherlands (see Appendix). (It is worth noting from the outset that those who chose to respond to our questionnaire did not come exclusively from literary and historical studies, but from gender, media and cultural studies.) Throughout the essay, our contention will be that the critical literatures of the Netherlands' *uneven diasporas* – that is, diasporas lacking a straightforward, colonial relationship to the one-time 'motherland' – represent at best a deeply belated writing, and is in the main a still-virtual discourse awaiting its moment of articulation (on belatedness, see Behdad 1996).

Dutch colonial legacies and the contemporary 'Multicultural Drama'

The Dutch East Indies embodied the prized colonial possession of the Netherlands. The colony was not only a 'prolific Frisian cash cow' – as one of several European commentators labelled it – but it also constituted a source of national pride and served as a model to other colonizing nations (Beaulieu 1872: 293). As the French expert on colonization Georges Henri Bousquet advised his compatriots as late as the 1930s: 'I can't too strongly advise French colonists to go and study Dutch material accomplishments in the Indies on the spot... such investigations could only benefit the French empire' (Bousquet 1940: 119). Bousquet perceived what more recent commentators on the Netherlands multicultural arena have so far failed to acknowledge: the productive critical analogies that may be drawn between colonial (and also postcolonial) contexts. Without its enormous and lucrative empire in South East Asia, the Dutch nation in the modern era would have been little more than an insignificant small European democracy 'on a par with Denmark' (as the popular Dutch platitude has it). From the mid-nineteenth century, the experience and perceived success of the Netherlands in governing the Indies was tied to Dutch national identity. It provided the Dutch nation with its sense of being a *gidsland* (a guiding nation) by displaying nothing but 'superior energy and intelligence in the demanding work of empire' (van Eerde 1914: 54).

Of particular pertinence for the present-day was that this demanding work took place in a predominantly Muslim though multi-ethnic context. The ethnically and culturally diverse population of the former Dutch East Indies was 90 per cent Muslim: the Netherlands colonial regime had therefore ruled over more Muslims than any other European imperialist nation, as has Bousquet indeed observed. In consequence, a reservoir of Orientalist scholarship and political expertise concerning Islamic religion, law and social practices informed Dutch colonial administration in the Indonesian archipelago until the transfer of sovereignty to the independent Indonesian nation took place in late 1949. Moreover – of further relevance to the present-day – the guiding principle of Netherlands colonial mastery had been cultural association or synthesis: a conscious policy designed to maintain the integrity and 'authenticity' of ethnic cultures by adjusting Western norms and forms to local circumstances (Gouda 1995; Stoler 2002). As this implies, colonial civil servants communicated not in Dutch but in Malay or other regional languages with the indigenous elites who were co-opted into the Dutch colonial administration. As late as 1961 A. D. A. de Kat Angelino, a theorist of efficacious colonial governance, hailed this allegedly unique system of cultural synthesis as flowing 'naturally from the lifeblood of the Dutch nation.' He noted: 'only a people who had embraced in their daily lives a variety of autonomous institutions, languages, dialects, religions, sects, mores, habits and customs, dress and architecture, were capable of such an accomplishment' (Baudet and Brugmans 1984: 49). Its embarrassing hyperbole aside, de Kat Angelino's celebration of the 'Dutch' virtues of cultural synthesis and respect for the 'autonomous circles' of distinct cultural and religious groups, has lingered on into the postcolonial era, and into contemporary popular understandings of Dutchness and national identity in the Netherlands (Gouda 1995: 40–1).

Since World War II, the Netherlands is said to have transformed itself from a monolithic colonial nation into a self-proclaimed multicultural society. Successive waves of ethnically diverse immigrants were greeted with the official reassurance – developed from that same laboratory of colonial rule in South East Asia and the Caribbean – that they might integrate into the body politic of the Netherlands on their own terms (Hoving 2005). In other words, in the postcolonial era the so-called Dutch habit of cultivating respect for the unique cultural authenticity and religious traditions of former colonial subjects was formally encouraged and perpetuated, on home ground. This created a civil society in which Islamic schools and religious organizations, for example, were incorporated into the publicly financed network of socio-cultural 'pillars' on a par with traditional Dutch institutions (a kind of separate-but-equal development). Until the late 1990s, Netherlands society continued to celebrate its policies of accommodation, association and cultural synthesis-instead-of-assimilation vis-à-vis Muslim and other non-Christian immigrants, thus underlining the ideological linkages between the colonial past and postcolonial present. However, at the beginning of the new millennium, and certainly since the killing of filmmaker Theo van Gogh, the ideological tenor began to alter (see, for example de Leeuw and van Wichelen 2005 and especially 2007 *passim*). The new era of what Paul Scheffer calls 'the multicultural drama' was inaugurated, in which once-time-honoured notions of respect for otherness were undermined by populist fears of Islamism and its apparent fifth-column presence in the Netherlands.

As in fellow EU countries such as Britain or France, the globalization of the world economy, and the growing transnational mobility of peoples, produced the effect in the Netherlands that a relatively large proportion of the population is of immigrant descent or is itself immigrant. In high-density areas like Amsterdam or Rotterdam close to 40 per cent of people are resident migrants, whereas ethnic minority children in elementary schools in the four major cities – Amsterdam, Rotterdam, The Hague and Utrecht – comprise more than 50 per cent of the student population. In previous decades the Netherlands welfare state projected a well-known if not always well-substantiated reputation for offering shelter and eventually a home to economic and political migrants from a range of countries. Certainly, between 1970 and 1995, the annual number of asylum seekers coming to the Netherlands grew at a steady pace. Even though this trend began to stabilize after 1995 and has even declined during the past five years, the Central Bureau for Statistics in the Dutch nation estimates that between 1972 and 2003 as many as three million foreign immigrants were added to the Dutch population (de Jong 2004).

The prevailing situation of relatively tolerant accommodation was disrupted by a sharp shift to the right in the early twenty-first century, following firstly on an animal rights activist's murder of the populist political candidate Pim Fortuyn in May 2002. The shooting of maverick filmmaker Theo van Gogh on 2 November 2004 by a Muslim extremist further aggravated public anxieties concerning the putative danger represented by 'terrorists' in the Dutch midst, a situation allegedly fuelled by Dutch permissiveness. (Henceforth right-wingers inaugurated the date of Van Gogh's death as the Netherlands' equivalent to '9/11'.) From that point onwards the country began to chart a contested but ineluctable retreat from its vaunted open-door policy. Among the followers of the neo-conservative Partij van de Vrijheid (PVV/Freedom Party, under the controversial leadership of Geert Wilders), these events have given rise to what Australian political scientist Ghassan Hage describes as white anxiety masking as aggressive self-assertion. Fantasies of 'white supremacy' are expressed in self-justificatory refrains of the nature of: 'I-am-white-and-therefore-I-worry-about-the-state-of-my-nation' (Hage 1998, *passim*). The retreat from openness and tolerance has been expressed legally as well as politically. It has led to the introduction of mandatory ID cards in 2005, and produced a far more intensive screening of applications for immigration and asylum. The 'conservative turn' also inaugurated compulsory language and culture classes for all newly arrived, non-Dutch-speaking immigrants.

Despite the fact that these concurrent practices of cultural accommodation and discrimination were self-evidently informed by the Netherlands colonial project, it is striking that, as against conditions in Britain or France, the new immigrants in this case were not former subjects of the (former) empire. This represents the nub of why their experience is deemed resistant to conventional postcolonial analysis. In the Netherlands, as in Germany and the Scandinavian countries, immigration in large numbers began from the 1960s with the influx of unskilled workers from southern Europe and North Africa. It is to their descendants that immigration problems now are seen to relate – in particular they relate to second- and third-generation Turkish and Moroccan immigrants and, to a lesser extent, asylum-seekers from places as diverse as Somalia, Ethiopia, Ghana, the former Yugoslavia and, more recently, Iran, Iraq and Afghanistan. All of these newcomers have little or no previous linguistic or cultural connection with their country of arrival. It is therefore perceived to be complicated to acknowledge the inevitable role that colonial histories play whether in the harmonious or the dissonant integration of these people, and subsequently difficult to insert a postcolonial perspective drawn from a different pedagogic tradition into the public debate. The hypothesis is that Indians and Pakistanis in Britain, or Algerians and Moroccans in France, have an easier time adjusting to their new homeland due to their long-standing familiarity with the political style, social mores and language of their former colonizers. Their funds of usable cultural capital are simply greater. Whereas in Britain and, to a lesser degree in France, debates about colonial legacies engaged by migrant spokespeople have entered the public domain and the academic arena, in the Netherlands, by contrast, questions concerning the 'empire striking back' are not perceived to have a comparable critical purchase.

An important factor contributing to the Netherlands migrant disconnect is grounded in the manner in which the inflow of immigrants from Dutch colonial territories in the East and West Indies has been represented in public culture. Immigrants from the Dutch East Indies who arrived after independence was granted in 1949 and citizens of the Dutch colony Suriname which achieved independence in 1975, are regularly celebrated as successful immigrants: their initial problems with discrimination, social adjustment and unemployment are glossed over (Kopijn 2007). The relative success of 'Indies' and Surinamese immigrants emerges especially prominently when their integration is compared and contrasted with Turkish and Moroccan newcomers who arrived in the Netherlands as guest workers during more or less the same period.

The latter are earmarked as a problematic social group, whose Muslim identity – often defined in an imprecise way – is constructed as a hindrance to their productive adjustment to Dutch society.

It is symptomatic of the disconnect that we are attempting to describe, that what gets lost in the shuffle is the Netherlands political experience of having governed a vast Muslim region in South East Asia for more than three centuries. When the Western press reports on modern Indonesia, the observation 'more Muslims live in Indonesia than in the entire Middle East' will crop up as a kind of truism. In the early twentieth century, this demographic reality prompted Dutch administrators to develop a fund of sophisticated knowledge about Islamic religion, law and social conventions – as we have observed – yet in the treatment of Moroccans and Turks in the present-day Netherlands none of this residual expertise is brought to bear. Netherlands government officials succumb to a wilful blind spot when it comes to Islam. Muslim immigrants are routinely represented as recalcitrant and ominous strangers incapable of accepting the core values of Dutch culture – values with which millions of Muslims in colonial times came into various forms of contact. Moreover, in populist and neoconservative circles they are habitually represented as dangerous freeloaders, who abuse the generosity of the Netherlands welfare state by both their 'idleness' and their (fundamentalist-related) 'ungratefulness'.

In sum, contemporary policy approaches Turkish, Moroccan, African and Middle Eastern immigrants within a recognizable colonialist matrix of segregation disguised as social accommodation ('pillarization'), alongside a promiscuous labelling of difference. Migrants are promised that their 'un-Dutch' religious traditions and social conventions will be safeguarded, thereby recycling the motto of cultural synthesis that sustained colonial rule in Indonesia and in Suriname. Paradoxically, however, new immigrants are simultaneously urged to embrace the Dutch work ethic by integrating as productive, self-reliant citizens. Such representational practices self-evidently reify the cultural distance between 'their/other' and 'real' Dutch civic virtues. So, while Muslim immigrants are often depicted as fully-fledged citizens with equal rights and obligations, they are as frequently portrayed as 'Others' congenitally incapable of mastering the basic lexicon of Dutch cultural norms and values. This contradictory vision – which is itself quintessentially colonialist – distorts a clear-sighted understanding of the continuities between the colonial past and the postcolonial present, and hence circumscribes any appreciation of the relevance for the Netherlands (academy and public sphere) of a postcolonial hermeneutic.

The belatedness of postcolonial studies and the bastion of *Indische Letteren*

Based on information provided by the Central Bureau of Statistics, in 2004 the combined total of first- and second-generation immigrants from the Netherlands' former colonies in South East Asia and the Caribbean was 860,000, comprising 5.3 per cent of the Dutch population. In comparison, in 2004 the combination of first- and second-generation immigrants from other countries in Europe or the Middle East, Asia, Africa and Latin America, comprised a grand total of 2,228,000 people or almost 14 per cent of the total population. These very rudimentary numbers indicate the extent to which a diverse immigrant population from elsewhere overtops the demographic presence of former colonized subjects in the Netherlands.

The Netherlands, in short, presents a situation of extremely heterogeneous diaspora. In comparison with a former colonial power like Britain, migrant conditions are anomalous and, relative to imported postcolonial paradigms, aberrant. There is little equivalent to the situation where the former colonial metropolis draws cultural influences and practitioners from around the world into a dominant yet broadly intelligible 'Europhone' hub. There is also little equivalent to the celebration of a hybridized English or a mongrelized Britishness. Especially given the fact that the British imperial experience is generally taken as definitive for postcolonialism, postcolonial paradigms such as borrowing, mimicry and translation do not attach in the same way. Moreover, even if these or related trends did in fact exist, they have not yet been isolated, defined or theorized as such, *on their own terms*, within academic and critical institutions, as modes of adaptive exchange *particular to* the Netherlands' migrant situation, although also bearing comparison with ex-colonial contexts elsewhere. The situation of anomaly has arguably interrupted or frustrated the creation within the Dutch critical establishment and academe of a home-grown vocabulary through which postcolonial insights might be generated and developed. Postcolonial discussions there certainly are – such as those generated by a small group of literary critics in select academic departments in Leiden, Amsterdam, Utrecht and Nijmegen or as in the Book Week example cited below – but these are framed in borrowed, Anglophone terms, and largely carried on *outside* literature departments, in the cultural pages of newspapers and the domains of cultural studies, under the heading of the investigation of the 'Other'.

At a theoretical level, postcolonial concepts of mimicry and hybridity – as has been widely described in the Anglo-American academy – draw on the language-based approaches of poststructuralism. Therefore a crucial way of accounting for their lack of critical purchase in the Netherlands must be with reference to the absence of linguistic continuities between the one-time colonies, their native élites and the present-day ex-colonial power. As will be made clear below, disruptive slippages of meaning or resistant re-readings simply do not operate in the same way between distinct language groupings as they do between groups with differing yet convergent relations to a shared dominant language.

To expand with reference only to the largest former colony, the erstwhile Dutch East Indies, the Dutch language never displaced Malay as the primary lingua franca of the multiethnic, multilingual Indonesian archipelago at any point during the colonial period. A borrowed or 'chutnified' Nederlands does not therefore form the medium of cultural expression of any social group in Indonesia today.[2] In the archipelago, the Malay language, originating in the coastal regions surrounding the Malaka Straits and eastern Sumatra, has long since been the medium of inter-island trade and communication, binding together commercially and culturally regions colonized by the Dutch, one-time British territories in Malaysia and Burma as well as the Philippines. As a mark of Malay's prominence, even the day-to-day administration of Dutch colonial power was conducted in Malay as well as other regional languages such as Javanese. The colonial state in fact encouraged popular literacy in Malay and regional languages rather than in Dutch, working through the *Balai Pustaka* – a government agency founded in the 1920s designed to increase the publication of Malay translations of classics in Dutch literature. As a result, Dutch as the language of colonial power and prestige was learned by only a small percentage of the native élite. In 1928 a strategic decision of the Indonesian nationalist movement was to proclaim that the lingua franca Malay – rather than the demographically dominant Javanese – would be the mother language of the independent nation of the future. And, during the twilight years of the Dutch East Indies, when a group of multiethnic, self-consciously modernist writers – the *Pujangga baru* (new writers) – began to contemplate the nature of the new 'Indonesian literature', they chose Malay as a medium in order to invoke a hoped-for, inter-ethnic solidarity (Watson 2000, *passim*).

With respect to the Netherlands postcolonial context, therefore, we find no France *d'outre mer* or language hexagon. There is no equivalent to a Commonwealth of Anglophone nations in which colonially educated élites are able to refer back to a repertoire where English school songs, nursery rhymes and well known, canonical poems (Wordsworth's

'Daffodils' poem comes to mind) are held in common. The greater part of the one-time empire does not write back: it has no linguistic over-turning to accomplish and postcolonial concepts of semantic recalci-trance or 'sly civility' inevitably seem imposed and difficult to integrate. The fact that the postcolonial vocabularies to analyse social and cultural processes – like racial marginalization and discrimination – by contrast *do* often relate closely to the Netherlands context, is something that is erased by an overriding appearance of disconnectedness and belat-edness. The erasure is further upheld by a conservative, philological tendency in academic institutions – a tendency that finds no relevance in the seeming a-historicity of postcolonial critical thought, as will again be seen.

Netherlands belatedness is sharply focussed on by a debate that took place in 2001 – on the occasion of the so-called Netherlands Book Week – as is insightfully discussed in a study by the critic Sarah de Mul (2001). As de Mul describes, the Book Week each year takes a particular theme, which, as will be familiar from many contexts, shapes the nature of the readings and the other events organized. Each time, too, a single book published in that year is selected as promotional material, to be sent to sponsors, event convenors, participants and so on. In 2001 the keynote theme was the impeccably postcolonial: 'Het Land van Herkomst: Schrijven tussen twee culturen' / ['Land of ori-gin: Writing between two cultures']. And the accompanying book was Salman Rushdie's *Fury*, translated into Dutch as *Woede* (which was in fact published before *Fury*).

Despite Rushdie's standing as a respected, widely read author in the Netherlands, the selection of his novel as a mascot book provoked heated protest and fierce debate – a debate that continued well beyond the bounds of Book Week. In a nutshell, the contention crystallized around the nature of that quintessential postcolonial concept of 'inbe-tweenness' as it related to the Netherlands. The British-identified, New York resident Rushdie was rightly taken to typify the neither-nor of the diasporic borderline condition, yet the choice of his novel was at the same time perceived to signify an Anglophone, postcolonial hegemony. That is, its nomination again implied – through no fault of Rushdie's of course – a belatedness to the Dutch postcolonial condi-tion. 'Where was the Dutch instance of "inbetweenness", of writing between cultures?' commentators asked. Rushdie's novel had been set up as representing a mode of metropolitan yet postcolonial authority, a gold standard against which the diasporic expression of a smaller, once-colonial nation, conversant in a minority European language, was being forced to measure itself; inevitably, to appear as lacking by contrast. Netherlands writing of the in-between was, ironically, 'not quite' right, not definitively borderline. As one critic put it, migrant writers in Dutch suffered from having to respond to the wrong sort of colonizers – less influential, less globally hegemonic. They were doubly disadvantaged, both by the marginality of the Netherlands colonial condition and by their marginality to postcolonial writing in English.

The Book Week debate raised interesting questions concerning the image of the Netherlands nation and nationality: how definitions of Dutchness or Netherlands identity (not necessarily the same thing) were impacted alternately by foreign and by home-grown postcolonial work; how such identities were shaped by multicultural and migrant productions (in this case, novels). The discussion had recourse to a perceptibly nationalist concept of a homogeneous Netherlands culture and literary tradition, to which migrant writers in Dutch belonged, or belonged to a certain extent – or more self-evidently than did Rushdie. As the critic Danilo Verplancke put it:

> Was er now echt geen andere keuze te maken? Mischien één die dichter bij het Nederlandse klimaat staat? Desnoods een die eventueel niet in het Nederlands schrijft, maar er wel tenminste woont en bekend is met een beeld van ons land. [Could no other choice have been made? Of a writer who at least stands a little closer to the Netherlands atmosphere or climate? If necessary one who does not perhaps write in Dutch, but who is familiar with the image of our country.]
>
> (de Mul 2001)

Would the selection of multicultural writing as a Book Week theme not have been an appropriate occasion, asked a third commentator, Roland Fagel, to champion a migrant writer working in the Netherlands language? In this there was the interesting implicit admission that the Netherlands merited the appellation 'postcolonial', at least at the level of embracing a sufficiency of 'in-between' writers.

As this suggests, the linguistically interrupted, historically anomalous 'Netherlands postcolonial' represents a far from established terrain: it is in fact, we submit, something curiously defensive and undefined. Who are its authors? Who are its critics? It is not easy to tell – even in our own experience – from the course reading lists submitted by our questionnaire respondents. Names like Hafid Bouazza (a Moroccan-origin Dutch novelist), Ayaan Hirsi Ali (the Somali-origin activist) and Mieke Bal (the cultural critic), are cited but remain in the minority relative to the more usual Anglophone suspects – Said, Spivak, Bhabha, Loomba, Huggan, McClintock and Hall. Among critics and teachers there would appear to be a shared preoccupation with migrant subjectivity, with what it is to be marginal and lack a recognized voice. Yet this exists side-by-side with a concern to escape from a condition of theoretical and writerly after-effect, or, within a differently post-colonial space, of offering little more than a reiteration of the already-known.

On one level, to be sure, as the very term belatedness suggests, the situation may be differently interpreted. The borrowed landscape of post-colonial criticism in Dutch and in the Netherlands adds a potentially interesting further level of translation to the epistemological frameworks through which the postcolonial is generally understood. Postcolonial writing is famously a liminal writing, composed of metaphors that have historically been 'borne across': articulated through layers of cultural and linguistic translation. In the Netherlands context the multiply translated condition of postcolonial writing is arguably especially prominent, or unavoidable, in that postcolonial critical discourse is largely undertaken, and conceived of, through the medium first and foremost of the English language and must therefore be translated. What might seem from one point of view as a restrictive commitment to an Anglocentric focus, could equally be regarded as an invitation to examine the transmission and translatedness of critical discourse itself, while also propagating the further adaptation of postcolonial terminologies. A further frame of transfer and translation is added on to the discussion of writing that is always-already seen as migrant, carried across and borrowed.

To date however this potential for the flexible adaptation of post-colonial terms has not been mobilized. Instead, postcolonialism's 'translatedness' in the Netherlands context is allowed to get in the way of applying critical insights imported from academic debates elsewhere to the country's untypical diasporic cultural materials. The situation is of a piece with the noticeable paucity in Dutch literary and cultural studies of an independent, home-grown critical discourse of otherness, *allochtoon* minority and so on, as well as of a discourse of national identity of what comprises Dutchness. With Mieke Bal, Isabel Hoving, Ieme van der Poel and Pamela Pattynama as clear exceptions, the frequently cited names are, as was seen, derived from Anglo-American and French cultural criticism. Obviously we are dealing here with an instance of the cultural cringe of a self-perceived small country. Yet perceptions of a derivative local postcolonial field have as an inevitable consequence the embedding of a certain academic parochialism – as reflected in the Book Week commentator's abject plea for a writer 'who stands closer to the Netherlands atmosphere or climate'. Under such conditions adaptive yet innovative postcolonial re-readings tend not to be quickened into being. Moreover, a licence is given to those in the academy hostile to postcolonialism – due to its lack of empirical specificity or borrowed culturist paradigms – to dismiss its hermeneutic richness with regard to colonial representation or its interventions in the study of migrant subjectivity.

In order to move on to what this institutional resistance in fact entails, we venture a provisional summary. The wholesale import of a postcolonial critical vocabulary into the Netherlands academy is, as has been intimated, circumscribed for several overlapping reasons. First, as suggested, postcolonialism based on the British imperial experience is seen to disregard the insights that Dutch diasporic and nominally postcolonial writing might offer – in that it is unable to respond to the historical and linguistic anomalies of the Netherlands ex-colonial context. Furthermore, as some of our questionnaire's respondents suggested, students and even academics in many tertiary institutions are sufficiently convinced of the success of the multicultural experiment in the Netherlands to fail to see how postcolonial concepts of cultural difference and otherness, say, might relate to their day-to-day reality. That is to say, their context is perceived to lack postcoloniality.

In departments of Dutch specifically, there remains a strong tendency to refuse to accept postcolonial perspectives on any terms. This tendency emerges in particular from scholars of Indies writing, a coterie identified with the journal *Indische Letteren*, whose intellectual antecedents lie in philology, and whose concerns with colonial *belletrie* are noticeably moved by a defensive nostalgia that expresses at times as anti-Foucaultian empiricism. Their remarkable point of view is that writing of the Netherlands colonial experience in Dutch, even that produced today, is strictly speaking a colonial writing (informed by the historical and linguistic hiatus described in this and the previous section). The colonial experience as articulated in Dutch represents a period frozen in time: a reality that does not recede. Especially for those who are more than merely baffled by postcolonial questions, there can be no possibility of writing back or sly civility, by definition, as the idea of the non-colonial writer who deals in colonial experience is an impossibility (d'Haen 2002: 7–29).

Then again, it must be conceded that in departments of Dutch in the Netherlands there is at least some consideration given to colonial representation. In departments of English literature, by contrast, outside Conrad criticism, postcolonial scholars and teachers are conspicuous by

their absence. Yet this is in a country where most students are techni-
cally bilingual English-Nederlands, and therefore, potentially at least,
sensitive to the issues of border crossing that postcolonialism raises,
and sufficiently confident of their proficiency in English, too, to explore
beyond canonical boundaries. In the Netherlands, it is clear that literature is regarded as closely involved in unitary constructions of the
nation (whether Britain, France or the Netherlands) – constructions
from which the colonial experience is evacuated. Against this backdrop
it is significant that, to the knowledge of the writers, the Netherlands
does not at this point in time have formal involvement as a participating country in the European Association of Commonwealth Literature
and Language Studies (EACLALS), which is part of worldwide ACLALS.
EACLALS remains for all its old-fashioned entitling as one of the primary forums within which postcolonial literary discussion is held
within Europe and across the globe. When weighed against the active
participation of Germany, France, Spain, Italy, Denmark, Belgium as
well as Britain, Dutch non-membership is revealing of some form of
institutional resistance. Also revealing is that most of the colleagues in
literary studies in the Netherlands whom we approached with our short
questionnaire, did not respond.

Postcolonial pedagogy in the Netherlands

In this section we move to relate our somewhat speculative and gener-
alizing observations above, to specific findings raised by the questionnaire on postcolonial teaching we put to a number of Netherlands
academics with experience of tertiary education in the humanities –
specifically in literary, language and cultural studies. The questionnaire
set out to discover, as the covering letter put it, whether postcolonial
studies 'remains poorly supported institutionally, and marginalized as
a literary discipline'. Of the 25 questionnaires sent out, there were nine
respondents, of which one was a Dutch postcolonialist currently working outside the Netherlands, while another was a freelance writer and
critic. Their findings were combined with observations from a postdoctoral student of comparative literature, and anecdotal verbal remarks
gleaned from an academic with a history of teaching in the Netherlands
currently also working outside the country.

Our survey found that postcolonial critical discourses tended to be
widely taught as part of gender and cultural studies, seemingly on
the basis of the analogy that both gender and postcolonial perspectives
are perspectives on forms of difference. Several colleagues had some

background in comparative literary studies, but had moved away from this discipline in order, it seemed, to work more freely with critical theoretical approaches. The postdoctoral student described being introduced to postcolonial issues ('intersectionality', migrant writing) in eye-opening ways in a department of gender studies. Novels by, especially, women writers from other cultures (Mariama Ba, Jamaica Kincaid) were universally regarded by the respondents as sensitizing students to experiences of otherness, though, interestingly, such experiences were generally seen as taking place away from home, in other countries. Nearly all the respondents remarked on this in one or other form.

Although the pedagogic focus of the respondents tended to be on race, difference and minority discourses, most commented that little more attention than a seminar or two was paid in the courses on which they taught to the Netherlands diaspora as such. For this they blamed institutional and course structures. Netherlands postcolonial topics generally featured in their curricula in a comparative frame, alongside examples drawn from other postcolonial areas: they tended not to be addressed in and for themselves. Equal prominence was given to film texts and life-writing as to literary texts as instances of key postcolonial issues. The situation that emerged corresponded to that schematized by Isabel Hoving in 2004 where she outlined two 'postcolonial' approaches in the Netherlands academy. The first, as we have also noted, arose out of a traditional Orientalist philology, with its focal point in Leiden, which claimed intense faithfulness to the historical record and to indigenous cultural perspectives, to which it deemed itself uniquely privy through linguistic knowledge. The second was a more critical theoretical group that allied itself to cultural studies perspectives as developed within the Anglo-American academy.

Yet, from the evidence of the questionnaire, even this receptive second group had not taken significant steps to adapt their borrowed approaches in a sustained way to diasporic postcolonial conditions in the Netherlands itself – to look at representations of Islam past and present, for example, or at examples of cultural 'inbetweenness'. Their seminar discussions – arguably unlike that of the first group – were not informed by work on the ground. Although the postcolonial teaching of the second group raised topics of multiculturalism and race, it did not as often raise its critical accompaniment, that is, questions of the nation, national identity and narratives of the colonial past. Where there was discussion of Dutchness it appeared that this was rarely tied to debates on the Netherlands' status as an ex-colonial power. As one respondent observed, in response to Mieke Bal's caustic theorization of the patronizing Zwarte Piet (Black Peter) tradition in Netherlands culture, students were resistant, 'simply [refusing] to see this tradition as other than innocent play' (Bal 2002).

Against this, the freelance respondent outside the academy wrote that a foremost aim in her work was to demonstrate that migrant writers were 'part of the national history too'. Concurring, another respondent sought in her classes – at least in principle – to demonstrate the 'deconstruction of the Dutch canon as merely white and univocal Dutch'. We are committed to 'embedding' theories in the location and context of teaching, said yet another. These remarks illustrated something of Hoving's own bracing analysis of Dutchness, which she sees posited as an empty and excessive ideal of openness, cited by Dutch citizens as 'an impassable obstacle to integration' (Hoving 2005). If this is taken as true, however, then the power of migrant writing must be that, like developer fluid in photography, it casts into relief the boundedness as opposed to the openness of Netherlands society. As this might suggest, it is from Dutch diaspora writing that new concepts of belonging, divided identity, resistant emotion, relationality and even Dutchness can be subversively drawn.

To close with a provocation, we suggest that it is in the Netherlands' heterogeneous diasporic writing – many-tongued, palimpsestic, only jaggedly connected to the former colonial project – that the deep belatedness of the Dutch postcolonial condition might prolifically and tumultuously generate new meanings. So newness enters the world: generated out of the anomalous, noisy and unlikely Netherlands of the multiply translated migrant condition.

Appendix

QUESTIONNAIRE, by Elleke Boehmer and Frances Gouda. 5 November 2007.

[Our thanks to those who responded, several of whom preferred to remain nameless]

1. Please describe your academic discipline. (1–2 lines)
2. Within the remit of your discipline, which postcolonial approaches do you teach, and/or which theorists and writers?
3. In which language or languages do you teach postcolonial material? And under which subject headings (as defined by your institution)?
4. At which level (undergraduate, masters, postgraduate) do you tend to introduce postcolonial perspectives to students?
5. Do you teach Neerlandophone counterparts (Bourassa, Buruma) alongside or as well as Anglophone or Francophone writers and theorists?
6. If so, which writers and theorists?
7. What kinds of resistance if any have you encountered whether in structures or in students to teaching postcolonial writers and approaches? Please describe fully.

If your experience has been without resistance, please describe your situation fully also.
8. Would you say that the coverage of theories and approaches relating to race and racism, migration, identity and nationalism within your department or institution relates to or bears correspondence with conditions in the country at large?

Notes

1. Translations are ours throughout, unless stated otherwise.
2. A situation more comparable to that of English in India operates in Suriname, in the positioning of Dutch, the one-time language of colonial administration, vis-à-vis Sranantongo, the Surinamese creole.

Bibliography

Bal, M. (2002) *Travelling Concepts in the Humanities* (Toronto: University of Toronto Press).

Baudet, H. and Brugmans, I. J. (eds) (1984) *Balans van beleid. Terugblik op de laatste halve eeuw van Nederlands-Indie 1961* (reprint Assen: Van Gorcum).

Beaulieu, P. L. (1872) *De la colonization chez les peoples modernes* (Paris: Privately published, 1872).

Behdad, A. (1996) *Belated Travelers: Orientalism in the Age of Colonial Dissolution* (Durham, NC: Duke UP).

Boehmer, E. (2005) *Colonial and Postcolonial Literature: Migrant Metaphors*, 2nd edition (Oxford: Oxford University Press).

Bousquet, G. H. (1940 [1939]) *A French View of the Netherlands Indies* (trans. New York: Institute of Pacific Relations).

d'Haen, T. (2002) 'Inleiding' in T. d'Haen (ed.) *Europa Buitengaats: Koloniale en postkoloniale literaturen in Europese talen* (Amsterdam: Bert Bakker), pp. 7–29.

de Jong, A. (2004) *Schatting aantal westerse en niet-westerse allochtonen in de afgelopen dertig jaar* (Centraal Bureau voor de statistiek, 2004): www.cbs.nl/nl.NL/menu/themas/bevolking/publicaties/artikelen/archief/2003. Date accessed: 9 May 2008.

de Kat Angelino, A. D. A. (1984 [1961]) 'De ontwikkelingsgedachte in het Nederlands overzees bestuur' in H. Baudet & I. J. Brugmans (eds) *Balans van beleid. Terugblik op de laatste halve eeuw van Nederlands-Indië* (Assen: Van Gorcum), pp. 28–49.

de Leeuw, M. and van Wichelen, S. (2005) '"Please, Go Wake Up!": Submission, Hirsi Ali and the "War on Terror" in the Netherlands', *Feminist Media Studies*, 5.3, 325–40.

de Leeuw, M. and van Wichelen, S. (2007) 'Transformations of "Dutchness": From Happy Multiculturalism to the Crisis of Dutch Liberalism' in G. Delanty, P. Jones and R. Wodak (eds) *Identity, Belonging, and Migration* (Liverpool: Liverpool University Press), pp. 261–78.

de Mul, S. (2001) 'De Nomade ontwapend: De politiek van het nomadisme in *Woede* van Salman Rushdie en de pragmatiek van de institutionalisering in de Nederlandse Boekenweek 2001: "het land van herkomst: schrijven tussen twee kulturen"' (unpublished MA thesis: University of Antwerp).

Fanon, F. (1986 [1961]) *The Wretched of the Earth*, trans. Constance Farrington (London: Penguin, 1986).

Gouda, F. (1995) *Dutch Culture Overseas: Colonial Practice in the Netherlands Indies 1900–1942* (Amsterdam: Amsterdam University Press).

Gouda, F. (2007) 'Gender en Etniciteit, gisteren en vandaag' in E. Geudekker, F. Gouda (guest editor), S. Poldervaart, K. Steenbergh and A. Tijsseling (eds) *Gemengde Gevoelens: Gender, Etniciteit en (Post)Kolonialisme. Jaarboek voor Vrouwengeschiedenis no. 27* (Amsterdam: Aksant), pp. 7–31.

Hage, G. (1998) *White Nation: Fantasies of White Supremacy in a Multicultural Society.* (Sydney: Pluto Press).

Hart, J. (2003) *Comparing Empires: European Colonialism from Portuguese Expansion to the Spanish-American War* (Basingstoke: Palgrave Macmillan).

Hoving, I. 'Circumventing Openness: Creating New Senses of Dutchness' in *Transit. Migration, Culture and the Nation-State*, 1.1 (2005): http://repositories. cdlib.org/ucbgerman/transit/vol1/iss1/art50909. Date accessed: 9 May 2008.

Hoving, I. (2004) '"Niets dan het heden": Over Jamaica Kincaid, de postkoloniale literatuurstudie, en wat er van ons terecht moet komen' in M. van Kempen, P. Verkruisse and A. Zuiderweg (eds) *Wandelaar onder de palmen: Opstellen over koloniale en postkoloniale literatuur en cultuur* (Leiden: KITLV), pp. 15–28.

Kopijn, Y. (2007) 'Duizend-en-één verhalen van een nacht: Representaties en interpretaties van Indische vrouwelijkheid' in E. Geudekker, F. Gouda (guest editor), S. Poldervaart, K. Steenbergh and A. Tijsseling (eds) *Gemengde Gevoelens. Gender, Etniciteit en (Post)Kolonialisme. Jaarboek voor Vrouwengeschiedenis no. 27* (Amsterdam: Aksant, 2007), pp. 107–133.

Maussen, M. (2006) *Ruimte voor de Islam? Stedelijk beleid, voorzieningen, organisaties* (Apeldoorn/Antwerp: Het Spectrum).

McLeod, J. (2004) *Postcolonial London: Re-writing the Metropolis* (London: Routledge).

Nasta, S. (2002) *Home Truths: Fictions of the South Asian Diaspora in Britain* (Basingstoke: Palgrave Macmillan).

Procter, J. (2000) *Writing Black Britain* (Manchester: Manchester University Press).

Scheffer, P. (2007) *Het land van aankomst* (Amsterdam: De Bezige Bij).

Stoler, A. L. (2002) *Carnal Knowledge and Imperial Power: Race and the Intimate in Colonial Rule* (Berkeley: University of California Press).

(2006) Symposium van de Stichting Koninklijk Paleis Amsterdam, *Nederlands buitengaats; een taalreünie* (Amsterdam: Stichting Koninklijk Paleis).

van Dis, A. (2006) 'Vrijtaal', *Optima literair tijdschrift*, 21.4: 5–9.

van Doorn, J. A. A. (1995) *Indische lessen: Nederland en de koloniale ervaring* (Amsterdam: Bert Bakker).

van Eerde, J. C. (1914) *Koloniale volkenkunde: eerste stuk: Omgang met inlanders* (Amsterdam: De Bussy).

van Herten, M. and Otten, F. (2007) 'Naar een nieuwe schatting van het aantal Islamieten in Nederland' (Den Haag: Centraal Bureau voor Statistiek): www. cbs.nl/nl.NL/menu/themas/bevolking/publicaties/artikelen/archief/2007. Date accessed: 9 May 2008.

Watson, C. W. (2000) *Of Self and Nation: Autobiography and the Representation of Modern Indonesia* (Honolulu: University of Hawai'i Press).

3
Transcultural Encounters in Contemporary Art: Gender, Genre and History

Siobhán Shilton

Postcolonial studies of diaspora have tended to privilege literary genres, or have often evaded the question of genre entirely. Anglophone scholarship has only recently attended to visual works emerging from primarily British diasporic contexts (See Hall 1990; Lloyd 2001; Mercer 1994; Mirzoeff 2001). However, Francophone postcolonial studies – despite an emerging interest in film – reveals a marked absence of criticism focusing on the visual arts.[1] This chapter aims to address this absence by comparing work in different visual genres by artists living in French diasporic contexts.

Specifically, the chapter will focus on two Paris-based artists whose work articulates gendered versions of what Avtar Brah terms 'diaspora space' in particular cross-cultural contexts. Majida Khattari (b. Erfoud, Morocco, 1966) designs *vêtements-sculptures* ('dress-sculptures') inspired by diverse types of *hijab*, which she then presents in *défilé-performances*, performances which take the form of fashion catwalks. The multi-sensorial experiences she creates draw on 'Western' art forms and fashions, which are combined with music, dance and crafts from a range of 'Arab' cultures. By contrast, Marjane Satrapi (b. Rasht, Iran, 1969) is a graphic novelist best known for *Persepolis* (2000-03), an autobiographical work which depicts her upbringing in the context of the Iranian Revolution and the Iran/Iraq War, the four years she spent in Austria and her return to Iran. While her juxtaposition of text and image recalls, at times, the Persian art of miniature, *Persepolis* engages primarily with an emerging strand of *bande dessinée* (the French term for comics, literally 'drawn strip').

The work of Khattari and Satrapi – along with that of artists such as Zoulikha Bouabdellah (b. 1977, Algeria), Zineb Sedira (b. 1963, France), Shirin Neshat (b. 1957, Iran) and Ghada Amer (b. 1963, Egypt) – reflects the generic heterogeneity and the cultural specificity of work depicting

56

women who originate in cultures which have often been constructed and amalgamated in the Western imagination as 'Oriental', and indeed 'Arab'. The work of these diverse artists in a range of media – including photography, video, installation, performance and *bande dessinée* – highlights regional and local specificities such as Persian or Berber languages and heritages[2]; it also indicates distinct histories of relations with Europe and the US. This wide-ranging artwork reveals a common aim to challenge both neocolonial and patriarchal attempts to impose identities upon women, and to articulate the specificity and complexity of postcolonial female identities.[3]

Art that renegotiates the relationship between cultures in ways that avoid attempts either to unify or hierarchize them might be characterized specifically as 'transcultural'. In contrast to the aim of colonial traveller-painters or writers such as Delacroix or Pierre Loti, the objective of the artist or writer who travels metaphorically and/or literally 'between' cultures is not to exoticize an 'other' culture, in the sense of positing the 'other' as irremediably different. Art and literature depicting immigrants and their descendants most frequently reveals the protagonist's aim to be integrated into a dominant culture without abandoning his or her culture of origin. Within much French political rhetoric, 'integration' emerges as a one-way process of assimilation. However, in accordance with Mary Louise Pratt's definition of 'transculturation', many immigrants and their descendants aim to select and adapt elements of 'metropolitan' culture (1992: 6). Pratt's analysis of colonial encounters reminds us that subjugated peoples determine to varying extents what they absorb into their culture and how they use it. She equally emphasizes that the 'metropole' may be determined by the 'periphery'.[4] 'Transcultural' art, whether or not it focuses on the artist, depicts any cultural encounter as a two-way or *multi*directional process of reciprocal, non-hierarchical influence and exchange.

While the process of transculturation – both as social phenomenon and as aesthetic strategy – can occur in a range of 'contact zones', this chapter will focus on specific instances of its emergence as an aspect of postcolonial diasporic art. The demonstration of exchange, but also of resistance, between the multiple distinctive cultures to which the artist is affiliated emerges partly in response to reductive mainstream perceptions – particularly of women – in countries such as Iran and Morocco, as well as their diasporic communities in France. Both Khattari and Satrapi pose a challenge to rigid constructions of female identity in their culture of origin and in the diaspora, a challenge which is partly enabled by their multiple viewpoints: their indication of the process of exchange between porous cultures – as well as their emphasis on the subjective, sexual, travelling female body – disrupt patriarchal attempts to preserve a cohesive identity of which 'woman' is posited as the guardian.

Transculturation emerges at the level both of content and form. In specific cultural contexts, and in divergent ways dependent upon the exigencies of their chosen medium, the work of Khattari and Satrapi engages with, and contests, a range of 'Western' and 'non-Western' art forms and cultural references. Corresponding with Pratt's emphasis on selection and adaptation, they hold disparate elements in tension, rather than hybridizing or fusing them; reflective of cultural identities in perpetual states of 'becoming', such elements are endlessly combined and re-combined (Hall 1990: 225). In this way, they also recall what Jean Fisher (following Marcos Becquer and José Gatti 1991) has characterized as the 'syncretic turn' – to distinguish such practices from 'hybridity' and the resolution of contradictions that this term implies (Fisher 2006: 233–41). In the work of both artists, the cross cultural spectators/readers are drawn into what might be called a 'transcultural encounter', becoming aware of their own role in the construction and reconstruction of identities.

In addition to countering both neocolonial and patriarchal discourses, both Khattari and Satrapi emphasize women's corporeal presence and agency. Rather than avoid the difficulties inherent in depicting women who have often been referred to as 'doubly' alienated (see Mohanty 1988), both artists confront the problem of how to 'represent the unrepresentable' (Salloum 2001: 358). Zineb Sedira quotes this phrase to refer specifically to the problems involved in representing the veil (Sedira 2003: 58). Both Khattari and Satrapi deal with veiling: re-using what, in Europe and the US, has become an overdetermined sign – a 'visual shorthand' (Donnell 2003: 122) – to indicate variously, and contradictorily, exoticism, oppression, fanaticism or (in France) anti-Republicanism.[5] However, both artists demonstrate – in relation to particular cross-cultural, postcolonial contexts – that it is possible to re-present women without reifying stereotypes. A comparison of their works across cultures and genres will highlight the dissonance – yet also the interrelatedness – of postcolonial feminist agendas.

Representing the unrepresentable: Majida Khattari's *Défilé-Performances*

While adopting the convention of the fashion catwalk, Majida Khattari's *défilé-performances* are staged as exhibitions within art venues. Her first performance took place in June 1996, at the *ENSBA* (*École nationale supérieure des beaux-arts*) at an open day following the artist's graduation from this Paris art college. She has since staged two new such perform-ances, at the Pompidou Centre in July 2001 within the context of the annual arts festival *Paris quartier d'été*, and again at the *ENSBA* in July 2004, as well as presenting variations on all three performances in diverse locations in France and in Britain (as part of the touring INIVA exhibi-tion 'Veil', 2003). In this essay I will focus primarily on her first *défilé* of 1996. Khattari designs what she calls *vêtements-sculptures*, which she then presents in performances that take the form of fashion catwalks. The dresses are inspired by different types of *hijab* and are designed to restrict or emphasize bodily movement. The non-professional performers animate or 'perform' the *vêtements-sculptures*, highlighting the restric-tive or liberating qualities of the forms and materials employed through the use of action, gesture and facial expression, while also interacting with the spectators as they move up and down the 'catwalk'. They are accompanied by music from France and a broad range of Arab countries.

The idea to design dresses which demonstrate the situation of women in contemporary Islam came to the artist in 1995, during debates surround-ing the headscarf in France. Khattari's aim was to provide a counterpoint to narrow (particularly French) perceptions of the veil:

> There has been a lot of talk about the Islamic headscarf, the veil and the tchador [...] There has been a particular tendency to dramatise, but not to attempt to look more closely and to understand what lies behind it. I have tried to put this vision into material form to bet-ter understand the complexity of the issue at the same time as the ambiguity of the veil and of the gaze brought to bear on the body of women in the Arab and Muslim world.
>
> (Khattari, 1997a: 12; translation mine)[6]

However, the artist's critique is aimed not only at the West, but at restric-tions imposed upon women in the name of religion: 'I am a Muslim liv-ing in France, I adhere to Islam, but I am absolutely against repressive uses of faith and ignorance (55% illiteracy in Morocco) in all theocratic regimes' (Khattari 1999: 41). Khattari's work counters different types of extremism and attempts to widen the debate by going beyond the headscarf polemic: 'I am neither for nor against, I want to demonstrate the possibility of a third way' (Khattari 2004: 1). By complicating and continually renegotiating the relationship between cultures and gen-ders, the *défilé-performances* destabilize both neocolonial and patriarchal attempts to polarize and hierarchize them.

Plate 3.1   'Robe serpent' with audience – 60 © Majida Khattari

This 'double' critique is characteristic of literary works depicting women of Maghrebi descent in a French diasporic context. Such works constitute a testimony to the difficulties experienced by these women while also disrupting attempts to impose static identities upon them both in the Maghreb and in the diaspora. Literature by writers such as

Leïla Houari and Faïza Guène shows that in certain Maghrebi families in Belgium and France the patriarchal imperative to separate genders is inextricably tied to an attempt to separate French and Muslim cultures (Shilton 2007). In these narratives, expressions of the protagonist's sexuality – along with her individuality and freedom of movement – are a threat to the cultural cohesiveness that the authoritarian father strives to preserve. Female sexuality is perceived in Islam as dangerously active (Mernissi 1975). As I will show, Khattari's visual work diverges from literary representations, while it similarly indicates the instability of cultures by challenging the separate gendered spaces central to Muslim societies (Mernissi 1975). The artist's adoption of the genre of performance art allows an emphasis on the actual body: its physicality, mobility and sexuality, in real time, for these postcolonial feminist purposes.

The performance is a highly provocative, ambivalent 'game' of veiling and unveiling, concealing and revealing, which draws the spectator in only to abruptly subvert their expectations. The predominantly French, art-going public for whom it is staged is presumably surprised, unsettled or amused – but also disconcerted – when observing the ambiguity cultivated around a sign which they thought they knew and understood. A contemporary review from a Francophone magazine aimed at the Maghrebi diaspora in France suggests that the performance has a similarly disturbing effect on members of this community (Khattari 1997a).

The dresses come in a range of colours, from muted tones to bright blue and neon pink, countering the recurrent image of the black tchador, and exacerbating what is perceived in France and other European countries, as the excessive visibility of the veil. Some are cumbersome forms that hide the contours of the body and restrict the performer's movement as in 'Kacha' (covering), 'La Robe serpent' or 'La Robe boulets' where the garment is weighed down by metal balls chained to the hem. Others are skin-tight costumes which, in some cases, constrain the body, as in 'Makane Makhdoude' (or 'Espace limité'): a bright blue velvet costume which covers all but the face, and lacks sleeves or leg room, as the performer's exaggerated walk emphasizes. In other cases they highlight freedom of movement and seductiveness: in 'Le Tchador moulant', the black tchador becomes a figure-hugging, veil-less dress with triangular spikes emerging from its seams. Seduction is combined ironically with potential danger; the spikes imply an assertive (penetrative) sexuality that questions stereotypes of the passive, conservative or sexually timid Muslim woman. While certain performances evoke uneasiness in the spectator, others provoke amusement. The performer, who wears black platform shoes, exaggerates a seductive walk and smile, and engages the audience with a beckoning finger just before leaving the stage.[7]

The performance foregrounds the ambiguous position of the Muslim woman, situated between the sacred, the seductive and the threatening. 'Mahjouba', or 'La Robe Sacrée', is a black tchador over a cubic form alluding to the *Kaaba* (the central, and most sacred, point of Mecca), worn by an unveiled model. Around the cube is a green band with an Arabic inscription in gold Islamic calligraphy. The use of Arabic is meant to alienate French spectators, most of whom will not be able to read the language. The work also challenges patriarchal relations in its combination of the art of Islamic calligraphy (traditionally practised by men) and the unveiled female body, given that traditional Islamic art forbids figuration and that certain Muslim societies forbid the circulation of unveiled women in the public sphere. This dress challenges attempts to posit women as sacred by representing that which it is forbidden to represent. For those who can read Arabic, this further transgression becomes clear; it is a phrase from the great mystic Hallaj, which says 'Glory be to the one who has hidden [women] from name, fantasy and representation'. Khattari's use of calligraphy to resist the Western spectator's desire to know and dominate the 'other' recalls that of Iranian-born artist Shirin Neshat, who overlays photographs of veiled women with – in her case – Persian female-authored poetry.

The dresses are ambiguously suffocating or protective. This ambiguity in the costumes' function is dramatized by the performance of the 'Robe serpent', in which the performer (enveloped in a bright orange phallic shape made of satin, which narrows above her head) battles frantically to escape, her arms and head emerging alternately from the narrow opening at the top of the object. While the woman's body is hidden by the 'sculpture', its contours can be imagined through exaggerated actions, which begin with circular hip movements, characteristic of a belly dance, before turning into desperate convulsive movements as she struggles to throw herself out of this protective/suffocating cocoon. While the belly dancing movements ambiguously posit the hidden woman as object, her attempts to escape, or to shed this chrysalis, can be seen as a metaphor for the woman as emerging subject.

The dramatic tension intensifies with the dress named 'Sésame, ouvre-toi', a reference to *Ali Baba and the Forty Thieves* (part of *The Book of a Thousand and One Nights*), a text steeped in exoticism in the Western imagination. The performer – whose face is covered by a black veil, contrasting with her heavily padded and rounded orange velvet dress – pulls on seemingly decorative strings to expose her naked body for a split second. The voyeuristic gaze is almost satisfied but immediately denied; this fleeting moment of self-exposure also threatens the order established by gendered spaces in certain Muslim societies, including diasporic communities. 'Sésame, ouvre-toi' plays on the fear of female sexuality and with the identification of women with disorder and chaos (see Mernissi 1975); it disrupts the habitual power relationship between men and women. However, it avoids a straightforward reversal; as the artist states: 'The more her dress reveals her, through small openings or through sudden exposure, the more the woman becomes dangerous for the man looking – but also for herself, against whom the costume turns' (Khattari 1997b: 128–9). An extreme example of the costume turning against the woman emerges in the 'Robe Maout' ('Mort'), in which each of the woman's attempts to loosen the dress by pulling on the strings strangles her.

These dramatic moments, which culminate in the performance of the 'Robe Maout', are followed by a more light-hearted – though no less ambivalent and ironic – dress which draws attention specifically to questions surrounding the place of the veil, and 'otherness' more generally, in France. The shift in tone is aided by the change in music: Charles Trenet's nostalgic, traditional French song 'Douce France' (1942) accompanies the walk of a smiling woman wearing a red, white and blue 'Tchador de la République'.

The tchador's shape – which turns into culottes towards the bottom – and the large blue buttons, recall a clown's suit, which appears to ridicule those who would attempt to separate French and Islamic identities, and provides a humorous counterpoint to constructions of women as sacred or threatening. When a repeat of the first *défilé-performance* was shown in Montreuil at the *Ecole Jean Jaurès* in 1998, another dress was added to the sequence: the final performer – in a white Christian wedding dress and veil adorned with plastic-covered *cartes de séjour* (residence permits) – was introduced as 'La Mariée de l'Eglise de Saint Bernard'. This title refers ironically to the eviction by riot police of more than 200 undocumented workers from this church on 23 August 1996. The dress provocatively alludes to the idea that French nationality can be gained through marriage; again, the tendency to polarize cultures is questioned by the demonstration that veiling belongs to Christian as well as Muslim traditions.

By cultivating ambiguity around dress codes, interpretations of which have posited Muslim women as irredeemably 'other', Khattari's *défilé-performance* goes beyond the simplistic for/against debate concerning the veil. The work foregrounds a process of transculturation: the artist

Plate 3.2 Tchador de la République – 64 © Majida Khattari

chooses to retain what for many in France has become a signifier of communitarianism and anti-Republicanism; however, she renegotiates the relationship between cultures in ways that avoid the extremes of hierarchization or assimilation (that is, integration into French society seen as necessarily synonymous with the rejection of the veil). The ambivalence produced by the perpetual oscillation between concealing and revealing, imprisonment and liberation, suffocation and protection – in addition to the combination of symbols of 'Frenchness' and symbols of perceived absolute 'otherness' – generates radical diversity, that is, non-reducible, heterogeneous 'otherness' that cannot be absorbed, domesticated or defined and located 'outside' (see Edouard Glissant on the concept of *Opacité* 1990: 203–9). It is this insistence upon radical otherness that allows the transcultural encounter to take place.

The performances posit the woman simultaneously as both object *and* subject. Discourses of voyeurism and fetishism are present in the work, seemingly to signal the persistence of stereotypes and the effects they have on women's lived experience. However, they co-exist with discourses of resistance; the women are shown to struggle against attempts to enclose them within static, immutable roles. Despite attempts to reduce women to passive objects, they emerge and re-emerge as active, embodied subjects. The artist's use of the performance mode enables an emphasis on their physical presence and corporeality. Identities are shown to be in a constant process of renegotiation, and the spectators are forced to recognize their own role in this process. Contrasting with (neo-)Orientalist representation – which allows the spectator to assume the comfortable role of passive, disembodied eye – this interactive experience affects and interpolates the spectator both mentally and physically.

Art as transcultural encounter

The sense of tension and flux between cultural and gendered identities in the art of Khattari is enhanced by the 'clashes' produced by unusual juxtapositions of form, material, texture, colour and gesture, as well as the contrasting sensations and emotions these evoke in the spectator. The *défilé-performance* is, of course, itself a syncretic, hyphenated form. The first of its kind, it brings a form associated with American and European avant-garde art together with the fashion industry. Khattari's re-deployment of the performance tradition seems appropriate given the political uses to which this has often been put: one thinks of the use of the medium to foreground feminist issues in the 1960s, when the traditional space of the gallery – and the arts it would accommodate, such as sculpture and painting – were male-dominated. This history of the medium heightens the ambivalence produced by its hyphenation with a form associated with the objectification of women and the perpetuation (through the cycle of advertising and consumption) of a monolithic image of women. As shown above, Khattari re-appropriates this form in which women are voiceless to articulate the subjectivity of women; instead they 'speak' through gesture, action and expression – this process becomes a means of resisting attempts at objectification and is simultaneously a critique of the fashion industry as well as of mono-lithic perceptions of Muslim women. The *vêtements-sculptures* similarly bring together modes that are habitually opposed: sculpture, traditionally conceived of as a 'high' or 'masculine' art and the dress, the 'feminine' item of clothing. However, the opposition is destabilized; sculpture, which in its traditional forms is static and rooted, becomes animated and mobile; the woman's movements are ambivalently controlled by the dress or vice versa, in a perpetual reversal of the dynamic of possession characteristic of both (neo-)colonial and patriarchal power relations.

Further contradictions are produced through the combination of rigid and pliable, heavy and light materials with opposing textures, qualities and associations. The first dress to be presented, 'Kacha', is made pre-dominantly of felt – an allusion to the work of Joseph Beuys[8] – which is sewn together with iron wiring and which rests on the performer's head through the use of thick, white elastic bands 'to ensure a certain flexibility', as the announcer tells us ironically.

The name of the dress and the materials employed in its fabrication are announced as the performer walks onto the stage. This functions to draw the spectator's attention to the materials used, appealing to their sense of touch; the spectator is familiar with the texture of the materi-als, as well as the uses to which they are normally put. Felt is known to be heavy and rough, and to conserve heat, reinforcing an impression of claustrophobia, suffocation and discomfort against the skin (this dress has also been referred to as 'La Robe étouffante' or 'La Robe irritante'). The contrast is sensed between the warmth generated by the felt – itself reminiscent of an animal's skin – and the sharp, cold, industrial iron thread with which the 'skin' is sewn together.

Contradictory associations, sensations and emotions are similarly produced through the use of opposing materials in the performance of dresses such as 'Les Mille et une epingles'. This time, the exoticism with which *Les Mille et Une Nuits* is associated in the Western imaginary is disrupted by a potentially violent material – the silver, simply-cut dress is covered in circular holes bordered with outward-facing pins which seem to invite and deny the gaze or touch. The contradictory responses evoked in the spectator are compounded by accompanying dance music that a European audience might customarily connect with the colonial 'exotic'. However, the discrepancy between the sensations and images

Plate 3.3   Kacha – 67 © Majida Khattari

evoked disrupts the processes by which the 'Orient' is constructed (Said 1995 [1978]) and habitually feminized (see Yeğenoğlu 1998). Moreover, the multi-sensorial experience produced by the *défilé-performance* challenges the hierarchy of the senses inherent in (neo)colonial exoticist representation and other contemporary stereotypical imaging in which primacy is given to vision. Power relations maintained by discourses of surveillance are disrupted (Spurr 1993); rather than being defined and dominated by the neocolonial and/or male gaze, the 'other' is freighted through multiple and often conflicting sensory and emotional effects, which are produced and renegotiated through the interaction between the embodied performers and spectators.

The renegotiation of the relationship between porous, interconnected cultures is effected also on a formal level, through the engagement with, and contestation of, a range of European and American art forms, which are brought together with music, dance and crafts from a range of Arab cultures. The work is in itself a site of travel, since it is 'traversed' by multiple cultural forms and references.[9] The combination of dance, costume and music is reminiscent of Oscar Schlemmer's Bauhaus theatre. However, the work incorporates belly dance – particular to Arab cultures – and the music played is specifically Moroccan, Lebanese, Pakistani as well as French. European references for the costumes can again be found in Schlemmer's theatre: in particular, his exploitation of costume to emphasize the identity of the body, or to transform it; or in the Surrealist-influenced fashions of Elsa Schiaparelli. The 'clashes' produced by the juxtaposition of opposing materials – the rigid and the pliable, the machine-made and the handcrafted – recall Eva Hesse's work, as well as *Arte Povera*; the influences of this anti-consumerist art is ironically combined with the fashion catwalk. However, the costumes also incorporate Islamic calligraphy and Moroccan caftan materials (see 'Sésame, ouvre-toi'); some dresses are named in Classical Arabic and one in Moroccan Arabic ('Kacha').

References to diverse cultures through form and material were even more apparent at the second *défilé* (2001), which saw the creation of dresses based on traditional Moroccan wedding dresses, as well as a series interpreting the *hijab* in a range of cultures: the Moroccan hayek, the Moroccan berber gna, the Iranian tchador and the Afghan tchadiri – taking further the artist's aim to demonstrate the plurality behind monolithic perceptions of Islam. Other dresses have referred to, and critiqued, American culture through the use of the flag and denim in 'La Robe puissance' (2002), or again through icons of globalization in a Saudi dress embroidered with the *Coca-Cola* logo in Latin and Arabic script (1999).

The re-use of Western forms is reminiscent of what Said has called the 'voyage in', to describe the re-use of elements of the former colonizer's culture for postcolonial purposes (Said 1994 [1993]: 260). However, this work goes beyond the 'voyage in': engaging not only with French and other European and American forms but also with specific Arabic forms, effecting a conversation between cultures reflective of the artist's diasporic viewpoint. Moreover, Khattari's multimedia *défilé-performances* make connections between ranges of national, local, pan-Arabic and global cultures by going beyond a France/Morocco binary and illustrating the diversely transnational nature of postcolonial identities.

Travelling identities in Marjane Satrapi's *Persepolis*

Diverging from Khattari's performance work, Marjane Satrapi's *Persepolis*, originally published in four volumes (L'Association 2000–3), is an autobiographical depiction of her journeys between 'Western' and 'Eastern' cultures, against the backdrop of the Iranian Revolution, and the Iran/Iraq War. Published to wide critical acclaim in France, *Persepolis* has now sold over one million copies and has been translated into several languages (though not into Persian). The story has reached an even wider audience since the emergence of the film based on the *bande dessinée* (produced by Satrapi and Vincent Paronnaud), which won the *Prix du Jury* at the Cannes Film Festival in 2007.

While Khattari's performances unsettle the spectator, the predominantly European or American reader of *Persepolis* is encouraged – at least initially – to identify with the protagonist, even if their expectations of 'sameness' are subsequently subverted by the introduction of elements with which they are unfamiliar (see Naguibi and O'Malley 2005). In a French diasporic context, Satrapi's work is less provocative than that of Khattari: in addition to employing a genre that encourages identification as opposed to confrontation, it does not engage specifically with issues of integration in France. Moreover, while Khattari's performance explicitly signals the continuing legacy of French colonialism in France, *Persepolis* focuses on Iran and Austria. This geographical particularity – as well as the work's critique of Austrians, the British and 'the West' in general – arguably enables the French reader to maintain a clear(er) conscience.

The use of the mode of the graphic novel results, of course, in a very different presentation of travel, owing to its specific temporal and spatial dimensions, as well as the ways in which it engages the spectator. However, like Khattari's work, it can be seen to foreground a process of transculturation in which the reader is implicated. Both artists question the very terms 'East' and 'West' by highlighting their diversity and intertwined histories. With different emphases, Satrapi shares Khattari's motivations to counter reductive images of non-Western (in this case, Persian) cultures, particularly as they appear in the media. Moreover, both works challenge neocolonial and patriarchal attempts to reduce the complexity

Plate 3.4 Marji and her parents on a magic carpet – 70 © L'Association/Marjane Satrapi

of postcolonial female identities through an emphasis on their diversity and on their status as embodied subjects.

Like Khattari, Satrapi combines syncretically both Western and non-Western forms and references. While *Persepolis* engages consciously with a particular, emerging strand of the European *bande dessinée* tradition, connections can be made to the Persian tradition of juxtaposing text and image in ways that depend on their interaction. While certain comic books make regular use of full pages without the use of panels, most rely on panels for the forward movement of the narrative sequentially, from left to right, and from top to bottom. The majority of Satrapi's narrative follows this convention. However, the sequence is, at times, 'interrupted', and the reader is provided with large or full-page panels for contemplation.

Such panels are often employed to magnify an idea, a sensation or an emotion, or to convey the passing of time. An example can be found in the section entitled 'Le Voyage' (Volume 2: 6).[10] A sequence of small and medium-sized panels conveying the increasingly repressive nature of the new regime is followed by an entire page depicting a three-week journey made by Marji and her parents to Spain and Italy. While the panel retains Satrapi's minimalist style, the suggestion of a sense of perspective by gently inclining buildings on either side is reminiscent of a Persian miniature, as are the swirling arabesque patterns (a recurring motif in *Persepolis*) that stylize the movement of clouds. In contrast with the legends and romances conveyed by the textual and visual poetry of Persian miniature, traces of this tradition are re-used in *Persepolis* to depict subjects such as war (see Volume 2: 'La Cigarette': 6) or exile (see Volume 3, 'La Pilule': 6), from a female perspective.

The juxtaposition of text and image is characteristic of other Iranian-born artists, such as Shirin Neshat, whose calligraphic texts are combined with a 'Western' mode – in her case, photography – to produce a syncretic form. Specific to an Iranian diasporic context, Neshat's practice additionally highlights and challenges the tendency, in Europe and the US, to conflate Persian and 'Arab' identities: many will 'misinterpret' her text as Islamic and Arabic, until they read the translation she provides of a Persian poem, written by a female author. Similarly, Satrapi's *Persepolis* explicitly signals the differences between Persian and 'Arab' identities on a number of occasions: for example, when Marji is obliged to take the 'ideological examination' to get into university in Tehran and is asked whether she prays, she justifies her negative response by affirming that 'like all Iranians, I don't understand Arabic. If praying is talking to God, I prefer to do it in a language I know. I believe in God, but I address him in Persian' (Volume 4, 'Le Concours': 9).

In *Persepolis* transculturation emerges primarily through the sequential depiction of Marji's personal itineraries. Critics have tended to compare *Persepolis* to the genre of autobiographical memoir, especially in relation to a new wave of such writing by women of the Iranian diaspora in the US, such as Azar Nafisi's *Reading Lolita in Teheran* (2003) and Azadeh Moaveni's *Lipstick Jihad* (2005).[11] While links can be made with literature and art produced by women in the Iranian diaspora in the US, Satrapi's Francophone text can also be situated specifically in relation to Francophone postcolonial production. *Persepolis* shares its structure, and certain tropes, with many Francophone narratives of immigration, exile and 'return'. While distinct from novels arising from specific legacies of French colonialism, Satrapi's graphic novel similarly emphasizes the omnipresence of 'other' cultures, regardless of her geographical location.

Marji's experience of being 'torn between' cultures begins before her literal journey to Austria as a result of the replacement of her French, secular education by an Islamic one, following the revolution. Her experience of exile as an existential condition will only be compounded by her journey to Austria. She attempts to integrate by denying her origins, but fails to forget the past. An illustration, headed: 'I wanted to forget everything, make my past disappear, but my unconscious was catching up on me', shows her sleeping, surrounded by memories of her childhood in Iran. The feeling of having to 'choose' one culture over another, and the failure to forget the past, are recurrent themes in Francophone literature depicting immigrants and their descendants. Francophone examples are particularly prevalent in literature by writers of Maghrebi descent, such as Leïla Houari's *Zeida de nulle part* (1985). However, while rare, Francophone examples by Iranian-born writers do exist: the Iranian immigrant protagonist of Chahdortt Djavann's *Comment peut-on être français?* (2006 [2005]), describes a similar exilic experience of the (personified) past catching up on her, despite her efforts to leave it behind and become Parisian (63–4).[12]

Following the failure of her attempts to integrate, Marji decides to go back to Iran; however, like other Francophone narratives of 'return', in diverse cultural contexts, *Persepolis* questions the very notion of 'return' by illustrating the 'impossibility of homecoming' in the sense of reintegrating into the community (Said 2000: 179). Back in Iran, Marji attempts to forget her years in Austria; but again, 'my past was catching up on me' (Volume 4, 'Le Ski': 2). Her feelings of alienation and exile are compounded, leading to depression and suicide attempts: 'I was nothing. I was a Westerner in Iran, an Iranian in the West. I had no identity. I didn't even know anymore why I was living' (Volume 4, 'Le Ski': 6).

Her experience of 'betweenness' as loss and absence is reminiscent of Zeida's experience of return (from Belgium to Morocco), as the title

Plate 3.5   Image of self in negative – 73 © L'Association/Marjane Satrapi

of Houari's novel suggests. A visual corollary to the sense of 'being nothing' is found in the stark, negative image of her white silhouette against a black background. However (also like Houari's protagonist), she gradually begins to accept that the discrepant components of her identity cannot be reconciled. Her decision to take control begins with her physical transformation. A sequence of several small panels – conveying the speed of her self-transformation – humorously depicts her waxing, buying clothes and shoes, getting a hair cut, applying make-up and exercising (Volume 4, 'Le Ski': 8–9). This attention to different parts of the body, and then to physical actions, emphasizes her corporeal presence, in contrast to the negative (white on black) image, which conveyed a sense of hollowness and absence. Despite differences in genre and style, and the autobiographical content of *Persepolis*, this emphasis on corporeal presence, subjectivity and agency is a feature shared with Khattari's *défilé-performances*.[13]

Marji struggles to construct a life for herself in Iran for several years, but her constant battles with the restrictions imposed by the political regime eventually lead to her decision to go to France. The concluding departure scene at the airport, which depicts the protagonist in transit 'between' cultures (Malek 2006), is also a recurring trope of Francophone narratives of travel.[14] Here, it highlights the complex, transnational dimensions of 'home' in a postcolonial diasporic context. Marji eventually renegotiates the relationship between the cultures to which she belongs in ways that avoid the extremes of assimilation and alienation.

Departures, arrivals and transits

The process of transculturation emerges additionally from the presentation of Iran's perpetually evolving connections to cultures outside its geographical boundaries. *Persepolis* challenges attempts (both by the regime and by a reductive Western perspective) to impose a static identity on Iran by emphasizing its status as a site of departures, arrivals and transits (Clifford 1997: 30): it highlights ethnic and religious diversity within Iran. *Persepolis* focuses on Marji's Zoroastrian family; it also draws attention to the Jewish community, most of which fled the country following the revolution (the tragic episode which recounts the death of Marji's Jewish friend in an explosion exposes the extremism of attempts to maintain a cohesive 'national' Islamic identity). A new community is formed by the arrival of refugees from Kuwait after the war with Iraq. Iranians themselves are shown to be in perpetual motion, despite efforts to contain them. In addition to Marji's journey to Austria, and with her parents, to Spain and Italy, her parents travel to Turkey; movement across borders is not limited to exchanges with the perceived 'centres' of Europe or the US. In contrast to tourism, or Marji's journey as a student and exile, the novel also depicts coercive journeys of escape, such as that of the family who crawl across the border hidden within a flock of sheep (an episode reminiscent of Odysseus and his men escaping from Polyphemus by tying themselves to the undersides of sheep; see Volume 1: 'Les Moutons'), or the young boys sent off by their families before the age of thirteen to avoid being enlisted in the army (Volume 2, 'La Dot': 9).

Inevitable links to 'global' cultures are particularly evident in the section entitled 'Kim Wilde' (Volume 2), in which Marji's parents smuggle goods back from Turkey into Iran for her, including clothes, as well as posters of English pop singer Kim Wilde and heavy metal band Iron Maiden. Marji goes out wearing her new Nike trainers, denim jacket and Michael Jackson badge (together with her veil) to buy contraband tapes of Kim Wilde and English progressive rock band Camel on the black market.

Throughout Satrapi's work, global, transnational elements combine with specific facets of daily life for Iranian women under the Islamic Republic, as well as with references to pre-revolutionary Iran – which recur through the exposure of discrepancies between public and private life – both of which underlie the work as a whole through the use of

Plate 3.6   Image of Marji in veil and denim jacket with Michael Jackson badge ('Kim Wilde' (volume 2)) – 75 © L'Association/Marjane Satrapi

the title *Persepolis*.[15] Furthermore, in both cases unusual juxtapositions of the global and the local emphasize the historical specificity of Iranian women, while exposing their affiliations to cultures outside, thus countering continued attempts to deny their contemporaneity and subjectivity.

Marji emphasizes the diverse and evolving ways of wearing the veil in Iran. She demonstrates, through the use of a humorous diagram of differently shaped women, how a woman's form – and even her political allegiances – can be discerned through the veil, again emphasizing women's physical presence and agency. She also shows how women perform small but significant acts of resistance on a daily basis: by wearing make-up (or coloured socks, on one occasion), exposing a fringe or a wrist and by listening to a walkman or laughing loudly (Volume 4, 'Les Chausettes': 4).[16] As in Khattari's performances, attempts to constrain women co-exist with their resistance to such attempts; they are shown to manipulate the boundaries surrounding what has been constructed as an immutable symbol.

Satrapi highlights resistance to repressive uses of *hijab*, among other forms of repression in the name of religion, such as censorship, restrictions on travel and bans on the importation of cultural products. However, also like Khattari, her critique of extremism within Iran is always 'doubled' by her critique of Western extremism. Indeed, Iranian and Western distortions of 'otherness' come together explicitly in a discussion between Marji and her parents, in which Marji tells them that just as the media in Iran produce anti-Western propaganda, 'the Western media are against us too. That's where our reputation as fundamentalists and terrorists comes from!' As her mother replies: 'Between the fanaticism of some and the disdain of others, you don't know which to choose' (Volume 4: 'La Parabole', 3).

Concluding remarks

This chapter has demonstrated that while important differences emerge between Khattari's *défilé-performances* and Satrapi's graphic novel, they converge in their emphasis on distinctively *visual* processes of transculturation. Khattari's *défilés* – multi-sensorial experiences which take place in real time – renegotiate the relationship between cultures through a syncretic mingling of 'Western' art forms and 'Arab' forms and references. From Satrapi's graphic novel, which engages with the European tradition of *bande dessinée* but also recalls the Persian tradition of juxtaposing text and image, transculturation emerges primarily through the narrative demonstration of cultures and identities as sites of travel.

While visual arts presenting transculturation are reminiscent of postcolonial literature, they enable an *ocular* confrontation of stereotypes that are most emphatic in their visual forms. The counter-stereotypes that artists produce often re-appropriate visual clichés from the contemporary media or from Orientalist imagery, and rework them by combining them with visual symbols of 'the West' or specific 'Western' countries (such as the French or American flag, the denim jacket or the can of Pepsi). They also re-appropriate images, materials and/or techniques associated with a 'Western' history of art or comic books, or with 'non-Western' visual forms. However, the postcolonial visual arts often go *beyond* the visual, appealing to a range of senses in order to challenge the privileging of vision by (neo)colonial exoticism or other stereotypical imaging. They combine the visual with the auditory and the kinaesthetic to produce a multi-sensorial, multidimensional experience of 'opacity' and interaction.

While the graphic novel cannot produce the experiences of which performance (and installation) art are capable, Satrapi's work, like that of Khattari, does evoke an affective response in the reader through its emphasis on interactivity, triggered by specifically visual means. In *Persepolis*, as in Khattari's *défilé-performances*, the 'transcultural encounter' extends beyond the work to involve the reader. The graphic novel shares with Khattari the emphasis of performance on participation. Scott McCloud (1994) underlines the importance to *bande dessinée* of the 'gutter', the space between panels, in which the reader is required to produce links between actions and ideas. Reminiscent of Khattari's performances, the reader is drawn in, only for his/her expectations to be subverted. However, whereas at the *défilé*, it is the spectator's expectations of absolute difference (the veiled woman as exotic object to be dominated, or as repressed victim to be liberated) that are subverted, *Persepolis* subverts the reader's tendency to *identify* with the protagonist (see Naguibi and O'Malley 2005).

Both works highlight the interconnectedness of a range of local, national and global cultures, going beyond an 'East'/'West' binary, and illustrating the diversely transnational nature of postcolonial identities. They expose the relativity of 'here' and 'there', through the evocation of journeys that reverse or circumvent the 'centre'/'periphery' trajectory. Moreover, in addition to challenging both neocolonial and patriarchal extremisms, both artists emphasize the corporeal presence and agency of women, re-presenting them without reifying them; they convert their 'double alienation' into a double – or multidirectional – critique.

Notes

1. An exception can be found in the work of Joe McGonigle on the French-born, London-based artist Zineb Sedira. While work foregrounding issues of diaspora has only recently received support in Britain, from the Institute of International Visual Arts (INIVA, founded in 1994) and the international journal *Third Text* (since 1987), there is no equivalent organization or critical apparatus in France.
2. While *Persepolis* has often been compared to literature, this chapter will compare it to both the visual arts and literature, as well as emphasizing the specificity of *bande dessinée*.
3. Cultural production foregrounding gender issues demonstrates that gender co-exists and interacts with a range of other factors, including culture, religion, class and generation.
4. More recent reinterpretations of transculturation, a term originally coined by Fernando Ortiz in 1940, can be found in Silvia Spitta (1995), Felipe Hernández, M. Millington and I. Borden eds. (2005) as well as Alicia Arrizón (2006).
5. In France, the veil is commonly perceived as being incompatible with *laïcité* (secularism, a founding pillar of the Republic since 1905), and is associated with a refusal to 'integrate' in the sense of assimilating (see Blank 1999).

6. Translations are mine throughout, unless stated otherwise.
7. My interpretation of this performance is informed by a recording owned by the Pompidou Centre (seen in September 2007), in addition to reviews and my own conversations with Majida Khattari. The recording is, of course, in itself a work of art, and the experience of it will necessarily differ from that of the original performance in 1996. Interpretations of the work (in its original form or as filmic document) will always be plural and – in the case of the recording – are affected by the knowledge of the development of the headscarf debate, and of events such as 9/11, since the specific moment in which the performance was produced.
8. In his performances, installations and sculptural objects Beuys (1921–86) employed non-conventional materials such as felt and fat, expanding the sensorial possibilities of art.
9. For a literary precedent, see Rachid Boudjedra (1975).
10. As *Persepolis* (L'Association, 2007) is unpaginated, I will number the page within each section.
11. See, for example, Naguibi and O'Malley (2005); and Malek (2006). Diverging from this tendency, Jennifer Worth analyses the work in terms of a performance. Regarding the engagement with Western and non-Western forms, Worth asserts that while theatre as conceived by the Western world took root in Iran only in the nineteenth century, street performance and public storytelling are long-established traditions (2007: 144).
12. Djavann's novel illustrates the specificity of Franco-Iranian relations; the protagonist ironically 'writes back' to Montesquieu, who assumed the role of an Iranian in France in *Lettres persanes*.
13. Worth's article analyses Satrapi's focus on embodied experience as the primary means of understanding. Her argument that the protagonist comes to regard embodied experience as more reliable than language that can be manipulated, might also be applied to Khattari's *défilés*, in which the performers communicate through action, gesture and facial expression.
14. See, for example, Camara Laye's *L'Enfant noir* (1953, written a few years before independence in Guinea), or again, Houari's *Zeida de nulle part* (1985). The panel depicting Marji's departure recalls that depicting her earlier departure to Austria, though this time her journey is undertaken positively.
15. Naguibi and O'Malley have shown how this combination disrupts attempts to identify with the protagonist (2005).
16. A comparison can be made with Leïla Sebbar's *La Jeune fille au balcon* (1996), which, while its context is specific to *intégrisme* (Islamic 'integralism') during the Algerian Civil War, demonstrates similar 'daily' acts of individual resistance.

Bibliography

Arrizón, A. (2006) *Queering Mestizaje: Transculturation and Performance* (Ann Arbor, MI: University of Michigan Press).

Becquer, M. and Gatti, J. (1991) 'Elements of Vogue', *Third Text*, 16/17, 65–81.

Blank, D. (1999) 'A Veil of Controversy', *Interventions*, 1.4, 536–54.

Boudjedra, R. (1975) *Topographie idéale pour une agression caractérisée* (Paris: Denoël).

Clifford, J. (1997) *Routes: Travel and Translation in the Late Twentieth Century* (Cambridge, MA and London: Harvard University Press).

Djavann, C. (2006 [2005]) *Comment peut-on être français?* (Paris: Flammarion).

Donnell, A. (2003) 'Visibility, Violence and Voice? Attitudes to Veiling Post-11 September' in D. A. Bailey and G. Tawadros (eds) *Veil: Veiling, Representation, and Contemporary Art* (Cambridge, MA: MIT; London: INIVA), pp. 122–35.

Fisher, J. (2006 [2005]) 'The Syncretic Turn. Cross-Cultural Practices in the Age of Multiculturalism' in Z. Kocur and S. Leung (eds) *Theory in Contemporary Art Since 1985* (Oxford: Blackwell), pp. 223–41.

Glissant, E. (1990) *Poétique de la relation* (Paris: Gallimard).

Hall, S. (1990) 'Cultural Identity and Diaspora' in J. Rutherford (ed.) *Identity: Community, Culture, Difference* (London: Lawrence & Wishart).

Hernández, F., Millington, M. and Borden, I. (eds) (2005) *Transculturation: Cities, Spaces and Architectures in Latin America* (Amsterdam: Rodopi).

Khattari, M. (1997a) 'Un voile qui dévoile', *Salama: le Maghreb dans tous ses états*, 5 April, 12.

Khattari, M. (1997b) 'Majida Khattari: le défilé de mode', *Les Cahiers du GRIF*, 2, 128–9.

Khattari, M. (1999) 'Casablanca', *Des Territoires en revue*, 2 October, 30–41.

Khattari, M. (2004) 'Paris-Défilé: les voiles osés de Majida Khattari', http://www.yabiladi.com/article-agenda-133.html, accessed 8 July 2004.

Lloyd, F. (ed.) (2001) *Displacement & Difference: Contemporary Arab Visual Culture in the Diaspora* (London: Saffron Books).

McCloud, S. (1994) *Understanding Comics: Invisible Art* (New York: Harper Perennial).

Malek, A. (2006) 'Memoir as Iranian Exile Cultural Production: A Case Study of Marjane Satrapi's *Persepolis* Series', *Iranian Studies*, 39.3, 353–80.

Mercer, K. (1994) *Welcome to the Jungle: New Positions in Black Cultural Studies* (London: Routledge).

Mernissi, F. (1975) *Beyond the Veil: Male-Female Dynamics in Muslim Society* (London: Al Saqi Books).

Mirzoeff, N. (2001) *Diaspora and Visual Culture: Representing Africans and Jews* (London: Routledge).

Mohanty, C. (1988) 'Under Western Eyes: Feminist Scholarship and Colonial Discourses', *Feminist Review*, 30, 61–88.

Naguibi, N. and O'Malley, A. (2005) 'Estranging the Familiar: "East" and "West" in Satrapi's *Persepolis*', *ESC: English Studies in Canada*, 31.2/3, 223–48.

Pratt, M. (1992) *Imperial Eyes: Travel Writing and Transculturation* (London: Routledge).

Said, E. (1995 [1978]) *Orientalism: Western Conceptions of the Orient* (Harmondsworth: Penguin).

Said, E. (1994 [1993]) *Culture and Imperialism* (London: Vintage).

Said, E. (2000) *Reflections on Exile and Other Literary and Cultural Essays* (Cambridge, MA: Harvard University Press).

Salloum, J. (2001) 'In/tangible Cartographies: New Arab Video' in *19th Worldwide Video Festival: 2001* (Netherlands: Stichting World Wide Video Centre), pp. 354–417.

Satrapi, M. (2007 [2000–03]) *Persepolis* (Paris: L'Association).

Sedira, Z. (2003) 'Mapping the Illusive' in D. A. Bailey and G. Tawadros (eds) *Veil: Veiling, Representation, and Contemporary Art* (Cambridge, MA: MIT; London: INIVA), pp. 56–71.

Shilton, S. (2007) 'Gender, Generation and the Legacy of Immigration: Renegotiating Female Identities in Houari's *Zeida de nulle part* and Guène's *Kiffe kiffe demain'* in A. Georgio and J. Waters (eds) *Women's Writing in Western Europe: Gender, Generation and Legacy* (Newcastle: Cambridge Scholars Publishing), pp. 401–16.

Spitta, S. (1995) *Between Two Waters: Literary Transculturation in Latin America* (Houston, TX: Rice University Press).

Spurr, D. (1993) *The Rhetoric of Empire: Colonial Discourse in Journalism, Travel Writing, and Imperial Administration* (Durham, NC and London: Duke University Press).

Worth, J. (2007) 'Unveiling: *Persepolis* as Embodied Performance', *Theatre Research International*, 32.2, 143–60.

Yeğenoğlu, M. (1998) *Colonial Fantasies: Towards a Feminist Reading of Orientalism* (Cambridge: Cambridge University Press).

Section 2 Nostalgia and Longing for 'Home'

4
'Naturally, I reject the term "diaspora"': Said and Palestinian Dispossession

Patrick Williams

There is an initial double surprise, even shock, to be registered on reading Said's comment from an interview in 1999 (in Said 2004a); firstly, that someone so notable – and deliberately, as a matter of self-identification – associated with ideas of exile, should reject its cognate term diaspora, and secondly that such a rejection is deemed natural, to be expected. That shock is compounded by the fact that, according to the 2006 report by the United Nations High Commission for Refugees: 'By far the most protracted and largest of all refugee problems in the world today is that of the Palestinian refugees, whose plight dates back fifty seven years' (UNHCR 2006). If, however, it appears deeply paradoxical for Said to reject the idea of what is, in Kachig Tölölyan's well known formulation, the 'exemplary community of late modernity' (Tölölyan 1991: 4), then to an extent that might be seen to be in keeping with the nature of the individual in question – Said famously instantiated a number of paradoxes and contradictions – but even more so with the fundamental situation of Palestine itself, defined by Said in the 1992 preface to *The Question of Palestine* as constituted by paradox and irony. If the Palestinian condition is indeed characterized by contradiction, irony and paradox, then it is all the more understandable that Said's friend Mahmoud Darwish – whose work is deeply inflected by those very traits (discussed later in this essay) – should be regarded (much to his annoyance) as the poet of the Palestinian nation[1]. And indeed, Darwish agrees with Said's assessment of the Palestinian situation (see Darwish 1995: 73).

Leaving the apparent paradox aside for a moment, we could posit a number of reasons why Said might be less than happy with the term diaspora, indeed why 'comparing diasporas', postcolonial or otherwise, is precisely what he does not wish to do. One of these is no doubt the strong Jewish associations that the term carries: given the fact that historically the primary referent has been the Jewish diaspora, there is a definite sense of 'ownership', the feeling that other groups – Africans, for example – should look for alternative names for their experience and leave diaspora to the Jews. Another explanation, which would fit well with the activist side of Said, is the argument put forward by Bassma Kodmani-Darwish in *La Diaspora palestinienne* (1997) that the use of the term tends to depoliticize – and to allow the essential problem to remain unaddressed – in a way that talking instead about 'the refugee crisis' would not. A third possibility is that, from a certain perspective, diaspora does not adequately account for the Palestinian experience, since many Palestinians are precisely not 'scattered', living as they do in their Israeli-occupied homeland. (Two additional observations, or even counter-arguments, here would note, firstly, that the majority of Palestinians are now in the diaspora, and secondly, that even for those who remain in a state of internal colonization, the result of the new Israeli 'security wall' has been to create conditions of isolation and separation amounting to a kind of 'diaspora on the spot'.)

In the interview from which the quotation is taken, Said ruefully acknowledges that people will continue to use the term diaspora regardless, and here and elsewhere goes on to explain that he prefers a number of Arabic terms – *shatat* [dispersion], *ghurba* or *manfa* [exile], for example – but that dispossession seems to him to encompass Palestinian reality better than diaspora. In line with Said's preference, this chapter will examine some of the forms and histories of Palestinian dispossession – but only some, for the list is long, the issues frequently extremely complex and the sheer awfulness of the human misery involved is beyond the scope of an essay such as this to encompass. Before doing so, however, since we have already queried one of the two key terms in the title of this collection, it may be worth briefly mentioning the other, and registering what some will regard as the almost inevitably less-than-straightforward status of the postcolonial. This problematic positioning is the case both in terms of Said's own relation both to the concept and the field (for more on this, see Williams 2001), as well as in terms of the relevance of notions of the postcolonial to the colonial enterprise of Zionism and to the ongoing, colonized condition of the Palestinian people in the twenty-first century. In 'The Angel of Progress', for instance, Anne McClintock famously criticized the idea of the post-colonial as 'prematurely celebratory', especially if used in relation to Palestine and other peoples in similar circumstances (McClintock 1993: 294). Others, wishing for an example to highlight the strength of Palestinian resistance as an instance of post-colonial praxis, might in turn regard McClintock's comments as prematurely dismissive, but it is necessary to recognize that Palestine/Israel constitutes in many ways a more than usually testing case for the application of certain postcolonial analytic frameworks – especially those working with a notion of straightforward chronological succession, or with the postcolonial as an achieved space of freedom. A different way of understanding the possibly 'premature' nature of Palestinian postcoloniality would be in the context of the argument put forward by Childs and Williams (1996) that postcolonialism can be seen as an anticipatory discourse, adumbrating the liberated world which is yet to come. Certainly, one of the clearest lessons from Palestine is that, although the great age of the European colonial empires may be over, colonialism – European-inspired or European-supported – can continue to thrive, and that the struggle to be post-colonial goes on.

While Said's avoidance of any discussion of Palestinians under the heading of diaspora is principled (if paradoxical), the same avoidance by academic authors of studies of the topic is altogether less comprehensible. Thus, for example, Braziel and Mannur's *Theorizing Diaspora* has a chapter on the Jewish diaspora, but only a single passing mention of Palestine. Similarly, Kalra et al.'s more recent *Diaspora and Hybridity* manages only one mention. Robin Cohen's *Global Diasporas* does include half a dozen references, but again only in the context of a much more extensive analysis of the Jewish diaspora. While the reasons for this may be debatable, the fact of Palestinian absence remains incontrovertible, and the need for a fully comparative analysis of the Palestinian case becomes ever more urgent.

In terms of the modes of dispossession experienced by Palestinians, some of the most important include the territorial, the ontological, the narrative, the historiographical, the ethical and the dialogic. The territorial loss is the most fundamental, the most significant both materially and symbolically, the one from which many others derive, and the one therefore to which we will devote most attention in due course. Ontological dispossession has consisted of denials that an entity called the Palestinian people exists or that Palestine itself exists. The former occur most notoriously perhaps in the comments made in 1969 by the then Prime Minister Golda Meir – 'There was no such thing as Palestinians, they never existed'; 'How can we return the occupied territories? There is nobody to return them to' – but they are far from rare. A small but significant instance occurred a year or two earlier, when Mahmoud Darwish presented his poem 'A lover from Palestine' to the Israeli censors for permission to publish. The poem was approved, but returned with 'Palestine' crossed out and replaced by 'Eretz Israel'. Denials such as Golda Meir's have particular relevance in the context of mechanisms of colonial ideological justification – to which we shall return – but find curious contemporary forms in, for example, the removal of Elia Suleiman's film *Divine Intervention* from the 2002 Oscars shortlist because, the official explanation said, the film claimed to be from Palestine, and no such country exists. Two years later, one of the main websites for the Athens Olympic Games listed every team taking part – with the exception of the Palestinians.

Narrative dispossession, and the related historiographical version, are topics that Said has revisited on numerous occasions, most notably in his 1984 essay 'Permission to Narrate', where the Israeli blocking of the production of a narrative of Palestinian history and national identity is a crucial ideological dimension of their attempts to prevent the emergence of a Palestinian nation requiring a national homeland. 'What would need to be added [...] is that the "idea" of a Palestinian homeland would have to be enabled by the prior acceptance of a narrative entailing a homeland. And this has been resisted as strenuously on the imaginative and ideological level as it has been politically' (Said 1995: 256). The blocking of the narrative involves much more than rhetorical strategies and discursive manoeuvres, however: during the Israeli incursions into West Bank towns in 2002, for example, Palestinian archives stored on computers, particularly in the Palestinian Authority (PA) offices in Ramallah, were systematically removed or destroyed. While such actions might just be understandable as motivated by the deep Israeli dislike of Yasser Arafat as head of the PA and a desire to weaken him politically, how are we to make sense of the ransacking of the Khalil Sakakini Cultural Centre in Carmel – one of the most important in the country – and the destruction of its archives relating to Palestinian life and culture? The question irresistibly asserts itself: if, as the Israelis routinely claim, Palestinians have no history, why would they need to go to such lengths in systematically destroying something that does not exist?

The fact that the cultural centre is also the base for Mahmoud Darwish and his influential journal *Al Karmel* may have some bearing on the attack, particularly since – in the opinion of sections of the Israeli population – Darwish is regarded as the implacable cultural enemy of their people. In the furore over the suggestion that Israeli secondary school pupils might study some of Darwish's poems, the Likud Party whip denounced them as a threat to the existence of the state: 'In every word of every song, there is hatred of Zionism and the people of Israel' (Jaggi 2002). The idea that Darwish's work might represent an archive needing to be destroyed is supported by the novelist Anton Shammas's assessment of his importance:

> For through some eighteen collections of poetry, Darwish has constructed the annals of the Palestinian experience in such a manner that his insightful commentaries on the vicissitudes of that experience are now part of the virtual archive of Palestinian history since 1948 [...]. Fortunately, that interpretation, unlike some other Palestinian assets, could not be deleted in Oslo.
>
> (Shammas 1999: 15)

Or, one might add, deleted by Israeli vandalism. The practice of the systematic denial and destruction of history and memory is famously noted by Fanon in the context of colonialism – to which we shall return later in this chapter:

> Perhaps we have not sufficiently demonstrated that colonialism is not simply content to impose its rule upon the present and the future of a dominated country. Colonialism is not satisfied merely with hiding a people in its grip and emptying the native's brain of all form and content. By a kind of perverted logic, it turns to the past of the oppressed people, and distorts, disfigures and destroys it. This work of devaluing pre-colonial history takes on a dialectical significance today.
>
> (Fanon 1990 [1961]: 169)

The ethical dimension of dispossession relates to the refusal to accord any validity to Palestinian rights, claims and sufferings. Indeed, not only must they be refused any validity, they must not even be mentioned: Said recounts how, at a gathering in Washington in support of Israel, Paul Wolfowitz – then second in command at the Department of Defence, and as right-wing and pro-Israeli as the next neo-con – happened to mention in passing 'the sufferings of the Palestinians', at which point 'he was booed so loudly and so long that he was unable to continue his speech, and left the platform in a kind of disgrace' (Said 2004b: 178). Finally, the fact that Palestinians (supposedly) have no position – national, ontological, ethical – from which to speak is presumably one reason for the Israeli chorus, growing through the 1990s, that Palestine offers 'no appropriate interlocutors' for dialogue with Israel. This approach was principally elaborated as another means to undermine Arafat (despite – or precisely because of – his recognition by the UN and world leaders, cemented ironically in the famous handshake with Yitzak Rabin on the White House lawn), but has also continued to deny the existence of anyone from among the Palestinians with whom Israel could consider the possibility of negotiation.

While all the approaches to dispossession take different forms, they are alike in so far as they contribute to Palestinian dispersal by weakening the bonds of solidarity and collectivity – and in so doing, compounding the original dispossession: the loss of the land. 2008 marked the sixtieth anniversary of what the Palestinians designate as *Al Nakba*, the 'catastrophe' visited on them by the Israeli forces that drove them out of their homes, off their land, and, for three quarters of a million of them, out of their country, as part of what Ilan Pappe has recently called 'the ethnic cleansing of Palestine' (Pappe 2006). Although the *Nakba* figures as a terrible historical event, its apparent singularity arguably masks the ability of the catastrophic to continue, not least in the context of what the Israelis represent as unending progress for the country. The paradoxical or ambivalent relation of these two concepts is captured by Walter Benjamin's caustic assessments of modernity – 'The idea of progress is to be grounded in the catastrophe: the fact that everything just goes on and on *is* the catastrophe' (Benjamin 1985: 35) – as well as more famously in the 'Theses on the Philosophy of History':

> This is how one pictures the angel of history. His face is turned towards the past. Where we perceive a chain of events, he sees one single catastrophe, which keeps piling wreckage upon wreckage and hurls it in front of his feet. The angel would like to stay, awaken the dead, and make whole what has been smashed. But a storm is blowing from Paradise; it has got caught in his wings with such violence that the angel can no longer close them. The storm irresistibly propels him into the future to which his back is turned, while the pile of debris before him grows skyward. This storm is what we call progress.
> (Benjamin 1982: 259–60)

The idea of the relentless persistence of the catastrophic is also highlighted by Said: '[Israeli policy/governance] is a set of evil practices, whose overall effect is a deeply felt, humiliating injustice, and it is ongoing. Every day. In every conceivable way' (Said 2004a: 449). However, in case aligning analyses like Said and Benjamin's should seem a mere intellectual conceit, it is worth recalling that the catastrophe represented by the loss of the land in 1948 has indeed continued to this day, both steadily and incrementally – by means of stealth, brute force, illegality as well as Israeli legislation – and marked by other decisive dates – 1967, 1982, 1994, 2002 – all signalling in their different ways further Palestinian defeats and dispossessions.

Darwish is aware both of the ambivalent Benjaminian perspective and the more straightforward Saidian one, and includes the former in a poem on the latter: 'Advancing could be a bridge / Leading back / to Barbarism'. He also expresses, as a concern shared by himself, Said and the readers of his work, the following anguished query: 'What can poetry say in a time of catastrophe?' (Darwish 2004). While there may be echoes here of Adorno's famous comment on the barbarity of writing poetry after Auschwitz, Darwish's own affirmative reply, that poetry does indeed have something to say in such conditions, is amply demonstrated not only in his response to the immediacy of the catastrophic, as for example in 'State of Siege' (2002), but also by his chronicling of more than half a century of ongoing catastrophe, of whose persistence he is in no doubt:

> We are not looking back to dig up the evidence of a past crime, for the Nakba is an extended present that promises to continue in the future. We do not need anything to help us remember the human tragedy we have been living for the past fifty three years: we continue to resist its consequences in the here and now, on the land of our homeland, the only homeland we have.
>
> (Darwish 2001)

Indeed, the experience of recent years may have brought about a change in how Darwish conceptualizes the catastrophe, as – in line with the argument above about the Nakba as both singular historical event and enduring condition – the fact and image of a people under siege comes to encompass both the traumatic events of 2002 and the unchanging face of Israeli occupation. In Operation Defensive Shield in May 2002, Israeli forces attacked and occupied a number of West Bank towns, including Jenin, where they allegedly massacred a considerable number of the inhabitants, and Ramallah, where Darwish had lived since his return from exile. 'State of Siege' was Darwish's response to the latest assault on his people; of epic length, in keeping with other recent works such as 'Mural', it also had its paradoxical aspect, in so far as he had for some time been attempting to distance himself from immediate political commitment in his poetry, but felt that the attack left him no choice but to engage with the demands of the situation. At the same

time, the 2002 siege comes to stand for all the forms of militarized brutality the Palestinians have endured and continue to endure as a way of
life, as well as pointing towards a number of philosophical issues. The
intersection of the military and the philosophical can be brutal, too, as
in: 'Soldiers measure the gap between being and nothingness / Using a
tank's gunsights.../ We measure the distance between our bodies and
the shells with a sixth sense' (Darwish 2002). While the extension of the
cruel realities of life under siege to images of life as a siege might seem to
belong to the realm of rhetorical inflation proper to poetry, it is worth
recalling that critical sociologists may also take the same view, as for
instance in Zygmunt Bauman's *Society under Siege* (2002). More recently,
the Israeli government has demonstrated the precisely non-rhetorical
nature of life under siege, increasing both the extent and the cruelty of
its techniques as it has put the whole of the territory of Gaza under total
siege, both militarily and economically, blocking border crossings and
cutting off essential supplies of fuel, medicine and foodstuffs as well as
continuing to bomb and shell as it pleases.

In what could seem appropriately paradoxical fashion in the context of
the Palestinian Question, complete recovery of the land of Israel both was,
and was not, part of the plans of Zionism. Although resettlement of Jews
in 'interesting' places such as Madagascar or Argentina was considered
by Herzl and others, a particular Zionist mind-set stubbornly proposed
that the recovery of anything less than all of Eretz Israel was unthinkable.
Unfortunately for the Palestinians, it has been the latter approach that has
dominated their history, and to that end, how the land of Palestine was
represented was central to the dispossession of its people. As Said puts it:
'what specially interests me is the hold of both memory and geography on
the desire for conquest and domination' (Said 2000: 181).

As far as conquest and domination are concerned – and in spite of
later denials when Zionism attempted to portray itself as a movement
of anti-colonial national liberation, in keeping with the popular movements that had swept across the globe after the Second World War – the
Israeli *reconquista* proceeded according to classic colonialist protocols,
perhaps unsurprisingly, since the first Zionist Congress in 1897 had
set up both the World Zionist Organisation and a 'Programme for the
Colonization of Palestine'. Following the medieval papal declaration of
terra nullius, whereby unoccupied territory could legitimately be colonized, the land was declared empty, most notoriously in Israel Zangwill's
slogan from 1895, 'a land without a people for a people without a land'.
If, however, the existence of an indigenous population ever had to
be acknowledged, then, in full Orientalist fashion, it was in the same

moment discounted, its size diminished, its importance negated – as in the remarks made by a senior British official to Chaim Weizmann, head of the World Zionist Organization, and subsequently the first President of Israel: 'there are a few hundred thousand Negroes [i.e. Palestinians], but that is a matter of no significance' (cited in Chomsky 1992: 435).

The second aspect of colonialist ideology brought in to legitimate the Zionist project was the notion that land inappropriately husbanded could be counted available for settlement (although not strictly speaking empty, the fact that it was not made use of as it should be amounted to the same thing). Historically, the charge was deployed particularly against peoples whose way of life was insufficiently settled and sedentary, and whose forms of agriculture not intensive enough to meet Western criteria of the time. British use of this notion, for example, ranged from North America in the early seventeenth century to East Africa in the late nineteenth. Thus, Palestine, which had for centuries been renowned as fertile and productive, had now to be declared a desert, a wilderness, a wasteland: its fields, in the words of Chaim Weizmann, untilled since the time of the Romans. And it was not only Zionists who offered this bizarre-but-logical form of legitimation: according to Winston Churchill in 1936, there was no injustice involved in removing the Palestinians from the land, since '[t]he injustice is when those who live in the country leave it to be desert for thousands of years' (cited in Gregory 2004: 80). Unsurprisingly, 'making the desert bloom' became one of the most famous catchphrases of a redemptive, modernizing Zionism, which of course looked after the land 'properly'. Importantly, the colonialist arguments were not used simply to justify events in advance: in terms of *de post facto* rationalization, the supposedly liberal and progressive Shimon Peres, speaking in the 1980s, managed to compress a whole range of legitimating claims into a single paragraph:

> The land to which [the Jewish settlers] came, while indeed the Holy Land, was desolate and uninviting; a land that had been laid waste, thirsty for water, filled with swamps and malaria, lacking in natural resources. And in the land itself there lived another people; a people who neglected the land, but who lived on it. Indeed the return to Zion was accompanied by ceaseless violent clashes with the small Arab population.
>
> (cited in Said 1988: 5)

One of the many ironies here is the extent to which the various governments of which Peres has been a member have been responsible for turning the non-Jewish parts of the 'Holy Land' into desolate, uninviting semi-desert (or worse) through the practice of diverting increasing quantities of water to Jewish cities, settlements and farms; and while malaria may not currently be a major problem, a range of diseases, especially in Gaza, are on the increase as a result of the lack of clean water (see Zeitoun 2008).

A third standard colonial option for the achievement of an empty land is to make the population leave or disappear. Although something resembling 'persuasion' looks preferable to modern sensibilities, the forcible removal of indigenous peoples has historically been the method most frequently adopted. Once again, and despite denials, removal of the Palestinians has been – and continues to be – a basic assumption for Israeli politicians and Zionist thinkers. Herzl in the 1890s saw the process as essentially non-violent: 'We shall have to spirit the penniless population across the border by procuring employment for it in transit countries, while denying it any employment in our own country. Both the process of expropriation and the removal of the poor must be carried out discreetly and circumspectly' (Herzl, cited in Said 1992: 70–1). Forty years on, David Ben Gurion, later to become Prime Minister, viewed things very differently. In a letter to his son, he wrote: 'We must expel the Arabs and take their place, and if we have to use force, to guarantee our own right to settle in those places, then we have force at our disposal.' In his *War Diary* in 1948, he argued that: 'During the assault we must be ready to strike the decisive blow; that is, either to destroy the town or expel its inhabitants so our people can replace them.' And, finally, writing to the head of the Jewish National Fund, he stated: 'The war will give us land. The concepts of "ours" and "not ours" are peace concepts; only, in war they lose their whole meaning' (cited in Martin 2005).

As far as 1948 is concerned, one of the key legitimating historical accounts offered by the Israelis in terms of an empty land is that when their forces entered Palestinian territory, the Palestinians had simply left their homes and fled en masse. The principal reasons suggested for this somewhat unusual collective behaviour were that the Palestinians had been persuaded by their own leaders and those of neighbouring Arab states to run away, or that they had fled to avoid the Arab armies that invaded Palestine when the Israeli state was declared in May 1948. Despite having been routinely repeated over the years – and apparently still believed in certain quarters – this was a direct obfuscatory lie on the part of the Israeli government, disproved by a secret report produced by their army intelligence services as early as the summer of

1948, showing that the 'emptiness' of the land was in fact the product of successful Israeli military and terrorist actions, psychological warfare and propaganda campaigns. The fact that many of these predated May 1948 was a further indication of the nature of the lie being perpetrated. The ability – or perhaps the need – of ideology to resist contact with reality is further demonstrated by the fact that even in the 1990s the 'liberal' Shimon Peres was happy to repeat in his book *The New Middle East* the central Zionist lie that the Palestinian population ran away in 1948 because their leaders told them to (Peres 1993).

One of the central problems confronting the continuing Israeli desire for 'population transfer' in order to clear the land of unwanted indigenous inhabitants has always been the simple stubborn resistance of Palestinians to further dispossessions and displacements. Said has frequently highlighted the quality of *summud*, that is, the patient, unspectacular, refusal of the Palestinians either to give up or go away, no matter how oppressive the behaviour of the Israeli government, army and settlers may be. In Darwish's simple formulation in 'State of Siege', his people are: 'Standing here. Sitting here. Always here. Eternally here. / And we have one single united goal: To be. / After that, we differ on everything' (Darwish 2002). Merely staying put can in certain circumstances be a not inconsiderable form of resistance, and Said quotes Tawfiq Zayyad's poem 'Baqun' [We shall remain] in this context, where the Palestinian ability to endure literally sticks in the throats of the occupiers just as they themselves 'stick' to the land:

> Our roots are entrenched
> Deep in the earth
> Like twenty impossibles
> We shall remain

> (cited in Said 1992: 130)

The enigmatic 'like twenty impossibles' has more recently been taken as the title of a 2003 film by Annemarie Jacir, which also highlights the ability of culture to 'remain' and resist military occupation.

The most obvious step to be taken in the overcoming of the dispossession suffered by the Palestinian people would of course be to return to them some or all of the land stolen in 1948, or, failing that, in 1967 and on an ongoing basis since then. Despite being obvious, just, and, until recently a fundamental demand of most Palestinians, it remains – unsurprisingly – totally unthinkable and unacceptable to the majority of Israelis, and – slightly more surprisingly perhaps in the circumstances – a subject on which Palestinians have become both pragmatic and flexible.

The simple desire to return is one of the fundamental assumptions of diaspora theory. Stuart Hall's classic article on diaspora and cultural identity offers a somewhat different perspective on the question:

> Diaspora does not refer us to those scattered tribes whose identity can only be secured in relation to some sacred homeland to which they must at all costs return, even if it means pushing other people into the sea. This is the old, the imperialising, the hegemonising form of 'ethnicity'. We have seen the fate of the people of Palestine at the hands of this backward-looking conception of diaspora – and the complicity of the West with it. The diaspora experience as I intend it here is defined, not by essence or purity, but by the recognition of a necessary heterogeneity and diversity; by a conception of 'identity' which lives with and through, not despite, difference; by *hybridity*.
>
> (Hall 1993: 401–2)

Hall is quite correct to condemn the impact on Palestinians of the effects of the obsessive and frequently brutal policies of Zionism to return to and recover all of *Eretz Israel*. He is also probably correct in terms of the unavoidably hybridized nature of diasporic experience and identity. What is perhaps rather less certain is that Palestinians, even after so many years of dispersal, might be – indeed should be – ready to give up the idea of return to their homeland since that is allegedly not what modern diaspora is about. It could of course be argued that Hall is in fact not necessarily claiming such a thing; and that the qualifications in a phrase like 'those scattered tribes whose identity can *only* be secured in relation to some *sacred* homeland *to which they must at all costs return*' allow for more appropriately flexible, inclusive and secular modes of identity formation and diasporic belonging. Be that as it may, the question of the ability, or possibility, of Palestinians to return to Palestine is one of the most contentious issues in the whole 'Palestinian question' – a fact signalled by its relegation to the 'final status negotiations' category in the Oslo Accords, where its resolution remains as likely as the appearance of the famous 'last instance' of Althusserian Marxism.

Return is the site of possibly the most painful of paradoxes ('glaring injustice' or 'rank hypocrisy' would be other ways of describing it) in relation to Palestinian dispersion: the fact that the Israeli Law of Return allows any Jew, from anywhere in the world, to settle in Israel, while no Palestinian has the right to return. In the face of this blatantly discriminatory legislation, UN Resolution 194, which states the right of refugees to return to Palestine or to receive compensation if they do not wish to do so, has been regularly reaffirmed since it was first passed in 1948 – and to that extent might seem to stand in opposition to Hall's apparent downplaying of the importance of return. (Sadly, it doubtless goes without saying that both the original resolution and its repeated restatement have consistently been ignored by Israel and the United States, while at one of the most promising moments for progress on issues relating to Israel/Palestine the then-President Bill Clinton suggested that the time for measures such as Resolution 194 was past, and that new ways of thinking about the question were needed.) However, for a section of dispersed Palestinians, the essentially non-negotiable idea of return is symbolized by the heavy iron door keys which so many took with them as they were driven from their homes in 1948, and which they kept, in many cases worn round their necks, and handed on as necessary.

As well as actively blocking the possibility of Palestinian return, the Israeli government has typically argued that most Palestinians do not want to come back anyway; and while there may be a kind of logic to this (who would actually want to come back in order to be oppressed by the Israelis?), anything like solid evidence is lacking. In that context, a relatively recent survey, which claimed to show that a growing number of Palestinians were not interested in exercising their right of return, caused inevitable controversy. Carried out by the Palestinian Centre for Policy and Survey Research, the purported findings pleased opinion in the United States and Israel as evidence of growing Palestinian moderation, while among the Palestinians themselves they led to angry demonstrations and attacks on the author of the report (see *Middle East Intelligence Bulletin* 2003). The fact that the survey was simultaneously methodologically flawed and coincidentally representative of the 'mature' and 'moderate' position the Palestinian Authority – who had worked closely with the lead researcher – sought to project to the world did little to enhance its credibility. Clearly, the possibility and nature of return for dispossessed and diasporic Palestinians is not to be conjured away by the production of 'facts' such as these.

A paradigmatic figure in terms of the problems and paradoxes of return from the diaspora has been Darwish, for whom the fact of return is in itself no guarantee of an end to exile. In addition to the state of internal colonization in the Occupied Territories as a form of exile, there is the possibility of a more literally internal state of exile, of remaining in exile in one's mind: 'Even if I return to Haifa and Acre and live there, the exile within me, which can be considered a large human exile, will be my overriding human condition' (Darwish 1997a). Describing himself in 'Eleven planets in the last Andalusian sky' as 'An Adam of two Edens / Lost to me twice' (Darwish 2000: 154), Darwish has made two returns to Palestine. The first return was in 1949, after he and his family had fled to Lebanon in the wake of the *Nakba,* and found themselves as members of that category of profound contradictions, the 'present-absent' (that is, those who were not part of the 1949 Israeli census, and therefore lacked proper status under the new dispensation), faced with the loss of home and land – their village of Birweh was one of more than five hundred destroyed by the Israelis after the seizure of Palestine – as well as loss of national identity and civil status. Darwish eventually joined the diaspora in 1970, and made his second return in 1996 after more than a quarter of a century in exile. This return, too, was fraught with contradictions: while it was in a sense a return to the homeland, Ramallah was very much not Darwish's part of Palestine (to which he could not return); there remained, also, the question posed by one of his poems written after the return, 'What will we do without exile?':

> We have become weightless – as light as our dwellings in distant winds.
> We have, both of us, befriended the strange beings in the clouds.
> We have both been freed from the gravity of the land of identity.
> What shall we do?
> What shall we do without exile
> and long nights of gazing at the water?

> > (Darwish 2003: 113)

Despite having had to live in at least eight different countries during his time in the diaspora; despite having endured the brutal siege of Beirut by the Israelis (recorded in his remarkable *Memory for Forgetfulness*) and the subsequent expulsion of the PLO, Darwish – in many ways like his friend Edward Said – refuses to see exile as a purely negative condition. As the poem 'What will we do without exile?' suggests, exile can be a paradoxical form of liberation – 'We have both been freed from the gravity of the land of identity' – offering a certain kind of relief, although in other ways being cut adrift from the homeland is hardly desirable. For Darwish, however, the experiences of exile, as well as being formative and constitutive of so much that he has become, are simply too enriching to be peremptorily disavowed: 'Exile has been very generous and educational, providing culture, enlarging my human scope and the scope of my language, and enabling my poetic phrases to include dialogue between peoples and cultures' (Darwish 1997a). The important thing for him is that exile should be properly understood – including its contradictory aspects: 'The only thing we must guard against is that exile should not become a habit, but rather a way of looking at human existence and the isolation of beings in this existence. Therefore no homeland can cancel exile, and no exile can cancel the homeland' (Darwish 1999: 7). Adorno's comment in *Minima Moralia* that '[t]oday [...] it is part of morality not to be at home in one's home' (Adorno 1974: 39) is no doubt one with which Darwish would agree.

Given the current impossibility for most Palestinians in the diaspora of returning to any part of the Occupied Territories, the idea of return risks losing a certain power or relevance. In that situation, Said continued, right up until his death in 2003, to champion the principle of the right of return, and was one of a small number of people who attempted/dared to think about the issue differently. In *After the Last Sky*, for example, he says:

All of us speak of *awdah*, 'return', but do we mean that literally, or do we mean 'we must restore ourselves to ourselves'? The latter is the real point, I think, although I know many Palestinians who want their houses and their way of life back, exactly. But is there any place that fits us, together with our accumulated memories and experiences?

(Said 1986: 33)

The idea of 'restoring ourselves to ourselves' or 'returning to ourselves', is one to which he himself returned on various occasions, extending and refining the notion:

But what return does mean to me is return to oneself, that is to say, a return to history, so that we understand what exactly happened, why it happened and who we are. That we are people from that land, maybe not living there, but with important historical claims and roots. Many of our people will continue to reside there. But we have a common self-consciousness of not the most, but one of the most interesting twentieth century experiences of dispossession, exile, migration.

(Said 2004a: 429)

Part of the importance for Palestinians of 'returning to ourselves' historically, as Said indicates, is the continuing fact of historical and historiographical dispossession – a process which in various ways is as 'grounded' or territorial as the theft of the land, and one which also separates and disperses. Just as the land of Palestine was to be cleared of the unwanted presence of its inhabitants, so the period after 1948 witnessed the 'clearing' of evidence of non-Jewish cultures: in the shape of their historical and archaeological remains, from the landscape as well as the looting of their artefacts from museums and archives. Part of this was sanctioned – if secret – Israeli government policy; part of it unattributable (military) vandalism – again. Astonishingly, as well as the 'primitive' cultural relics of the Palestinian past – with something like eighty per cent of village mosques demolished in this period – the destruction also included remarkable Roman remains, as in the city of Tiberias, which happened even when Israeli officials had specifically asked for them to be spared (see Rapaport 2007). Once again, just as the Nakba contrived to be both punctual historical event and persistent catastrophic condition, so the obliteration of historic non-Jewish sites in Palestine proved to be not simply a product of the destructive ecstasy of the moment of victory in 1948, but much more of a calculated, consistent approach, a policy that is still being carried out today, in pointless demolition, bulldozing and dynamiting in cities such as Nablus and Hebron.

At the same time, while one area of historical and archaeological evidence was being actively suppressed, another – Jewish – was being even more energetically discovered – or, as Said would argue, invented and constructed, in particular through the medium of archaeology and Biblical studies. The historical narratives they produced became a particularly effective means of dispossessing the Palestinians in this field:

> For years and years an assiduous campaign to maintain a frozen version of Israel's heroic narrative of repatriation and justice obliterated any possibility of a Palestinian narrative, in large part because certain key components of the Israeli story stressed certain geographical characteristics of Palestine itself.
>
> (Said 2000: 184)

For Darwish, also, the domination of one narrative – especially historical – over others brings in its train the domination of the land to which the narrative refers (see 'Qui impose son récit hérite la Terre du Récit', in Darwish 1997b). As a result, as Said goes on to say:

> Perhaps the greatest battle Palestinians have waged as a people has been over the right to a remembered presence and, with that presence,

the right to possess and reclaim a collective historical reality, at least since the Zionist movement began its encroachments on the land.

(Said 2000: 184)

Unfortunately, despite certain advances and limited achievements this is not an area where Palestinians can yet claim any significant victories. Part of the reason for this lies in the already-mentioned ability of the Israeli narrative to override and deny legitimacy to their Palestinian counterpart. Part of it, however, lies in a particular kind of Palestinian failure: 'Yet the fate of Palestinian history has been a sad one, since not only was independence not gained, but there was little collective understanding of the importance of constructing a collective history as a part of trying to gain independence' (Said 2000: 184).

Questions of Palestinian responsibility for their lack of collective progress occur elsewhere. Although Darwish has examined the possibility of 'returning to ourselves' from different angles, the nature and condition of the Palestinian self or selves may not be a constant, still less a comforting, entity. In the wake of the fighting between Hamas and Fatah in Gaza and the West Bank in early 2007 – which also happened to be the fortieth anniversary of the Six-Day War, marking another crucial stage in Palestinian dispossession – Darwish wrote an angry poem entitled 'From now on you are not yourself', attacking the fratricidal conflict not only for its impact on Palestinian identity, but also for doing the Israelis' dirty work for them:

> June amazed us on its fortieth anniversary:
> If we do not find someone to defeat us again,
> We defeat ourselves with our own hands
> So as not to forget.

(Darwish 2007)

The development of a proper historical awareness in relation to issues of 'returning to ourselves' may produce paradoxical results. One of the central concepts in Said's discussion of colonialism in *Culture and Imperialism* is that of that the need for a contrapuntal reading strategy 'with a simultaneous awareness both of the metropolitan history that is narrated and of those other histories against which (and together with which) the dominating discourse acts' (Said 1993: 59). The contrapuntal strategy is appropriate in the context of the 'Overlapping Territories, Intertwined Histories' that Said sees as constituting the geopolitical framework. The Israel/Palestine conflict, however, is structured very much in terms of the exact opposite of the overlapping and the intertwined, particularly where culture and identity are concerned. Therefore, the idea of Palestinians 'returning to ourselves' would seem, on the face of it, to imply the recovery of a unitary, perhaps primordial, form of identity. Certainly, as far as Darwish is concerned, there is a pressing need to reject, or to escape from, an alien, imposed identity. In terms that recall both Sartre in *Anti-Semite and Jew* and Fanon in *The Wretched of the Earth*, he says: 'It is the Other who ceaselessly demands that I be an Arab – in accordance with his definition of Arabness, of course' (Darwish 1997b: 35). What is being escaped to, however, is a historically informed sense of intertwined identities, which Said would approve of – even if the (Israeli) Other cannot recognize this:

> Since this land has, throughout its history, been criss-crossed by strangers, and I myself at a particular moment have been a 'stranger' in it, I can accept that we should both be strangers. But he demands that I be the only stranger, the only intruder. And he insists on being the only 'authentic' one.
>
> (Darwish 1997b: 35)

'Returning to ourselves' therefore – in some ways paradoxically, in others quite logically – reveals itself to be a going forward rather than a going back, a movement in the direction of complexity, rather than simplification. An awareness of complexity, of shared humanity and cultural interconnectedness in the context of Palestine/Israel is something that has characterized Darwish's work at least since early poems, such as 'A soldier dreams of white lilies' from 1967, and which he retains even in the most challenging of conditions, such as the 2002 siege. At various moments in the poem 'State of Siege', Israeli soldiers and 'a quasi-Orientalist' are invited to recognize their shared humanity and cultural proximity to those whom they attack either with weapons or with words, while one of Darwish's optimistic visions of a possible lifting of the siege is precisely premised on cultural exchange: 'The siege will last until our enemies have been taught / Some of our *jahili* [pre-Islamic] poetry' (Darwish 2002). Unfortunately, on one side of the divide, any kind of infiltration by the alien culture is still seen as a major threat: when the besieged ask for a truce so that 'a bit of peace might seep into the soul', the response from their attackers is: 'Don't you know that peace with oneself / Opens the doors of our fortress to *hijaz* and *nahawand* music?' (Darwish 2002). A particular problem for Darwish in this respect is that everything is available to be shared – with the exception of history, which so far has remained an area of antagonism and irreconcilability in a way that individual and collective identities seem not to be. As he says in 'Qui impose son récit hérite la Terre du Récit' (Darwish 1997b), it is already difficult to agree over a history which is in fact incontestable, so what hope is there when faced with two histories apparently so implacably opposed?

As far as Said is concerned, however, apparently implacable oppositions are there to be worked through – however difficult the process involved – with the ultimate aim of overcoming both division and dispossession. As one possible means for healing wounds and bringing the two populations closer (ideally, *en route* to the establishment of a bi-national state), he was a long-term advocate of a local version of the South African Truth and Reconciliation Commission – though he later suggested that a Historical Truth and Political Justice Committee might be more appropriate (see Said 2004b). He was also part of movements such as the Palestine National Initiative which aim both to effect change within the Palestinian territories and between the Palestinians and Israelis. As an instance of what is closest to his heart – music – but which stands as what may be achieved within the broader cultural sphere, he founded the (now hugely successful) East-West Divan Orchestra with Daniel Barenboim to allow young Palestinian and Israeli musicians to play together for the first time.

Given so many years of belief in, and so many examples of determined commitment to, connectedness and coexistence, it is strange – at the very least – to find Said being accused of exactly the opposite by someone who might be expected to be on the same side or to interpret him better. In his book *Destroying the Other's Collective Memory,* Ilan Gur-Ze'ev ('one of the leading figures of the Israeli educational left') mounts an attack on Said, largely based on a few final comments in an interview with the Israeli newspaper *Ha'aretz,* where Said playfully claims, as true follower of Adorno, to be 'the last Jewish intellectual' (see Said 2004a: 458). For Gur-Ze'ev, however, this means that 'he wants to inherit their Jewishness', and that it somehow makes him 'part of a wider trend which represents the Zionist and very often any Zionist as a present-day Nazi' (Gur-Ze'ev 2003: 46). Further, Said is accused of having a 'colonialist project' in relation to Palestine/Israel (Gur-Ze'ev 2003: 47). At one level, such claims – however bizarre they might appear – could be seen as simply following Gur-Ze'ev's highly problematic zero-sum approach to understanding the situation in Palestine/Israel, where for him the two sides are locked into identical rejectionist positions by denying the 'Other' any validity whatsoever. While this ignores multiple instances of Palestinian accommodation to Israeli positions and demands (including unreciprocated recognition of Israel), its theoretical approach denies in advance – and therefore refuses to acknowledge – the sort of efforts made by Said and others in this field. As an unlooked-for instance of intellectual dismissal or dispossession perpetrated by a putative ally – devaluing arguably some of Said's most important contributions – it stands as a salutary reminder of the continuing greater dispossessions of his people. For Said, as for his people – dispersed, dispossessed, if not automatically diasporic – the struggle for justice and return in the liberated space of the post-colonial goes on. Their achievement, and the concomitant end of exile, would be just one of the reasons why, for Said, such a thing as a postcolonial diaspora could never exist.

Note

1. Mahmoud Darwish died on 9 August 2008, when this book was in its final proof stages.

Bibliography

Adorno, T. (1974) *Minima Moralia: Reflections on a Damaged life* (London: NLB).

Bauman, Z. (2002) *Society under Siege* (Cambridge: Polity).

Benjamin, W. (1982) 'Theses on the Philosophy of History' in *Illuminations* (London: Fontana/Collins), pp. 249–66.

Benjamin, W. (1985) 'Central Park', *New German Critique*, 34, 32–58.

Braziel, J. E. and Mannur, A. (2003) *Theorizing Diaspora: A Reader* (Oxford: Blackwell).

Childs, P. and Williams, P. (1996) *Introduction to Post-Colonial Theory* (Harlow: Longman/Pearson).

Chomsky, N. (1992) *Deterring Democracy* (London: Vintage).

Cohen, R. (1997) *Global Diasporas: An Introduction* (London: UCL Press).

Darwish, M. (1995) *Memory for Forgetfulness: August, Beirut 1982* (Berkeley, CA: University of California Press).

Darwish, M. (1997a) 'Home is more lovely than the way home', *Al Jadid*, 3 (19 June), www.aljadid.com, date accessed 1 May 2008.

Darwish, M. (1997b) *La Palestine comme métaphore* (Arles: Actes Sud).

Darwish, M. (1999) 'There is no meaning to my life outside poetry', *Banipal*, 4: 5–11.

Darwish, M. (2000) *The Adam of Two Edens: Selected Poems*. Trans. by Munir Akash and Daniel Moore (Syracuse, NY: Syracuse University Press).

Darwish, M. (2001) 'Not to begin at the end', *Al Ahram Weekly* (15 May 2001), weekly.ahram.org/eg, date accessed 1 May 2008.

Darwish, M. (2002) 'State of Siege', *Al Ahram Weekly* (11 April), weekly.ahram. org/eg, date accessed 1 May 2008.

Darwish, M. (2003) *Unfortunately, it was Paradise: Selected Poems*. Trans. by Munir Akash and Carolyn Forché with Sinan Antoon and Amira El-Zein (Berkeley, CA: University of California Press).

Darwish, M. (2004) 'Edward Said: a contrapuntal reading', *Al Ahram Weekly* (30 September), weekly.ahram.org/eg, date accessed 1 May 2008.

Darwish, M. (2007) 'From now on you are not yourself'. Extracts cited in *The Economist* (21 June), www.economist.com, date accessed 1 May 2008.

Fanon, F. (1990 [1961]) *The Wretched of the Earth* (Harmondsworth: Penguin).

Gregory, D. (2004) *The Colonial Present: Afghanistan, Palestine, Iraq* (Oxford: Blackwell).

Gur-Ze'ev, I. (2003) *Destroying the Other's Collective Memory* (New York: Peter Lang).

Hall, S. (1993) 'Cultural Identity and Diaspora' in P. Williams and L. Chrisman (eds) *Colonial Discourse and Post-Colonial Theory*, pp. 392–403.

Jaggi, M. (2002) 'Poet of the Arab world', *Guardian* (8 June), www.guardian.co.uk, date accessed 1 May 2008.

Kalra V., Kaur, R. and Hutnyk, J. (2005) *Diaspora and Hybridity* (London: Sage).

Kodmani-Darwish, B. (1997) *La Diaspora palestinienne* (Paris: PUF).

Martin, W. (2005) 'Who is pushing whom into the sea?' *Counterpunch* (11 March), www.counterpunch.org, date accessed 1 May 2008.

McClintock, A. (1993) 'The Angel of Progress: pitfalls of the term post-colonialism' in P. Williams and L. Chrisman (eds) *Colonial Discourse and Post-Colonial Theory*, pp. 291–304.

Middle East Intelligence Bulletin (2003) 5.8–9 (August–September).

Pappe, I. (2006) *The Ethnic Cleansing of Palestine* (Oxford: Oneworld).

Peres, S. (1993) *The New Middle East* (London: Element Books).

Rapoport, M. (2007) 'History erased', *Ha'aretz* (6 July), www.haaretz.com, date accessed 1 May 2008.

Said, E. (1986) *After the Last Sky* (London: Faber & Faber).

Said, E. (1988) *Blaming the Victims* (London: Verso).

Said, E. (1992) *The Question of Palestine* (New York: Vintage).

Said, E. (1993) *Culture and Imperialism* (London: Chatto & Windus).

Said, E. (1995) *The Politics of Dispossession* (London: Vintage).

Said, E. (2000) 'Invention, memory and place', *Critical Inquiry*, 26.2, 175–92.

Said, E. (2004a) *Power, Politics and Culture* (London: Bloomsbury).

Said, E. (2004b) *From Oslo to Iraq and the Roadmap* (London: Bloomsbury).

Sartre, J-P. (1995 [1946]) *Anti-Semite and Jew* (New York: Schocken Books).

Shammas, A. (1999) 'The Poet Goes Home', *Banipal*, 4, 14–15.

Tölölyan, K. (1991) 'The nation-state and its others: in lieu of a preface', *Diaspora* 1.1, 3–7.

UNHCR (2006) *State of the World's Refugees*.

Williams, P. (2001) 'Nothing in the Post? Said and the problem of post-colonial intellectuals' in B. Ashcroft and H. Kadhim (eds) *Edward Said and the Post-Colonial* (Huntington, NY: Nova Science Publishers), pp. 314–34.

Williams, P. and Chrisman, L. (1993) *Colonial Discourse and Post-Colonial Theory* (New York: Columbia University Press).

Zeitoun, M. (2008) *Power and Water in the Middle East* (London: Pluto).

5
Latin Americans in London and the Dynamics of Diasporic Identities

Patria Román-Velázquez

The migration of Latin Americans to Britain and the contribution of Latin Americans to London's distinct and varied cultural 'ethnoscape' have been conspicuously neglected in the literature on diasporas.[1] The aim of this essay is to make this presence more visible and in doing so I wish to contribute more broadly to debates about the movement and articulation of cultural identities across different geographical locations. This will be done firstly by exploring the ways in which Latin Americans develop routes through the city and establish connections to specific sites; and, secondly, the essay will focus on the ways in which Latin Americans contribute to the changing character of London by transforming these sites, thereby attributing specific Latin identities to them. Studies of diaspora have provided us with ways of understanding the types of connection that people establish with certain locations, as well as the ways in which identities are transformed in the process of relocation. These issues are often explored in relation to the nation-state (through ideas of national and cultural identity) and not in relation to specific sites within the territories in which these groups have relocated.[2] However, in approaching the issue of Latin identities in London I draw on the concept of diaspora as a way of understanding the relationship between place and identity. Diasporas all too often invoke movement across places and shifting identities – which in turn implies the idea of location and dislocation; diasporas are both dispersed and physically located, and as such imagined as belonging to various places simultaneously. This way of understanding diaspora challenges the idea of places as bounded and as a point of origin – as if people belong to these in a pure way (Hall 1995). Following Stuart Hall I treat places as porous and open to transformation – in the same way that identities are thought of as unstable, heterogeneous and fragmented. Approaching diaspora in this way 'does not depend on thinking about culture, identity and place in a closed unified or homogeneous way, as a return to roots, but instead redefines culture as a series of overlapping routes' (1995: 209). Thinking about Latin American identities in London through the idea of diaspora provides a way of exploring the relationship between place and identity as a series of overlapping routes through the city (in the manner traced by Hall).

I also draw on Hall's concept of identity as involving a constant process of change and transformation. I argue that cultural forms and practices (in this case Latin American) do not simply travel unproblem- atically from their 'original' location and then appear in the same form in other places; instead as 'global' movements (of people, images and things) take place so new identities are made, remade and articulated in new places (Hall 1991). I am not proposing an alternative argument about new, freely created 'diasporic' cultures, but wish to stress the ways in which Latin American cultural identities in London are constituted out of unequal power relations.

In connecting cultural identity to the issue of power, I draw on Doreen Massey's notion of 'power-geometry' to highlight that diaspora is not merely about 'who moves and who does not although that is an important element of it; it is also about power in relation to the flows and movements' (1993b: 61). In critiquing David Harvey (1989) and Anthony Giddens (1990) she stresses that the global movement of people around the world cannot be explained solely in relation to the economic development of capitalism or in relation to the spread of the institutions of modernity. Not everyone experiences global move- ment to the same degree: some are in a position of control, others are participating in that process but have little influence, some are on the receiving end, while others both contribute and are imprisoned by these movements (1993b). This is what Massey calls 'power-geometry' in order to highlight how 'different social groups and different individuals are placed in very distinct ways in relation to these flows and intercon- nections' (1993b: 61). Massey stresses that it is important to understand the ways in which people are both placed and assume a position in relation to a politics of mobility, access, international migration, trans- portation, ethnicity and gender. She adds that 'it is not simply a ques- tion of unequal distribution, that some people move more than others, some have more control than others. It is that the mobility and control of some groups can actively weaken other people' (1993b: 62). Thus, Massey argues that it is important to consider how social groups occupy different positions and how power is constituted through and as a result of the relations between these positions: 'Space is by its very nature full of power and symbolism, a complex web of relations of domination and subordination, of solidarity and co-operation' (1993a: 156).

This essay draws on the concept of 'power-geometry' by providing a focused discussion of how the evolution of immigration law in the UK has had a direct influence on the visible presence of Latin Americans in London, and discusses how Latin Americans manage to operate within these constraints by developing distinct spatial practices and routes through the city. The essay also explains how Latin Americans have contributed to the continual physical transformation and cultural associations of specific buildings, areas and resources; in this sense Latin Americans are developing links and establishing new relationships with existing places while contributing to, and becoming part of London's ethnoscape.

Negotiating routes through the city

Space is politically regulated and the movements of Latin Americans into and then across London is directly related to the attempts to classify, order and control the entry of people into Britain. Immigration controls in Great Britain have had a direct impact on the movement and visibility of Latin Americans across London. At the same time, Latin Americans have appropriated, transformed and used particular areas of the city for specific cultural practices. In this section I am concerned with the role of the nation state in defining its territorial borders and how these regulations have a direct impact both on people's mobility and their visible presence within the city. In the next section, I will discuss the ways in which Latin Americans have re-made parts of the city and given them a specifically Latin identity.

Latin Americans in London provide a particularly interesting focus for the exploration of diaspora, as they are not directly connected to the Commonwealth or Britain's ex-colonies. The arrival of Latin Americans in Britain as a large immigrant group started in the early 1970s, gradually increased in numbers and became more visible towards the end of the 1980s. The experience of migration has not been the same for everyone. Large numbers of Latin Americans arrived in Britain as migrant workers, some came as political refugees and others were escaping from political and civil unrest in their own countries.

During the 1970s, when Latin Americans began to arrive seeking employment, economic difficulties were starting to intensify in Britain: unemployment was rising, inflation was high and there was an increase in racial attacks and the mobilization of right-wing political parties around a xenophobic agenda (see Centre for Contemporary Cultural Studies 1982). However, many Latin American countries were enduring high external debt, civil war, invasion, dictatorship, economic instability and currency devaluation along with various related social problems; the immigration of Latin Americans to Britain during the 1970s was thus closely connected to the situation in Latin America. However, why did these migrants choose Britain as their preferred destination? The Immigration Act of 1971 played an important part in enabling Latin American immigration into Britain. This act allowed people from countries that had no relationship with the British Empire to enter the country. While the entrance of Latin Americans occurred prior to this act, most came as spouses or dependants of British subjects.[3]

In the early 1970s, many Latin Americans entered Britain with contracts of employment, most of them to work in hotels, factories, restaurants or as domestic employees. Those who came to Britain during this period and under the policies established by the Act of 1971 did not have problems with their visa because they arrived with work permits. After working for four years with the same employer the person could apply for residency and was then 'free' to look for another job. However, this did not necessarily mean that an individual's economic situation and employment circumstances would improve. Employment conditions, working standards, wages and lack of promotion were some of the problems faced by Latin Americans; added to this were the uncertainties of searching for new jobs, dealing with the cultural differences encountered in the host country, finding comfortable and affordable housing, as well as understanding how to obtain health care. In addition, many Colombian women between the ages of 18 and 23 came into Britain through an 'au-pair' scheme which provided an opportunity for Colombian women to get a job and learn English, which would have been difficult to do in Colombia. However, the situation changed in 1978 when new immigration controls were introduced that imposed restrictions on 'au-pair' immigrants (Juan Rincón, cited in Santiago Castrillón 1984).

Many Latin Americans came to Britain as political refugees, principally because of the dictatorships in Uruguay and Argentina. Chileans also arrived after Augusto Pinochet's coup d'état in September 1973. Unlike economic immigrants, political refugees were entitled to certain protections and benefits. However, in Diana Kay's (1987) account of Chilean refugees she notes that they had little say in decisions on where to live and most were unemployed. The initial period of settlement for refugees involved feelings of confusion; they felt unable to engage in political activity relating to their homelands and most thought of this as a transitory period. Asylum is an alternative for many Latin Americans escaping from political and civil violence in their countries. These groups have reorganized politically and established solidarity campaigns in order to maintain links with, and highlight the situation of, their own countries, and they have also played an important role in organizing and advising Latin Americans already in London.

According to estimates based on the 2001 census a total of 31,387 Latin Americans were registered as living in London: of these Colombians (9035) and Brazilians (8162) make up the largest groups, followed by Argentineans (2557), Ecuadorians (2301) and Chileans (2054). There are also a smaller number of Venezuelans, Mexicans, Cubans, Peruvians, Uruguayans and Bolivians (McIlwaine 2007).[4] However, these figures are misleading as according to unofficial estimates the number of Latin Americans in London could be as high as 700,000 to 1,000,000, if the figures were to include those people who have overstayed the expiry of their visas (McIlwaine 2007). If these estimates are correct, then most of the Latin American population in London live without the proper documentation. Not surprisingly, immigration status is high on the list of issues that Latin Americans have to confront in order to survive in the capital as reported in McIlwaine's (2007) study of Latin Americans in London. It is important to recognize that there is not a unified or homogenous Latin identity in London: Latin identities are often represented through national symbols, while specific practices are also defined by issues of class and regional differences. The examples presented throughout this essay highlight not just the contrasting, differentiated and multiple Latin identities present in the city, but how these are politicized through the power relations involved in creating the identity of the various Latin sites. Latin American identities in London must thus be understood in relation to how different groups have come to occupy different positions and how certain cultural practices are positioned in terms of particular power relations throughout the city.

Those who have overstayed their visas will have to negotiate their routes through London in quite distinct ways when compared with other immigrants who are legally settled in Britain. As soon as legal boundaries are transgressed, the worry is to operate without being caught, or to find a way to live legally in Britain. Undocumented immigrants do not have any employment rights and are often susceptible to exploitation in their workplace. Many of these 'invisible workers' come with the idea of working hard for a couple of years, saving some money and then returning to their home countries. But many never return as Britain offers economic stability not only to the immigrant, but also to the families they have left back home. For an illegal immigrant to return to their countries might mean, among other things, the risk of not being allowed back into Britain (a risk many people do not wish to take). The desire of employers to recruit a low-paid labour force, particularly in manual work and hotels, along with an awareness of the political, civil and economic situation in many Latin American countries, and the hopes for better living standards once back home, explain why many people operate as 'invisible workers'.

Undocumented immigrants live in constant fear of being caught by the immigration authorities; they are uncertain about the system and find it very difficult to integrate into the city. Their movements are constrained and this encourages the development of alternative spatial patterns and routes across London. For example Rubén Cárdenas narrates the spatial patterns he developed from his working place to his home once his visa expired:

> When the visa ran out and I had to leave work at midnight, every time I came across a policeman on my way home I began to shiver and shake, but I learned to calm down and worked out a way home through the back streets of Pimlico. Before that I used to get off in Victoria tube station, but you encounter many police in that area, so now I get off at Pimlico which is a longer walk but with less chance of coming across policemen.
>
> (cited in Castrillón 1984: 40)

As also noted by McIlwaine (2007) some undocumented Latin Americans avoid places such as Elephant and Castle shopping centre, Tiendas del Norte or Pueblito Paisa in Seven Sisters (known for their concentration of Latin American shops) for fear of being caught by immigration authorities. These places are visited for functional reasons such as purchasing Latin American products or sending money abroad, but they are not areas in which to spend a long time. For those who are undocumented their illegal status and fear of deportation tends to dominate most aspects of their social lives. This affects the jobs that they are able to choose, as well as access to health services, housing and other aspects of their social life, such as visiting clubs or restaurants in the capital. Visiting places like Elephant and Castle shopping centre and Seven Sisters market do not represent a threat for those who are legally resident in the United Kingdom; some might use these locations as a meeting place, an information centre or as a site where they can find Latin American products.

For those who are legally resident in the UK, the routes through the city are informed by personal and economic circumstances. For example, in a series of in-depth interviews that I conducted with Latin Americans in London throughout the summer of 2005, it became evident that their routes through the city were guided by issues such as workplace, economic and family circumstances. Claudia is a middle-class Argentinean woman who arrived in 1990 with a fiancé visa after having finished her BA in Canada where she met her English boyfriend. She explained how her routes through London have changed in relation to her altered circumstances. The first two years she experienced as difficult. Things got easier when she started working for Amnesty International and received a regular income, and when her social network widened. After fifteen years – having given birth to two children and with a more demanding job at another NGO – she was leading a more localized life around the area where she lives and works:

> There are zones that I never visit, I hardly ever visit the west of London, there are zones that I do not know. London is like a series of small villages all next to each other. Now that I am working near Angel I come to this area, but before I just used to visit the centre of London. I hardly ever go to Oxford Street now; I spend a lot of time near my zone. It is very regionalized... Also with the kids, it is more complicated, because things are more expensive you tend to carry water and so on. So, unless we take the kids to a particular museum, we tend to do things locally, we take them to the local cinema and that way we support it.
> (Personal interview with Claudia Rico, 20 June 2005)[5]

This experience of living a rather localized life in London was common among those I interviewed. For Rosario, also from Argentina, then unemployed, and resident in London since 2002, life revolves around Hackney:

> it is what I talk about with a friend, she also lives in the neighbourhood, you are always here in the neighbourhood, and we are always walking around, taking the boys to the park or to any other activity, and sometimes it feels as if we do not live in London. We are always here in the neighbourhood, after all you ask yourself, do I really live in London? I am half an hour away from the centre and I really do not feel like it at times.
> (Personal interview with Claudia Rico, 20 June 2005)

Visits to Latin American shops, clubs and restaurants in London tended to be more frequent not long after arriving in the UK and became less frequent as time went on, but still remain an important part of their social life. This was the case for example, with Claudia, who acknowledged that she rarely visited Latin American shops after the first years she was in London. Visits to shops, clubs and cafes were crucial for developing and maintaining social networks and were important during the initial settling process, but became less significant over time.

However, Latin American festivals have had a more enduring presence in the lives of those who have settled and for their children who are growing up in London. Festivals of music, dancing, food and culture provide occasions for affirming and celebrating a sense of Latin American cultural identity. Claudia for example narrated how she has taken her children to a Latin American festival to show them aspects of Latin American culture and allow then to hear and speak Spanish.

Latin Americans may take very similar routes across London. They might visit the same places, whether the tourist areas of central London or specific Latin American shops in outer regions, but their motives and reasons for taking such routes may be quite different. For example, for Claudia the routes and social networks that she developed were not based on a desire to belong to one place in particular, but of a sense of 'belonging a little bit in everyplace...One makes connections with the people who are around you with the interests that you have. Nationalism and the state issue are irrelevant' (personal interview with Claudia Rico, 20 June 2005).

The economic situation also shapes the possibilities for creating contact zones. For example, Claudia considers London to be a great city but only for those with money, and remarked: 'if you live in a bed-sit and work all day then it can be quite oppressive' (personal interview with Claudia Rico, 20 June 2005). Her view was confirmed by Angel who arrived from Ecuador in 1997, and who was working as a head waiter in 2005; of his first year and a half in London he says:

> When I first arrived I started washing dishes in a restaurant in Sloane Square. My brother-in-law worked there and that is how I connected with that. I worked there for about a year and a half, but at the same time I used to do cleaning in the mornings. That is, I used to have two hours of cleaning and then I went to the restaurant. After three months of being here I started studying, that was my break, and then back to work. That is, I used to work from six to eight, then from nine to three in the restaurant. From there I used to go to Victoria to the Westminster School from three to six and after that from six to

eleven at night again. That was the life that I had during a year and a half.

(Personal interview with Angel, 23 June 2005)

Thus, it is clear that the routes of Latin Americans in London are shaped by their economic, political and personal circumstances at any given period in their lives. However, as was noted above, for those who are undocumented their movements in the city are dominated by anxiety and fear over their legal status. Illegality means that people must think carefully about their movements in the city and negotiate the city in a different way to that of legal immigrants.

The legal status of Latin Americans has had an impact on their mobility and their visibility in London. For some, participating in activities in London's Latin locations involves confronting state regulation of citizenship and enforcement of immigration laws – most apparent when immigration officers raid premises used by Latin Americans. These regulations have an impact on people's mobility and influence their connections with the broader spectrum of Latin sites in London. However, policies and laws by themselves do not determine the movement of people; these are applied in certain ways and negotiated and subverted in others.

Constructing Latin locations and communicating Latin identities in London

London, we are told, is a 'world city': as a leading capital of culture it has been described as a multicultural and a cosmopolitan city due to the variety of people, products and practices that are present.[6] London's Latin locations contribute to – and at the same time transcend – conceptualizations of cultural diversity in the capital. Like many large cities, London contains numerous neighbourhoods that may be known locally as Afro-Caribbean, Irish or Chinese; and even though there is not a Latin American neighbourhood as such, a Latin presence can be detected in the numerous Latin-themed bars, restaurants and shops across the capital as well as by long-standing cultural events such as the Latin American carnival (Carnaval del Pueblo) in Burgess Park and the Latin American film festival (across various cinemas in London). Here I will concentrate on only a few manifestations of Latin identity in order to highlight the 'power-geometry' within which a Latin presence comes to be realized in the city. I shall provide an indication of this by referring to places that have been transformed and re-made as 'Latin' by both Latin Americans and non-Latin Americans.

I will focus on Latin American-owned shops at the Elephant and Castle shopping centre. One of the many other ways in which 'Latinness' is signified in the capital is through salsa music clubs, as is demonstrated in my previous research (Román-Velázquez 1996, 1999). My intention, in moving between these different types of locations, is to highlight the ways in which Latin Americans encounter (in creating routes through the city) a contrast between self-supporting attempts to maintain a sense of continuous, yet changing, identity and the different constructions of 'Latinness' that can be found in many of London's shops, bars, clubs and restaurants. My intention is not to raise issues about authenticity, but to highlight that despite the possibilities that cities provide for 'contact zones' and new hybrid identities, diasporic cultural practices often remain divided and separated.

Mapping out the location of Latin American-owned shops in London is not as easy as it was at the beginning of the 1990s, when I first conducted research about Latin Americans in London (Román-Velázquez 1999). During the 1990s most of the shops and restaurants established by Latin Americans were located south of the River Thames around the administrative boroughs of Lambeth and Southwark. Most of the retail activity was at the Elephant and Castle Shopping Centre with ten shops owned by Latin Americans. Another twelve shops could be found further down and around the ring of roads surrounding a shopping centre near to Brixton, Vauxhall and Clapham Common underground stations. Elephant and Castle, Camberwell, Peckham and Borough could be identified as areas where a Latin American presence was most obvious. It was in these areas that a visible Latin American economic and cultural activity was initiated in shops, bars, clubs and restaurants. However, by the end of the 1990s, Latin Americans were also running shops, restaurants and music clubs in other areas of north and east London, such as Holloway, Stoke Newington, Manor House and Seven Sisters. The 2008 edition of *Paginas Latinas* – a commercial guide catering for Latin Americans in London – provides an indication of the increase in the Latin American presence in the capital.[7] Elephant and Castle, Newington Butts and surrounding areas in South London still had the greatest concentration of Latin American-owned shops; however, Tiendas del Norte in Seven Sisters market has been emerging as another Latin American area, suggesting that in a period of about fifteen years (from 1992, when I first started doing research on Latin Americans in London to 2008) the distribution of Latin American-owned shops in the city has become more widespread and dispersed.

The Elephant and Castle shopping centre was one of the first in Britain when it opened in 1965. Apart from its location: 'Marooned by hurtling traffic on a life-threatening system of roundabouts in Southwark, south London' (Hall 1992: 18), and in one of the areas of highest unemployment, the Centre was also strongly affected by the economic recession at the end of the 1980s. Almost all the shops were closing or ceasing operations. By 1991, for example, there were hardly any shops open on the first floor of the Centre (Hall 1992). A year later Latin Americans started opening shops on the first level of the shopping centre. La Fogata opened in June 1992, followed by Inara Travels whose manager tried to encourage other Latin Americans to do likewise. By 1994 there were ten shops owned by Latin Americans including food shops, fritter stalls, a travel agency, a jeweller, an employment agency, a hairdresser and a tailor's shop. Fifteen years on, the presence of Latin Americans was still strong, with small snack places situated on the outside of the shopping centre (refer to Figure 5.1).

The economic situation was an important element stimulating the movement of Latin Americans into the shopping centre, while low rent was one of the most attractive features. Elephant and Castle showed the signs of a deprived inner-city shopping area that was frequented by low-income groups and that had been aesthetically neglected.

Figure 5.1 Elephant and Castle Shopping Centre (Photo taken by P. Román-Velázquez, May 2006)

Hence, Latin Americans started investing in a place when there was no guarantee of economic success, running businesses in areas that were in decline and which had been vacated at the end of the 1980s boom. This is not only an indication of how Latin Americans were located in an economically marginal position within the city, but also of how the economic decline provided possibilities for those who otherwise would not have the economic capital for investment. However, since land value in 'Zone One' has steadily been increasing and given its proximity to central London as well as its strategic location for commerce and businesses, plans were put in place for the redevelopment of Elephant and Castle. These development plans will include the demolition of the shopping centre in 2010 to provide new green spaces for recreation, play areas for children, a new open market as well as a new retail space.[8] Consequently, these plans raise a number of questions about the position and influence of Latin Americans within the planning of the new development. Latin Americans are represented in the committee meetings and have been offered financial compensation for their loss once the shopping centre is demolished. At the time of writing this essay, it is unclear whether the Latin American shops will have a place in the newly developed retail space or in the open market area.

The shops at the old Elephant and Castle shopping centre were constructed to create the illusion of being outdoors. Manufactured of wood, these shops were in a row in the middle of the corridor (previously the floor space of the centre) as if they were a row of shops in a little street. Towards the end of the 1990s the external appearance of the colourful row of shops was replaced with modular white metal structures, but the internal decoration and layout of the shops remained more or less unchanged. These shops are organized and decorated so as to resemble many of the little shops you can find in some rural areas or inner-country towns in many countries of Latin America. For example, 'La Tienda' (as it is commonly known, or 'Agencia los colorados su tienda Latina') sell products that are not otherwise available in the UK – for example the use of banana leaves to wrap the 'tamales', the distinctive flour for the 'arepas' of 'empanadas', 'frijoles' and boxes or ready mix desserts from Latin America, along with Latin American newspapers, magazines and handicrafts (refer to Figure 5.2).

There is also a music shop ('Sabor Latino') that includes a large collection of CDs from Latin American and sells greeting cards in Spanish as well. These shops not only make products available: the selection of products and the way in which these are displayed also constitute an important part of the way in which the identity of the shop is

Figure 5.2 Display window, La Tienda at Elephant and Castle Shopping Centre (Photo taken by Lucia Orellana, February 2008)

communicated to passers-by. A further way in which these shops mediate representations of a particular Latin American identity is through decoration. In the case of La Bodeguita, various Colombian icons are hung over the wall: including photographs of the Andes region and popular 'barrios' as well as handicrafts of the 'chiva' – a bus that travels around the rural areas of Colombia with fruits and people's luggage on top. Alongside the food and the icons, Latin music is also constantly played (refer to Figure 5.3).

Elephant and Castle shopping centre has become an information centre providing leaflets, newspapers, legal advice, currency exchange centres, services for cheap phone calls, Interflora services to Latin American countries as well as services for sending money and parcels to Latin America. For Latin Americans living in London, the Elephant and Castle has become not just a shopping centre to buy food, products from their home countries or gain information, but also a meeting point. During the week many people pass by the shopping centre to have their lunch or snack; perhaps to solve a problem or just to have a chat (refer to Figure 5.4).

Economically these shops are also important because they provide employment and income for many Latin Americans in London who

Figure 5.3 La Bodeguita in Elephant and Castle Shopping Centre (Photo taken by P. Román-Velázquez, May 2006)

are not only participating in the economy of the Elephant and Castle shopping centre, but have transformed it and have in the process created and communicated a particular Latin cultural identity. The identities represented in Elephant and Castle shopping centre are focused on national symbols represented by items such as the flag, local products and services. This is the case in 'Agencia los Colorados, Su Tienda Latina' (commonly known as 'La Tienda') where the Ecuadorian flag, the products on display and the postal services to Ecuador define the identity of the shop, while in 'La Bodeguita' a Colombian identity is defined through the use of the flag, products and menu. However, this is not the case for all Latin American owned shops housed in the shopping centre, particularly those where the name of the shop, the services and products cater for the general public such as 'Lucy's hairdressers', 'Inara Travels' or 'Nicole's Alterations and Repairs'. The different Latin American identities that come together on the first floor of the Elephant and Castle shopping centre make of this site a particularly complex Latin location in London.

The social experience of Elephant and Castle shopping centre is different for those Londoners or commuters who use it merely as a transit route, to visit a supermarket or to make a train connection. Latin Americans are

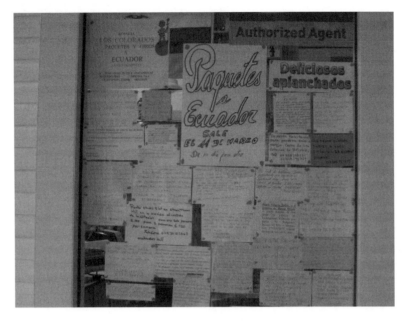

Figure 5.4 A notice board on the display window of 'La Tienda' (Photo taken by Lucia Orellana, February 2008)

establishing new social relationships across these places as an active part of creating and negotiating routes through the city. In this process Latin Americans are delineating new spatial boundaries in these places and establishing a new relationship with them.

There are numerous places in the more commercial, tourist oriented and wealthier parts of central and west London which are also deliberately constructed to communicate a specific Latin American identity. The most noticeable places with a Latin identity are clubs, bars and restaurants – with many operating as a combination of all three types of establishment. The physical presence of these clubs is often more visible to the tourist or resident who may be strolling through the city than are the Latin shops at the Elephant and Castle.

The making of Latin London at some of the capital's salsa clubs

In 1988 a small group of entrepreneurs co-ordinated the opening of several Spanish tapas bars in London (Bar Madrid, Bar Seville, Grey Camino and Bar Escoba). These included Flamenco (music from Spain) nights and little by little started incorporating salsa nights (music from the Caribbean regions of Latin America, although originally produced mainly by Cuban and Puerto Rican musicians in New York). The introduction of salsa music proved to be popular, and soon there emerged a series of clubs/ bars with a 'Latin', rather than a Spanish theme, although in many cases both concepts were mixed. Most notable here are Bar Cuba (opened in January 1992) on Kensington High Street; Bar Rumba (September 1993) on Shaftesbury Avenue; and Salsa on Charring Cross Road (March 1993). Bar Cuba's owner, Dave, relates the process of creating his club:

> I took it from a Spanish idea to a Caribbean idea. What can be Spanish Caribbean? Puerto Rico, well no. Cuba, well that is a good idea, it is basically Spanish. Not Puerto Rico, because it normally reflects fairly violent images. Puerto Rico is West Side Story, things like that, Puerto Ricans in America and I did not want to have that sort of image. I wanted a mysterious image of the Caribbean…I did some research, I went to Miami, to Little Havana…I didn't want what the Cubans have now because they don't have the resources, so I wanted to see what the Cubans have done in America. Then I went to Cuba to see what was happening in Cuba, which is not exactly how it would have been years ago…Nice old building, looking very old, very very different…We are pushing forward a certain idea…The whole identity of the place has to do with how it looks. It is smoky, noisy, it seems as if it is falling in parts, which it is not, but it's that sort of atmosphere, that is its identity.
>
> (Personal interview with Dave, 12 October 1993)

As Dave explained, Cuba was taken as a theme to construct a very specific Latin identity: one that attempted to recreate the style of pre-Revolutionary Cuba that the immigrant community had built up as 'Little Havana' in Miami rather than what he found in present-day Cuba. Hence, the Latin identity that was being constructed and communicated here was a 'mysterious' and nostalgic Cuba of the 1950s that drew on the way in which such an identity has been maintained by Cuban exiles and Cuban-Americans in Miami. Unlike the bars, stalls and restaurants at the Elephant and Castle – where music was often proudly played to identify specific Latin regions (Cumbia from Colombia, for example) – the music in Bar Cuba was one of the last considerations in constructing the identity of the place, as Dave mentions: 'You can get away with any type of music as long it has the right atmosphere' (personal interview with Dave, 12 October 1993). This is yet another way in which the construction and representation of Latin identities in London can be understood through Massey's concept of 'power-geometry'. The experiences and economic circumstances of both the shop owners at Elephant and Castle and the entrepreneurs setting up clubs in the West End are important when constructing the identity of a place. My intention here is not to raise issues about authenticity, but rather to highlight the relations of power involved in the making of Latin identities in London.

Another place constructed in a similar way was Bar Rumba: a tapas bar located in a corner of the Trocadero shopping centre on Shaftesbury Avenue in central London. Bar Rumba was not orientated towards the Latin population in London, although as the owner Eric Yu mentions, having some Latin Americans in the club 'gives authenticity', because after all 'it is a Latin bar' (personal interview with Eric Yu, 22 October 1993). Although Mexican and Spanish food and beer were sold on the premises, the 'Latin' identity of Bar Rumba was largely constructed through the music played on two dance music nights. One night aimed to attract a more cosmopolitan audience for whom salsa might be a part of various sounds from different places that have been labelled as 'world music', whereas the other attempted to attract those more interested in salsa as a specific type of dancing. Both nights were organized within the context of the owners' strategy of positioning Bar Rumba in relation to a wider network of bars, restaurants and dance clubs in London.

Closer to the Elephant and Castle, in south London, are working-class Latin clubs, not highly visible in the city (sometimes run illicitly without licenses), which often provide a refuge for working-class Latin Americans and particularly for undocumented immigrants. These places open and close regularly. At the same time, there are well known places (such as Club Bahia – a combined club, tapas bar and restaurant in Vauxhall run by a Chilean exile) that attempt to appeal to a middle-class Latin American clientele and maintain this identity through factors such as an admission fee, door policy, decoration and service. Latin identities are also found at Mambo Inn in Brixton where 'Latin' music features as part of a multicultural, Afro-Caribbean and politically alternative dance club. In the West End and in central London are the clubs, bars and restaurants that have been designed to appeal to middle-class Londoners, visitors and tourists. These places construct and communicate a Latin identity as part of London's 'cosmopolitan' nightlife where 'Latin' becomes another signifier of an 'ethnic' night out alongside Indian, Chinese or Thai restaurants.

The extent to which different people attend these clubs is affected by several factors including the days of the week that a club operates, the physical location in the city (many middle-class people are apprehensive about going to areas in south London, while some immigrants are apprehensive about the West End), the entrance fee, the manner in which the audience is addressed through advertising strategies, the music policy or music selection as well as through the granting and monitoring of licensing authorities. On this last point, I should note that certain Latin clubs and bars have occasionally been raided by the police and immigration officers, or have found it difficult to gain a license to operate legally.[9] This involves power struggles as entrepreneurs, disc jockeys, managers and local authorities all seek to influence the participation of different types of people at these various venues. These practices thus contribute to the mapping of a power-geometry of Latin sites in London.

Conclusion

This essay has explored how Latin American cultural identities in London are retained, transformed, negotiated and articulated within the context of specific relations of power. First, I highlighted the impact of nation and migration, stressing how immigration policies and the regulation of citizens affect the movement of Latin Americans into and then through London; and how the formation of specific identities within any one place cannot be addressed without considering the forms of regulation and laws of citizenship through which a sense of place-identity is constructed and transformed. The experiences of immigrants change as they adapt to the metropolis by adopting a more localized way of relating to the city, with more sporadic participation in the diasporic networks through which they initially oriented their lives in London. Thus, I argue that the micro-movements of people – through a shopping mall – are directly connected to the 'global' processes involving the regulated movement of citizens across national boundaries and through cities.

Drawing on those writers who have discussed the way in which the identities of places are created and re-made (Massey 1991; Keith and Pile 1993), I have focused on how, having entered a regulated national territory, Latin immigrant groups locate themselves within specific neighbourhoods of London. In doing so, places are transformed and given specific Latin identities (just as other places have been made as Afro-Caribbean or Jewish). The making of Latin identities in this way can be understood in terms of the 'power-geometry' (Massey 1993b) of the city, whereby Latin identities are re-made in a shopping centre in quite a different way to how a city centre restaurant may become Latin when the menu, music and decor is changed. Here, the topography of the city – encoded with meanings of class, ethnicity and gender – and lived according to feelings of safety, security and anxiety provides the conditions for different groups to establish particular routes and routines. Latin Americans have appropriated, transformed and used particular areas of the city for specific cultural practices, while providing these places with specific Latin identities. In this sense Latin Americans are developing links and establishing new relationships with existing places while contributing to, and becoming part of London's ethnoscape.

The Elephant and Castle shopping centre provided an example of a location where Latin Americans began positioning themselves in London in order to illustrate the particular ways that places have been given specific cultural identities. The shopping centre is not just a space for mediating representations of Latin America; it is actively being transformed and used as a meeting place and point of contact for social interaction and the sharing of information. Through the process of transforming places, and using them for different social practices, Latin Americans have created different routes through London. For those Latin Americans whose situation draws them to operate 'underground', the routes have to be negotiated in quite distinct ways. I contrasted this with some of the Latin venues operated by entrepreneurs in the West End of London, highlighting how bars and clubs that are constructing Latin America as a tourist site or as an exotic location also constrain and enable specific routes to be realized through the city. By stressing the contrasting meanings of 'Latinness' that are mediated in clubs, bars and restaurants, my intention is not to celebrate difference, or the appropriation and uses of places, or the multiplicity of meanings and hybrid identities; but, to politicize these issues in relation to the routes of Latin Americans in London. I have attempted to stress how participation in the making of Latin London has to be understood in relation to more than the characteristics of people who may visit a club or restaurant. Gender relations, class, national identity and ethnic background are important and complex elements that are at play simultaneously, but these have to be understood within the context of other power relations operating in the city (including immigration regulations, licensing laws and possibilities for economic investment and activity in different areas) and how these shape the movement of those participating in the making of Latin London.

Throughout the essay, I have highlighted how contact zones do or do not become possible. People create spatial routes through a city when visiting parks, shops, leisure facilities and sporting events and it is these that provide the possibilities for maintaining identities and creating contact zones where new identities might be made. Understanding participation across Latin London requires an awareness of how the routes of some might limit the movement of others who are involved in similar processes and movements. That is, through the specific dynamics that contribute to and are part of the way in which the power-geometry of Latin places is constituted. The routes and routines created by people as they move between different places are important for understanding the power-geometry within which individuals locate themselves and move across space when contributing to the making of Latin identities in London.

Notes

1. I take the term 'ethnoscape' from Arjun Appadurai to refer to the 'landscape of persons who constitute the shifting world in which we live: tourists, immigrants, refugees, exiles, guest workers and other moving groups and persons that constitute an essential feature of the world and appear to affect the politics of (and between) nations to a hitherto unprecedented degree' (1990: 7).
2. Some of the material presented in this essay draws on ethnographic research conducted throughout the 1990s, which is still relevant for understanding the initial setting and development of Latin London. This has been developed through in-depth interviews and ethnographic research conducted over the summer of 2005 and 2006. Further observations and updating of material have taken place preceding the writing of this essay.
3. As reported by the Immigration and Race Relations Committee for the House of Commons Reports (1986). The 1971 Act marked a significant change from previous attempts to control the entrance of certain people into Britain, which had started at the beginning of the twentieth century and continued to operate until the Act of 1971.
4. Excluding Suriname, Guyana and French Guiana (14,938), a total of 46,325 are registered, which constitutes an increase of 19,060 from the 12,327 recorded in the 1991 census. The 1991 census registered 9753 Brazilians and 5682 Colombians living in England (excludes Wales and Scotland). In total, there were 17,599 South Americans, 4062 from Central America and 2356 from the Caribbean (excluding those with any political or colonial relationship with Britain).
5. All translations from the Spanish, unless stated otherwise, are mine.
6. This has been asserted in financial, academic and governmental discourses. See for example some of the documents emanating from the Mayor's office.
7. A quick glance at the current version of the guide would take us to Walthamstow, Leyton, Putney and Croydon in search of Latin bars, restaurants and shops.
8. Elephant and Castle Development Framework, 2004. Elephant and Castle Development Team, London Borough of Southwark.
9. This is the case of Barco Latino, located on the River Thames, which was raided by police shortly after featuring in newspaper stories when Colombia were competing in the 1994 Football World Cup. For a more detailed discussion see Román-Velázquez (1996).

Bibliography

Appadurai, A. (1990) 'Disjuncture and difference in the global cultural economy', *Public Culture* 2.2, 1–24.

Castrillón, S. (1984) 'Latin Americans in London', *Ten 8*, 16.16, 38–41.

Centre for Contemporary Cultural Studies (1982) *The Empire Strikes Back* (London: Hutchinson).

Giddens, A. (1990) *The Consequences of Modernity* (Stanford, CA: Stanford University Press).

Hall, M. M. (1992) 'A nation of shoppers', *Observer Magazine*, 13 December, 16–29.

Hall, S. (1991) 'Old and new identities, old and new ethnicities', in A. D. King (ed.), *Culture, Globalisation and the World System: Contemporary Conditions for the Representation of Identity* (London and New York: Macmillan), pp. 41–68.

Hall, S. (1995) 'New cultures for old', in D. Massey and P. Jess (eds), *A Place in the World? Places, Cultures and Globalization* (Oxford: Oxford University Press/ Open University Press), pp. 175–214.

Harvey, D. (1989) *The Condition of Postmodernity* (Oxford: Blackwell).

Kay, D. (1987) *Chileans in Exile: Private Struggles, Public Lives* (London: Macmillan).

Keith, M. and Pile, S. (eds) (1993) *Place and the Politics of Identity* (London and New York: Routledge).

Massey, D. (1991) 'A global sense of place', *Marxism Today*, June, 24–9.

Massey, D. (1993a) 'Politics and Space/Time', in Keith and Pile (eds), *Place and the Politics of Identity*, pp. 141–61.

Massey, D. (1993b) 'Power-geometry and a progressive sense of place', in Jon Bird, Barry Curties, George Robertson and Lisa Tickner (eds) *Mapping the Futures: Local Cultures, Global Change* (London and New York: Routledge), pp. 59–69.

McIlwaine, C. (2007) 'Living in Latin London: How Latin American migrants survive in the city', Queen Mary, University of London and The Leverhulme Trust, http://www.geog.qmul.ac.uk/staff/mcilwaine.html, accessed 28 April 2008.

Román-Velázquez, P. (1996) 'The Construction of Latin Identities and Salsa Music Clubs in London: An Ethnographic Study', PhD thesis, University of Leicester.

Román-Velázquez, P. (1999) *The Making of Latin London: Salsa Music, Place and Identity* (Aldershot: Ashgate).

6
Constructing the Metropolitan Homeland: The Literatures of the White Settler Societies of New Zealand and Australia

Janet Wilson

The white settler: migration, exile and diaspora

> The sensitive nor'west afternoon
> Collapsed, and the rain came;
> The dog crept into his barrel
> Looking lost and lame.
> But you can't attribute to either
> Awareness of what great gloom
> Stands in a land of settlers
> With never a soul at home.
>
> (Allen Curnow, 'House and Land' (1941))

According to various diaspora typologies[1], settler-invader societies – notably the white dominions of Canada, Australia and New Zealand (which originated as migrations from Britain as the imperial 'mother country') – are defined as ethno-national diasporas: that is, dispersed groups that share a collective history, common ancestors, ethnicity and national traits; are associated with a specific homeland; and maintain a symbolical relationship with the homeland through these common constructs and shared affinities (Sheffer 2003: 9; Kokot, Tölölyan and Alfonso 2004: 3).

Yearning for and identification with Great Britain – the metropolitan homeland – are central features of white settler identity, contributing to the doubled and hybrid formations of white settler societies that are uneasily situated between the categories of colonizer and colonized, self and other, centre and periphery. Such 'ambivalence of emplacement' (Slemon 2006: 106) between the 'original world of Europe' and the indigene – that other source of authenticity and original belonging

(Lawson 1995: 29) – recalls the familiar argument that such colonies are not authentically postcolonial.[2] In Australia and New Zealand, as well as in Canada, the practice of 'complicit postcolonialism; an always present "underside" within colonization itself' (Mishra and Hodge 1991: 407) – whereby writers subliminally collude in 'territorial appropriation of land, voice and agency' (Slemon 2006: 106) – was for long masked by the articulation of anxieties about identity compounded by distance from Britain and slavish dependence upon metropolitan culture. An early expression of the 'cultural cringe' (Phillips 1997) – in the sense of deference to British culture – comes from the Australian writer Nettie Palmer in 1930:

> Waves of uncertainty sweep over us. Is this continent really our home or are we just migrants from another civilization [...] doomed to be dependent for our intellectual and aesthetic nourishment [...] on what is brought to us by mail from overseas?
>
> (cited in Rowley 1993: 64)

This schizophrenic state, encompassing both identification with and dislocation from the colonial society and the society of origin, is a defining feature of the 'unsettled' settler. Dream, memory and history blend in articulations of longing for the metropolitan homeland juxtaposed with images of the unhomely and alienation from the colonial world; all are discernible 'literary effects' of 'enforced social accommodation or historical migration and cultural relocations' (Bhabha 1997: 445).

This essay examines a variety of symbolic, mythological constructions of the originary homeland of Great Britain in New Zealand and Australian writing, arguing that the fixation on the metropolitan homeland as the object of frustrated colonial dreams belongs to a Europeanized romantic aesthetic. Such ahistoricized longing is based on essentialist ideas of the nation state and of a master race; it presupposes the white settler in exile as a coherent subject who experiences nation, home and homeland as primordial categories. The final sections of this essay also engage with the work of several contemporary Australian and New Zealand diasporic writers who revise and reposition subjective experiences of polarized geographical placement – a potent source of settler angst – and complicate notions of nation, location and identity by acquiring new reference points and plural subjectivities, as well as representing 'home' as living 'within the hyphen' (Radhakrishnan 1996: 175–6). In engaging with alternative overseas destinations to the original metropolitan homeland, such writing overrides the divisions of colony and empire and traverses the 'boundaries defining nation and diaspora' (Braziel and Mannur 2003: 5).

In terms outlined by Avtar Brah, these writers are accountable to more than one concept of home and homeland, expressing a 'homing desire' by contrast to 'the desire for a homeland', and showing 'the desire to rewrite and to reinvent home as much as a desire to come to terms with an exile from it' (1996: 16, 180, 193).

Contemporary diasporas can be seen both in terms of historical experience and the existential conditions that metaphorize post-modernity. But white settler manifestations of dislocation and nostalgia for the metropolitan homeland have traditionally been identified in terms of nation building rather than in relation to contemporary concepts of globalization and transnationalism. Longing for the homeland and the condition of estrangement belong to an earlier phase – according to accounts of evolutionary nationalism – preceding the development of a more locally-based nationalist consciousness (Said 1991: 359). Reconceptualizations of space such as Brah's 'space of diaspora' – where the 'genealogies of dispersion' are entangled with those of 'staying put' (181) – imply a challenge to those theories of the nation-state which focus primarily upon nineteenth-century migrations, for long dominated by white settler perceptions of remoteness, isolation and insignificance. In analysing early settler writing, therefore, I would argue that the prevalent sense of mourning and loss, for example, points towards a diversity of experience which can be associated with diasporic states of dislocation. Contemporary writers attest to the restlessness, uncertainty and fragmentation of identity that defined the white settler – so that even present-day 'diasporic' writing differs in its reorientation, but not in its 'essence' from that of the earlier tradition.

It is also true that the greater urgency with which the quest for home and homeland is being pursued recently (Hawley 2006: 4–5) is particularly pertinent to white settler diasporas for whom such urges have always been both persistent and deep-seated. To that extent, the contemporary diasporic consciousness was already a defining one for the white settler. In literary representations of the longing for home in both Australia and New Zealand, nostalgia and the desire for reconnection can be seen as constitutive of a literary tradition in which the apparently familiar, yet unknown world of 'overseas', represents a tantalizing, alluring ideal. However, Australian writing empirically tests the myth of a metropolitan homeland (because writers return to Britain in order to challenge it in an exclusive redefinition of whiteness), whereas New Zealand writing is more dependent on inherited literary structures, often romanticizing the indigene as 'other', and has remained 'disconnected' for longer (with 'dream' divorced from 'reality').

Representations of white settler nostalgia for 'Home'

As I have argued, the formation of white settler identities has often been marked by an ambivalence in which a local sense of belonging was predicated on a unitary myth of the country of origin as 'Home'. This has often precipitated, in white settler writing, a unique sense of loss and melancholy which sets it apart from much recent writing by postcolonial migrants who demonstrate an ability to live diasporically within the old imperial centre. Subscribing to the myth of common ethnic (European) origin, which is often invoked as a signifier of superiority, white settler writing is sometimes informed by racist ideologies such as the 'fatal impact' (Stasiulis and Yuval-Davis 1995: 20–1), that is, the inevitable supplanting of the indigene by the European; in some cases first peoples are ignored altogether and become the 'absent indigene' or 'excluded other' (Huggan 2007: 25). While much of the writing is Anglocentric, some writers appeal to Celtic traditions, particularly in recalling their origins. In Australian writer Miles Franklin's account of her childhood, for example, the sadness of her older cousin A is triggered by homesickness, a longing for the lost world of the Scottish past to which folk music and border ballad give voice:

> 'On the heights of Killiecrankie yestermorn our army lay'; and 'Come hither Euan Cameron, come, stand beside my knee'; 'Lochiel, Lochiel beware of the day.' There were others all heady with grief at leaving Scotland for ever. The poor old gentleman would forget he had a listener and nostalgia overcame him. Later I came to understand the poignancy of 'Only in dreams will they see again the outer Hebrides.'
>
> (1963: 89)

While Scotland and Ireland are mourned as lost homelands by first generation migrants from those countries – just as different regions of Italy were by Italian migrants to Australia – literary reconstructions centre primarily on England (the point of origin for the majority of early British settlers in New Zealand) as an imaginary homeland. Considerations of distance evoke sentimental nostalgia, as, for example, in the effusive preface by the New Zealander, Mrs C. Evans, to her novel *Over the Hills and Far Away* (1874): '[T]hinking of the mighty waste of water which separates me from the Homeland, I feel tempted to exclaim, "Oh mighty ocean which divides us, hush your roar awhile! Oh, wild winds, cease to moan! and let them hear my voice in England"' (cited in McCormick 1959: 45). Such affective utterances comprise a rhetoric of displacement in which the pioneering subject's identity is trapped in the essentialist binary oppositions of here and now (the host nation) versus there and then (the original homeland). This sense of disempowerment was so pervasive that it produced a kind of 'spiritual exile' of New Zealand poetry in the 1920s (McCormick 1959: 102–3), a situation lightly satirized by Bill Manhire in his recent poem 'Beach Life':

> you're reciting
> an early-twentieth-
> century poem – benign
> neglectful cadences, still
> pining to go home.

> (2001: 151)

The same strangulated mentality in which a contempt for the colonial habitus blends with nostalgia for the unattainable original homeland appears in Brian Penton's *Landtakers, The Story of an Epoch* (1935), an historical narrative focusing on the Australian gold rushes of the 1840s and 1850s. When speaking of the migrants who have come to Australia from Britain, the narrator reflects:

> Why I have often wondered, did men like Cabell, hating the country so much, keeping themselves going with the hope that every wretched day brought them nearer to England which their nostalgic fantasy had turned into a promised land – Paradise itself – why did they never go back?

> (21)

In this narrative, as in Henry Handel Richardson's trilogy *The Fortunes of Richard Mahony* (1930) – in which the gold rushes are the basis for a founding national myth – it is notable that the aborigine is 'an essential non-participant' (Goldie 1989: 13): instead, the tension is between two problematic nations and locations. This Anglocentric model of national identity was also, until relatively recently, true of New Zealand, which (as historian Keith Sinclair notes) 'grew up on an English dream' (1961: 41). In his memoir *Home: A Colonial's Adventure* (1929), author Alan Mulgan testifies to the imperial myth of England as 'home', held even by those who, like him, were not born there: 'As far back as I remember, it was "Home". In the little New Zealand community in which we lived it was as natural to talk of England and Ireland as "Home" as it was to call New Zealand a colony' (3).

The schizophrenic habit of thinking of 'home' as a place located half-way round the world contributed to the construction of a neo-British identity for antipodean colonial settlers at a time when there were limited discourses through which to articulate that other pole of settler non-belonging: the relationship with the indigene. At one level the national cultures naturalized the affinity with all things British; the obvious contradictions were tacitly tolerated. For decades the propaganda machine of Empire promoted Britishness as a concept in Britain's overseas colonies, which typecast New Zealand, for example, as a 'Better' or 'Brighter' Britain to encourage the more 'desirable' classes of British immigrant (Belich 2001). This ideology was reinforced by global networks of family, friends and professional or vocational associates; by the transport and postal systems which disseminated both textual and material forms of culture (such as domestic furniture, textiles, crockery, antiques, books and journals from British publishing houses as well as newspapers from British presses); by cultural markers such as cuisine and music – especially folk-songs and ballads; and by the self-familiarizing practices of settler culture, such as calendars and cards from the 'Old World' imaging an inappropriate 'white Christmas' with robins and snow. Other culturally cognate northern European images of flora and fauna or landscape and setting were introduced incongruously into the antipodean milieu, because the cultural and religious traditions they represented all reinforced the impression of continued and easy access to the culture they had departed from.

One of the most efficacious vehicles for expressing cultural affinity with the imaginary homeland was literature: the power of fiction to awaken readers' imaginations and to enter a more marvellous world was acutely felt. Propagandist colonial discourses were constructed by Wakefield's New Zealand Company[3] to entice migrants to the new world; but once there, settlers often satisfied a yearning for reconnection with the imaginary homeland by reading Victorian stories of adventure, romance or conquest. Alan Mulgan's romanticization of England, for example, arose from reading fable and fantasy: Arthurian legends and stories of romance and conquest made England – rather than Ireland (his parents' country of origin) – the subject of his imaginings:

> I had some affection for the country of my parents, but infinitely more for England. It was a huge, mysterious, awful, sacred, yet always lovable place, this England, a land of immemorial things, of shining heroes, of imperfectly understood but fascinating ritual, of marvellous romance, of world embracing authority and prestige.
>
> (1929: 7)

As stated earlier, this source of settler nostalgia has proved enduring; in Australian author Nikki Gemmell's 2001 novel *Lovesong*, the heroine, Lillie, describes England (her mother's birthplace) as 'that land I've read about all my life [...] and whose books I've read to a much greater extent than any from my own land' (49).

Ambivalence of location, both within the nation (where the settler is often alienated from the indigene) and beyond, is often identified with problematic powers of articulation: the Canadian poet Dennis Lee, for example, attests to the difficulties of writing authentically within colonial space (2006: 347–50), while theorist Stephen Slemon has suggested that the internalization of the conflicted self-other binary is primarily a source of creativity for the white settler, rather than an inspiration for critical writing (such as an anticolonial theory of resistance) (Slemon 2006: 106). Such bifurcated self-identification has a pathological side: the New Zealand cultural historian Eric McCormick notes 'the creation of an abstract, idealized often sentimentalized "literary" world, remote from both poles of reality, the English writer's and the colonial reader's' (1959: 103); while Australian writer David Malouf notes the effects of isolation: 'a particular intensity of the imagination, and a kind of contempt for everyday experience, that makes the *idea* for some of us, quite resistant to the strongest assaults of the actual. Real life happens elsewhere' (cited in Britain 1997: 13). Yet this sense of unreality, this belief in the power of the abstract, also paradoxically situates the white settler within the contemporary moment, the 'age of simulcra'; as Baudrillard argues, 'when the real is no longer what it used to be, nostalgia assumes its full meaning; there is a proliferation of myths of origin and signs of reality; of second hand truth, objectivity and authenticity' (Poster 2001: 174).

Provincial novels and poetry (written between the mid-1930s and the mid-1960s) which exploit this ontological dualism – the simultaneous inhabiting of both old and new worlds – dramatize the incongruities and misconceptions that occur when images of an established culture dominate an 'underdeveloped', dependent one. In New Zealand writer Robin Hyde's *The Godwits Fly* (1938) such a deception leaves the heroine, Eliza Hannay, feeling deprived of the 'real thing':

> One day with a little shock of anger you realised that there were no robins and no snow, and you felt cheated; nothing else was quite as pretty. [...] None of it happened, had ever happened, to your sight, hearing or taste, and yet everything else was unreal, because you had been weaned on it. The Antipodeans did truly walk on their damfool heads.
>
> (1974: 24, 102)

In Shirley Hazzard's novel *Transit of Venus* (1980), set in 1939, New World displacement is specifically attributed to literary discourse:

> What was natural was hedgerows, hawthorn, skylarks, the chaffinch on the orchard bough. You had never seen these but believed in them with perfect faith [...] Literature had not made these things true. It had placed Australia in perpetual, flagrant violation of reality.
>
> (31)

Hazzard's heroines travel to London, whereas Hyde's Eliza Hannay – who comes to understand the paradox that 'you were English and not English' and claims 'we belong there, don't we?' – stays at 'home' (1974: 34, 101). In an affected display of her sense of not being at home in either world, she composes a poem after John Masefield, echoing his patriotic invocation of England as the ultimate destination:

> There are white cliffs of England
> Where the sounding breakers speak,
> And he who never knew them
> Has yet his home to seek.
>
> (100)

England is exotic but unattainable; the godwits of Hyde's title – migratory birds that fly from New Zealand north to Siberia – become synonyms for a migration to the north (concomitant with England in the novel) that never takes place. In her foreword to the novel, Hyde posits the journey 'home' as a perpetual goal: 'Our youth [human godwits] must make the long migration, under a compulsion they hardly understand; or else be dissatisfied all their lives long' (xx). But in the novel only Timothy, 'the complete Godwit', realizes through travelling 'the great dream, the England dream' (163, 178). The novel's recurring images of journeying and travel – whether postponed, hoped for or dreamed of – typify the restlessness in settler writing of the early twentieth century.

As is the case in Miles Franklin's *My Brilliant Career* (1901) – where Sybylla Melvyn spurns marriage to the handsome, eligible, bachelor Harry Beecham in order to pursue an artistic career – *The Godwits Fly* illustrates one of the dominant colonial myths: that only through escape from their country of birth could artists gain access to the greater career opportunities offered by overseas metropolitan centres. The expatriate tradition includes distinguished antipodean women writers: Robin Hyde,

Miles Franklin, Christina Stead, Henry Handel Richardson, Katherine Mansfield and Fleur Adcock all followed their destinies overseas, seeking liberation from the parochialism of provincial society and the constrictions attendant upon their gender. This mentality is encapsulated in the dedication in New Zealand author Isabelle Cluett's novel, *Waif's Progress* (1929): 'To London The Dream and the Fulfilment' (McCormick 1959: 85), although the colonial theme of escape through travel was never so pivotal in New Zealand fiction as in Australian writing where such motifs subsequently became standard reference points. Shirley Hazzard's *Transit of Venus* alludes to such literary romanticizing: 'Going to Europe someone had written was about as final as going to heaven. A mystical passage to another life from which no-one returned the same' (37). And the heroine of Nikki Gemmell's *Lovesong* also sees herself as inheriting the tradition of distinguished, self-empowering expatriate women: 'it was Isabelle Eberhardt, Katherine Mansfield, Martha Gellhorn, Oriana Fallaci, travellers all, struggling, blazen [*sic*] women who'd seized their future and not had it shaped for them' (2001: 87).

Novels based on departures from the colonies and arrivals in the metropolitan homeland often involve some exposure of illusion or satire of human folly. The classic articulation of the experiences of the migrant who travels out to the colonial society and then back to the original homeland, making a home in neither and with a consequent loss of fortune and stability, is Henry Handel Richardson's trilogy, *The Fortunes of Richard Mahony* (1930). In the second, ironically titled volume, *The Way Home* (1925), the theme of the return as a utopian dream is explored against the dystopia of the present. England becomes the imaginary homeland for Richard Mahony, after he has made his fortune in Australia where he had arrived in 1852. Mahony's deluded desire to return incorporates a myth of archaic bonding and self-identification as 'the nomad son who, weary of beating up and down the world turns home at last to rest on the untravelled heart of his mother' (Richardson 1971: 7). He is also the traveller who, having 'heard and obeyed the home call' and now the 'richer for a goodly store of spiritual experience', enhances the vision of those who have remained (8). Brian Penton's hero in *Landtakers* similarly idealizes himself as a prodigal son who makes a 'triumphant return to some little English village which would be awestruck by the magnificence of the fortune of the returning native – remembered by the oldest inhabitant as an apple-cheeked boy setting out for foreign parts' (1935: 315). Mahony develops the myth of England's greatness, invoking the imperial concept of a master race – 'the guardian of a vast reserve fund of spiritual force' (Richardson 1971: 8) – and a grand scheme into which his individual life will fit. He epitomizes the disillusioned colonist who, according to Keith Sinclair, believed he was sailing towards civilization not away from it, yet on returning to England found himself a stranger in the land of his birth (1961: 80). Fundamentally estranged from his original homeland and unable to 'live diasporically' by exploring and negotiating differences between his past Australian experiences and present English habitation, Mahony becomes increasingly dependent on his Australian-born wife, and caught in a spiral of delusion and despair he returns to Australia in defeat.

In contrast to Mahony, who journeys between the imperial centre and the colony twice over, are heroines like Teresa Hawkins in Christina Stead's *For Love Alone* (1944) as well as Shirley Hazzard's Caroline and Grace Bell, who travel in pursuit of romance. Hawkins 'had never wanted to see England' (Stead 1978: 295), but deluded in love, she follows to England the university scholar, Jonathan Crow, only to be disconcerted by his misogynistic behaviour upon arrival. She judges her mistake: 'How remote was the foolish romantic girl, who had got on the boat six weeks ago' (343). Teresa views overseas travel as a route to success, and following Crow opens her access to the wider horizons of Europe: 'It isn't only him. I have a great destiny. If I stay here I will be nobody' (285). Caroline Bell in *Transit of Venus* similarly announces the sisters' arrival from Australia as though it is the fulfilment of a mission: 'London is our achievement. Our career. [...] Having got here is an attainment, being here is an occupation' (Hazzard 1980: 31).

Radical estrangement features strongly in the psycho-pathological experiences of the doubly displaced woman writer who, early in life, travels to the metropolitan homeland (usually to receive an education) and upon returning to the colony is overwhelmed by a malaise of 'unbelonging' prompted by intense desire for reconnection to the new spiritual home. Such conditions in younger women confirm that migration – the crisis of rupture and uprooting – is traumatic, creating feelings of helplessness modelled on the birth trauma, for it carries the threat of ego disintegration and the dissolution and blurring of boundaries. According to Vijay Mishra, 'imaginary homelands are constructed from the space of distance to compensate for a loss occasioned by an unspeakable trauma' (1996: 423–4).

This model provides a useful context within which to consider the work of Katherine Mansfield, who felt deeply dislocated upon her return to New Zealand after three years' education in England. She wrote in 1907:

My heart keeps flying off – Oxford Circus – Westminster Bridge at the Whistler hour – [...] It all haunts me all so much – and I feel it must

come back soon – How people ever wish to live here I cannot think –
[...] Tonight I feel too utterly hopelessly full of Heimweh.

(O'Sullivan 1989: 5)

In a similar vein, Fleur Adcock romanticized England upon returning to
New Zealand at the age of thirteen after seven and a half years in Britain
with her family during the Second World War. For long she was haunted
by a dream of going back 'and in this dream I'd walk up this hill and
see this village where we lived' (Ricketts 1986: 130). The 'placelessness'
of the poems in her first volume, *The Eye of the Hurricane* (1964), masks
the ongoing sense of dislocation from the halcyon world of her childhood that she experienced during her sixteen years of repatriation in
New Zealand. Lines in her earliest poetry (published between 1952 and
1963) such as 'Summer has gone to another country' and 'Always he
would inhabit an alien landscape' (in 'The Lover') are coded statements
of the trauma of separation and of longing (Wilson 2007: 20–1).

Inhabiting the metropolitan homeland

The 1950s and 60s were marked by increased emigration from the British
colonies to England; most potent was the generation of migrants who
arrived on SS Empire Windrush from the Caribbean on 22 June 1948.
A new wave of antipodean writers and entertainers shared this historic
moment of migration: these included the Australians Clive James,
Germaine Greer, Barry Humphries and Peter Porter; and New Zealanders
such as James Courage, Fleur Adcock, Kevin Ireland and Janet Frame.
Many remained in Britain, but some, like Frame and the Australian novelist Martin Boyd – whose novel *When Blackbirds Sing* (1962) was set in
England during the First World War – soon returned home or to alternative destinations. In the work of the returning postcolonial writers, new
perspectives acquired through extended habitation in the metropolitan
centre suggest the emergence of a diasporic consciousness; this includes
deconstruction of the original homeland and colony or 'centre' and
'periphery' binary, a capacity for doubled perceptions, relativized points
of view and multiple cultural reference points. All influence the generic
form and orientation of their fictions and verse.

Janet Frame – one of New Zealand's best-known writers – arrived
in Britain in 1959. In her third novel *The Edge of the Alphabet* (1962),
which was her second novel written in the UK, she adapts to the quest
framework the journey made by three travellers between the geographically polarized and culturally distinct locations of New Zealand and
England. In keeping with the tradition of antipodean travellers to the

northern hemisphere, Toby Withers suffers 'an affliction of dream called Overseas' while simultaneously 'dreaming of the Lost Tribe' (Frame 1962: 14). This 'Lost Tribe' could possibly be identifiable with the ancestral homeland, a place of Anglo-Celtic belonging – his mother had said 'if you ever go overseas [...] visit the places where your ancestors lived' (14) – or alternatively with the centre of New Zealand's South Island, near Toby's birthplace. In parallel to Stead's heroine's quest for love, Toby is searching for greater 'indigenization' (Jennings 2000) both in New Zealand and Britain (as the indeterminate location of the tribe suggests), and his journey across the world represents the white settler's quest for an elusive 'authentic' identity and sense of belonging. Toby's ambition to write 'The Lost Tribe' – associated with his journey – images that quest.

Although Toby writes no more than the title of his novel, these dual points of imagined belonging represented by his literary ambition contribute to his extreme disorientation in England. The arduous endeavour of writing (by contrast to Teresa's novel in *For Love Alone*, effortlessly completed in London (Stead 1978: 371)) provides new contexts for exploring the settler ambition of travelling, as well as anxieties about home and belonging. The white settler quest for identification may be Janus-faced, but Toby's failure to discover a viable new form of communication means that the world of fiction denies him a home just as his overseas destination does; this exclusion is disempowering. Toby's body becomes possessed or somatically defined by his unexpressed imaginings and ambition; the lost tribe (earlier seen as metaphorically inhabiting his head) becomes associated with a mysterious, poisonous sore on his arm (Frame 1962: 44–5, 149, 193). Unable to adapt to his new surroundings, Toby eventually returns to New Zealand. The interrogative 'Home?' followed by the conclusion: 'The edge of the alphabet where words crumble and all forms of communication between the living are useless' (224), suggests not only the failure of language but (as in the case of Mahony) the returning traveller's innate homelessness, his now radically reduced capacity to find a home in any society.

Frame's fifth novel *The Adaptable Man* (1965) – which she commenced during her seven-year stay in England and finished upon her return to New Zealand – is set in rural England in the imagined village of Little Burghlestatham in East Suffolk. As is the case in Christina Stead's *Cotters England* (1967), the focus is entirely on English society, although in *The Adaptable Man* the ontological state of dislocation and its opposite, adaptability, are dominant tropes. Frame's cast of middle class characters show the concept of a united, organic small community to be a 'false myth' (King 1992: 114). Many are travellers who experience difficulty in adapting their lives to time and place: most, like Vic Baldry – the farmer who desires to emigrate to Australia where he had spent his honeymoon – wish to escape or be somewhere else. This picture of self-delusion as the basis of village life mobilizes Frame's mockery of the nineteenth-century realist novel; in exploring migration as an end in itself 'made by man pursuing or fleeing from an idea' (Frame 1965: 10), the text projects the 'unreality' syndrome associated with colonial longings as discussed earlier in this essay. Repeated allusions to migratory birds possibly gesture towards Hyde's *The Godwits Fly*; but for Frame's narrator the seasonal migration of birds (and by implication the journeys to the imperial centre which these migrations symbolize in Hyde's novel) is insufficient to quell the flux of time and the chaos of undirected, confused and colliding movement: 'This everlasting movement back and forth in time without the stability and guidance of a visible world, recognized seasons, shared sun, is enough to make a man mad with the thought that he is not a migratory bird' (1965: 10). The novel presents a bleak picture of modernity: the dehumanizing machinery of air-traffic, public transport and identity cards whose overlapping stamps paradoxically blot out individual identity. Rod Edmond claims that in showing the 'unreality of English country life and writing', with dislocated characters like Vic Baldry whose house – a simulacrum of Australia with themed wall hangings and images projected through slide shows – symbolizes his thwarted desire to relocate there, *The Adaptable Man* 'can be read as a further step in the process of Frame's decolonization' (1995: 169); it might also mark another stage in her quest for 'an area of universal belonging' (Frame 1967: 177).

Where Frame's novel typifies a crisis of identification in mid-twentieth-century diasporic writing, work published by 'relocated' antipodean writers from the 1970s begins to renegotiate the relationship between 'colony' and 'metropole'. A sense of 'diasporic' belonging, demonstrating the ability to inhabit more than one location simultaneously, is represented through a consciousness of parallels and doublings, and of differences as well as similarities as determinants of identity. Fleur Adcock, for example, whose return to England in 1963 was marked by an initial unsettledness and (in two of her poems) overt rejection of New Zealand (Adcock 2000: 43–4) began in the 1970s to balance her dual allegiances: to friends and family in New Zealand, and to vocation and life in England. Landscape and place become vital markers of a new sense of belonging in her poetry, and in 'Letter to Alistair' (1978), for example, she says of the Lake District: 'You'd love this place; it's your central Otago, /in English dress – the bony land's the same' (2000: 122). After returning to New Zealand in 1976 – after thirteen years away – belonging, exile and estrangement emerge in her reconfiguring of 'home'. In 'Instead of an Interview' (from *The Inner Harbour* (1979)) she asserts that 'home is London; and England, Ireland, Europe' (2000: 115); both worlds remain inhabited, however, because the shells and souvenirs she has brought back in her suitcase symbolize her continued attachment to New Zealand. She reflects on the way in which her journey complicates and problematizes the categories of 'home' and 'away':

> But another loaded word
> creeps up now to interrogate me.
> By going back to look, after thirteen years
> have I made myself for the first time an exile?
>
> (2000: 115)

Moving back and forth between nations and classes as a diasporic subject enables Adcock to form multi-locational attachments, and to occupy more than one point of view: an outsider's insider knowledge of England appears in her satire of the British in poems such as 'England's Glory' and 'The Genius of Surrey' (163–4), while poems in the 'Thatcherland' section of *The Incident Book* (1986) – set in her local district of East Finchley – constitute locally-informed interventions into national politics. Poems in *Time-Zones* (1991) explore a more interstitial habitation of in-between spaces, celebrating her 'to and fro' movements between hemispheres in which, as the hyphenated title implies, temporal distinctions of 'zones' as periods of time are coordinated with time zones as spaces experienced in travelling (Wilson 2007: 86, 93).

Moving a step further from Adcock's poetry of dual locatedness, work by other antipodean writers published in the late 1970s and 1980s offers newly revised perceptions of the colonial home and of Britain's insignificance, rather than the processes of adjustment and the sense of 'in-betweenness' that come from living diasporically. Elizabeth Jolley's novel *Miss Peabody's Inheritance* (1983), for example, playfully subverts earlier narratives of escape to Europe, as well as reversing the polarities of 'English centre' and 'Australian colony': its heroine Dorothy Peabody (living in Weybridge, England) reads instalments of a novel about Australian schoolmistresses seeking culture and sexual adventure in Europe, sent to her by an Australian novelist. Only when she escapes England and arrives in Australia does she come into her inheritance: to complete the novel left unfinished at the novelist's death in what she perceives will be her new home. As Gay Raines points out, 'the draw of imaginative vitality and creative power comes, for once, from the Antipodes, pulling the provincial and marginalized spirit of England towards and into itself' (1995: 189). Similarly, in a reversal of earlier narratives in which Britain is posited as the object of settler self-fulfilment, in Murray Bail's novel *Homesickness* (1980), Australian tourists who come to Europe and visit the mummified versions of Europe's past in museums experience new insights into their Australian identity.

White settler postcolonial diasporas

Over the last thirty years, demographic changes such as an increase in the number of non-white immigrants, and resulting reassessments of antipodean race-relations, have led Australia and New Zealand to redefine themselves as multicultural societies. Increasing globalization and transnational connections between settler societies and other parts of the world continue to displace the imperial centre and colonial periphery model associated with the so-called 'monocultural' settler societies of the early twentieth century. As the British Empire has waned, and as global forces generate multidirectional movements of people and capital, writers have found alternative centres of pilgrimage, and are just as likely to travel to cities like Tokyo, Berlin, Prague, New York or Bombay (with which they have no prior attachment or affiliation) as they are to the former cultural capital of London. In these overseas destinations the society of origin is now represented as the place of belonging. Relocation in these new societies – which cannot be claimed as 'imaginary homelands' in the way that Britain originally was for the white settler – continues to overturn and complicate the earlier divisions of home and abroad.

Likewise the pursuit of indigeneity – which (according to the writers of the *Empire Writes Back*) was the white settler's principal undertaking – has been politicized and redefined (Ashcroft et al. 2002: 134; see also Goldie 1989: 13). Debates over ethnicity, sovereignty and nationalism have led to an acknowledgement of cultural hybridity rather than uniformity. In New Zealand in the 1990s, for example, a more complex post-settler Pakeha nationalism emerged as groups of sympathetic Pakeha (descendants of European settlers in New Zealand) developed affiliations with Maori, hoping to overcome the legacy of colonial guilt by embracing biculturalism (Williams 1997: 27); while in Australia, texts such as Peter Read's *Belonging: Australians, Place and Aboriginal Ownership* (2000) point towards a similar reassessment of the relationship between settlers and aborigines. The emerging field of Settlement Studies – spearheaded by antipodean researchers – draws on ethno-historical work undertaken in the Pacific with the aim of exploring the mutual transformation of colonizer and colonized in 'the complexities of encounter and exchange' (Calder and Turner 2002: 8). Yet the concept of indigeneity has also been sharply contested, claimed by some Pakeha on the grounds of their having developed distinctive Anglo-Celtic cultural traditions of equal value to those of the Maori, and invoked in arbitration cases over land ownership by white farmers in both New Zealand and Australia on the grounds that their length of land-tenure makes their claims supersede those of the indigene (Read 2000: 1).

Further, white settler identities are becoming increasingly relativized by proximity to and alignment with other races, as the category of whiteness – for long the dominant cultural reference point for both nations – becomes subject to a new scrutiny in the multicultural, transnational present. The presence of ethnic groups other than those of settler and indigene, both within the antipodes and beyond, necessitates a rethinking of 'whiteness' as a purely unmarked category, and also as 'a normative structure, a discourse of power, and a form of racialised identity' (Ware and Back 2002: 13). In the writing of antipodean postcolonial diasporic subjects, new formulations of identity cut across the divisions of ethnicity and gender, reconfiguring the relationship between the 'global' and the 'local'. Within these plural contexts, the longing for the metropolitan homeland which mobilized journeys to the imperial centre in search of greater indigeneity or self-discovery is now 'a past narrative' (Edmond 1995: 171); when these themes reappear they are usually invoked in order to critique or reposition mythologies of origin and belonging, or to provide new and expanded formulations of the ontological quest.

For example, the motif of longing for the metropolitan homeland of Britain is redeployed within a contemporary frame in Janette Turner Hospital's short story, 'The Bloody Past, The Wandering Future' (1987) in which the narrator recollects a walk she took with her grandfather as a child. The narrative constructs a palimpsest-like layering of her memory of this moment in her childhood over that of her grandfather, who is suddenly overcome by a sensation of loss for his own childhood in the company of his father 'who used to take me walking on the Eastbourne Pier. Just like this'. The narrator comments 'Eastbourne is in England and that England is on the other side of the world, a place as easily imagined and as fabulous as Persephone's Underworld' (1995: 162). The reference to myth here draws specific attention to the constructed nature of settler narratives of the metropolitan homeland. Jane Westaway's novel *Good at Geography* (2000), on the other hand, complicates the earlier pattern of migration from Britain to the antipodes with the story of the Midwinter family who migrate to New Zealand in 1964. The parents, believing that their expectations of a better life in a 'Man's country' have been betrayed, soon return to the 'Old Country', while their daughter Isobel, sixteen on arrival, marries and remains, but is unsure of where her cultural allegiance lies:

> 'Listen to your accent. You sound like a New Zealander.' She spooned instant coffee into cups. 'I am. You don't have to be born here, you can…make yourself one.' She paused, spoon in mid-air – England and childhood, time and distance were so hopelessly muddled that surely it meant that she was a New Zealander.
>
> (94)

As Isobel's marriage dissolves so does any certainty about the 'right' location – 'Man's country – she wondered how she had ever come to call it home' (236) – and the novel concludes ten years later with her visiting her family in England.

The myth of home is most fully reconsidered in Janette Turner Hospital's meditation, 'Litany for the Homeland' (1991). Like Shirley Hazzard, Hospital has lived outside Australia for most of her life and divides her time between Canada, the US and her original home in Brisbane. Her story gives shape and credibility to this diasporic existence: her Australian-born narrator unsettles the 'margin' and 'centre' model of colonialism by reclaiming marginality as a new centre of consciousness. In her cosmic concept of homeland – as existing through extended concepts of time and space – the earth 'spins in the margins of space'; the threat of extinction from a supernova links 'our homeland' to human existence more generally, enabling her to demonstrate the concept of homeland as both intimate and universal. Homeland is also described as existing before Captain Cook came with his maps, for the Aborigines made 'all of us' visitors, 'those who came in 1788 and those who came later' (1995: 411) – thereby acknowledging an indigenous presence marginalized in many former literary representations of antipodean settler societies. The medieval manuscript tradition is cited as a metaphor for the experience of finding home within the margins, as 'In the margins one is ignored, but one is free. That is where homeland is' (415). The narrator's current location near the St Lawrence river which 'subtracts from Canada here, depositing American silt there' situates her 'at the desiccating edge of things, on the dividing line between two countries, nowhere, everywhere in the margins' (422). These references illustrate the complex interstitial location of the white Australian-born woman narrator, who acknowledges that her literal and intuited homeland – 'Wherever I am, I live in Queensland' – is just one position on the map she draws; and this very inclusiveness makes the 'Litany' enact her ontological habitation of home in several ways simultaneously.

Today the concept of the metropolitan homeland has diminishing importance as the myth of cultural homogeneity dissolves and the Celtic elements of the migrant populations are increasingly acknowledged in novels like Peter Carey's *True History of the Kelly Gang* (2000) – a reconstruction of Australian Irishness – and Fiona Kidman's study of the Protestant mission of the Scottish preacher Norman McLeod, which eventually settled in Waipu in New Zealand's Bay of Islands, *The Book of Secrets* (1987). Diasporic writers, situated both within and outside the antipodes, write less of homelands and nations than of states of being which testify to different degrees of belonging as oppositional locales are reduced and new habitations affirmed: for example, Beverley Farmer's Australian protagonist in her story 'Place of Birth', set in Greece, suddenly yearns for Australia as 'home' as a result of her desire to give birth there near her ageing parents (1990: 7–8). This engagement with other metropolitan centres demands a rethinking of home and origin: Helen Garner in *Postcards from Surfers* (1985) and David Malouf in *Antipodes: Stories* (1985) write stories which are situated in both Europe and Australia; Gail Jones in *Dreams of Speaking* (2006) writes about Brisbane and Japan. From New Zealand, the Bulgarian-born writer, Kapka Kassabova, writes about Bulgaria and Greece; Sarah Quigley about Germany and the US; Carl Shuker about Tokyo.[4] Writing from antipodean and other postcolonial diasporas, therefore, continues the displacement of the binary, oppositional model of empire and periphery which postcolonial writing in general has inaugurated over the last half century by providing new models of interconnectedness, affiliation and cross cultural dependency. The proliferation of more dynamic types of relatedness between the home of origin and the new societies of relocation arguably show that postcolonial and global diasporas, in shrinking the distances between worlds far apart, have substantially broadened the ways we can think about home.[5]

Notes

1. See, for example, Cohen (1997); Safran (1991); and the critique by Kalra, Kaur and Hutnyk (2005).
2. Graham Huggan (2007: vi) claims this 'bitterly contested issue' is one that he addresses, but cannot quite resolve.

3. Founded in 1838 by Edward Gibbon Wakefield (1796–1862), and largely responsible for the establishment of settler communities in South Australia and New Zealand.
4. See, for example, Kassabova's novel *Reconnaissance* (1999) and poetry collections *Love in the Land of Midas* (2001) and *Geography for the Lost* (2007); Quigley's poetry in *AUP New Poets I* (1999) and novels *After Robert* (1999), *Shot* (2003) and *Fifty Days* (2004); and Shuker, *The Method Actors* (2005).
5. I should like to thank the Rothermere American Institute at the University of Oxford for the award of a Senior Research Fellowship for 2007–8, Cristina Sandru for reading a draft of this essay, and the editors of this volume for their helpful editing and comments.

Select Bibliography

Adcock, F. (1964) *Eye of the Hurricane* (Wellington: A.H. & A.W. Reed).

Adcock, F. (2000) *Poems, 1960–2000* (Newcastle-upon-Tyne: Bloodaxe).

Ashcroft, B., Griffiths, G. and Tiffin, H. (2002) *The Empire Writes Back: Theory and Practice in Post-colonial Literatures*, 2nd edition (London and New York: Routledge).

Bail, M. (1980) *Homesickness* (London: Faber).

Belich, J. (2001) *Paradise Reforged: A Story of the New Zealanders from the 1880s to the Year 2000* (London: Allan Lane and Penguin).

Bhabha, H. (1997) 'The World and the Home' in A. McClintock, A. Mufti and E. Shohat (eds) *Dangerous Liaisons: Gender, Nation and Postcolonial Perspectives* (Minnesota: University of Minneapolis Press), pp. 445–55.

Brah, A. (1996) *Cartographies of Diaspora: Contesting Identities* (London and New York: Routledge).

Braziel, J. E. and Mannur, A. (eds) (2003) *Theorizing Diaspora: A Reader* (Oxford: Blackwell).

Britain, I. (1997) *Once an Australian* (Melbourne and Sydney: Oxford University Press).

Calder, A. and Turner, S. (eds) (2002) *Journal of New Zealand Literature*, 20. Special issue: 'Settlement Studies'.

Cohen, R. (1997) *Global Diasporas: An Introduction* (Seattle, WA: University of Washington Press).

Curnow, A. C. (1997 [1941]) 'House and Land' in J. Bornholdt, G. O'Brien and M. Williams (eds) *An Anthology of New Zealand Poetry in English* (Auckland: Oxford University Press), p. 398.

Edmond, R. (1995) '"In Search of the Lost Tribe": Janet Frame's England', in A. Robert Lee (ed.) *Other Britain, Other British* (London: Pluto), pp. 161–73.

Farmer, B. (1990) *Place of Birth* (London: Faber).

Frame, J. (1962) *The Edge of the Alphabet* (New York: Braziller).

Frame, J. (1965) *The Adaptable Man* (London: W. H. Allen and Christchurch: Pegasus Press).

Frame, J. (1967) *A State of Siege* (Christchurch: Pegasus Press).

Franklin, M. (1901) *My Brilliant Career* (Edinburgh and London: William Blackwood and Sons).

Franklin, M. (1963) *Childhood at Brindabella* (Sydney: Angus and Robertson).

Gemmell, N. (2001) *Lovesong* (London: Picador).

Goldie, T. (1989) *Fear and Temptation: The Image of the Indigene in Canadian, Australian and New Zealand Literatures* (Kingston: McGill-Queens University Press).

Hawley, J. C. (2006) 'Theorising Diaspora' in C. A. B. Joseph and J. M. Wilson (eds) *Global Fissures: Postcolonial Fusions* (Amsterdam and New York: Rodopi), pp. 3–16.

Hazzard, S. (1980) *The Transit of Venus* (London: Macmillan).

Hospital, J. T. (1995) *Collected Stories* (Brisbane: University of Queensland Press).

Huggan, G. (2007) *Australian Literature: Postcolonialism, Racism, Transnationalism* (Oxford: Oxford University Press).

Hyde, R. (1974 [1938]) *The Godwits Fly*, ed. Gloria Rawlinson (Auckland: University of Auckland Press and Oxford University Press).

Jennings, O. (2000) 'Seeking Indigeneity: The Search for the "Lost Tribe" in Janet Frame's *The Edge of the Alphabet*', *World Literature Written in English*, 38.2, 80–93.

Jolley, E. (1983) *Miss Peabody's Inheritance* (Harmondsworth: Penguin).

Kalra, V. S., Kaur, R. and Hutnyk, J. (2005) *Diaspora and Hybridity* (London: Sage).

King, B. (1992) 'The Adaptable Man' in J. Delbaere (ed.) *The Ring of Fire: Essays on Janet Frame* (Sydney: Dangaroo Press), pp. 110–19.

Kokot, W., Tölölyan, K. and Alfonso, C. (eds) (2004) *Diaspora, Identity and Religion: New Directions in Theory and Research* (London: Routledge).

Lawson, A. (1995) 'Postcolonial Theory and the "Settler" Subject', *Essays on Canadian Writing*, 56, 20–36.

Lee, D. (2006) 'Writing in Colonial Space' in B. Ashcroft, G. Griffiths and H. Tiffin (eds) *The Post-Colonial Studies Reader*, 2nd edition (London: Routledge), pp. 347–50.

Manhire, B. (2001) *Collected Poems* (Manchester: Carcanet).

McCormick, E. H. (1959) *New Zealand Literature: A Survey* (London: Oxford University Press).

Mishra, V. (1996) 'The Diasporic Imaginary: Theorizing the Indian Diaspora', *Textual Practice*, 10.3, 421–7.

Mishra, V. and Hodge, B. (1991) 'What is Post(-)Colonialism?', *Textual Practice*, 5.3, 399–414.

Mulgan, A. (1929) *Home: A Colonial's Adventure* (London: Longmans, Green and Co.).

O'Sullivan, V. (ed.) (1989) *Katherine Mansfield: Selected Letters* (Oxford: Oxford University Press).

Penton, B. (1935) *Landtakers: The Story of an Epoch* (London: Cassell and Co.).

Phillips, A. (1997 [1950]) 'The Cultural Cringe' in I. Salusinszky (ed.) *The Oxford Book of Australian Essays* (Melbourne: Oxford University Press), pp. 112–15.

Poster, M. (ed.) (2001) *Jean Baudrillard: Selected Writings* (Cambridge: Polity).

Radhakrishnan, R. (1996) *Diasporic Mediations: Between Home and Location* (Minneapolis, MN and London: University of Minnesota Press).

Raines, G. (1995) 'England from the Antipodes: Images of England in Australian Fiction, 1960–88', in A. Robert Lee (ed.) *Other Britain, Other British* (London: Pluto), pp. 174–93.

Read, P. (2000) *Belonging: Australians, Place and Aboriginal Ownership* (Melbourne: Cambridge University Press).

Ricketts, H. (ed.) (1986) 'Fleur Adcock' in *Talking about Ourselves: Twelve New Zealand Poets in Conversation with Harry Ricketts* (Wellington: Mallinson Rendell), pp. 124–33.

Richardson, H. H. (1971 [1925]) *The Way Home*, vol. 2 of *The Fortunes of Richard Mahony* (3 vols.), ed. L. Kramer (Harmondsworth: Penguin).

Rowley, H. (1993) *Christina Stead: A Biography* (London: Secker and Warburg).

Safran, W. (1991) 'Diasporas in Modern Societies: Myths of Homeland and Return', *Diaspora*, 1.1, 83–99.

Said, E. (1991) 'Reflections on Exile' in R. Ferguson et al. (eds) *Out There: Marginality and Contemporary Cultures* (New York and Cambridge, MA: New Museum of Contemporary Art and the MIT Press), pp. 357–66.

Sheffer, G. (2003) *Diaspora Politics: At Home Abroad* (Cambridge: Cambridge University Press).

Sinclair, K. (1961) 'Life in the Provinces: The European Settlement' in K. Sinclair (ed.) *Distance Looks our Way: The Effects of Remoteness on New Zealand* (Auckland: Paul's Book Arcade for the University of Auckland), pp. 27–41.

Slemon, S. (2006) 'Unsettling the Empire: Resistance Theory for the Second World' in B. Ashcroft, G. Griffiths and H. Tiffin (eds) *The Post-Colonial Studies Reader*, 2nd edition (London: Routledge), pp. 102–6.

Stasiulis, D. and Yuval-Davis, N. (1995) *Unsettling Settler Societies: Articulations of Gender, Race, Ethnicity and Class* (London: Sage).

Stead, C. (1978 [1944]) *For Love Alone* (Sydney: Angus and Robertson).

Ware, V. and Back, L. (2002) *Out of Whiteness: Color, Politics and Culture* (Chicago: University of Chicago Press).

Westaway, J. (2000) *Good at Geography* (Harmondsworth: Penguin).

Williams, M. (1997) 'Crippled by Geography? New Zealand Nationalisms' in S. Murray (ed.) *Not on Any Map: Essays on Postcoloniality and Cultural Nationalism* (Exeter: University of Exeter Press), pp. 19–42.

Wilson, J. (2007) *Fleur Adcock* (Plymouth: Northcote House and The British Council).

Section 3 Comparative Diasporic Contexts

7
Exile, Incarceration and the Homeland: Jewish References in French Caribbean Novels

Celia Britton

From Desmond Dekker's 'The Israelites' (1969) to Bob Marley's 'Exodus' (1977), the Caribbean story of exile and the struggle for freedom has frequently compared itself to the Old Testament account of the Jewish people. In the early twentieth century, the Jamaican Marcus Garvey's 'Black Zionism' movement used Jewish Zionism as a template for the Caribbean aspiration to return to Africa; and some Rastafarians consider themselves to be 'the Twelfth Tribe of Judah'. In 'Deux figures du destin' – his introduction to 'Mémoire juive, mémoire nègre: deux figures du destin' (the 1998 issue of *Portulan*) – Roger Toumson points out that this parallelism extends to the whole of the Americas: 'The Old Testament narrative of exile has, since the first chronicles of transportation, become an obligatory reference for the destiny of black people in the Americas' (11). On the narrower issue of France's attitude towards its Caribbean colonies, Toumson shows how these two exemplary manifestations of the Other have long been closely interconnected: the 'Code noir' of 1615 is mainly concerned with regulating the treatment of African slaves in the French Caribbean, but its first article '[enjoins] all our officers to chase out of the Islands all the Jews who have established their residence there' (11); conversely, the Abbé Grégoire in the eighteenth century became famous as much for his castigation of anti-Semitism as for his defence of Negro slaves, and, as Toumson describes it, for 'arguing by analogy, posing and resolving in the same terms the problem of the civil condition of the Jews and that of the servile condition of the Negroes' (12).

In the aftermath of the Second World War, however, these parallels assume a rather different form. In the 1950s and 1960s, Europe was both coming to terms with the Jewish holocaust and witnessing the beginnings of large-scale immigration from the Caribbean. Now, in other words, the focus is less on Jewish exile in Egypt and more on Jewish incarceration in concentration camps; and the Caribbean experience of diaspora is less that of the original exile from Africa than the new migrations from the Caribbean to Europe. In France, the racism encountered by Caribbean immigrants has obvious similarities with – as well as important differences from – an older anti-Semitism. Frantz Fanon's analysis of the anti-black racism of the French in *Black Skin, White Masks* (1986 [1952]) makes frequent use of Sartre's *Réflexions sur la question juive* (1947) – and Sartre himself followed this text, published in 1947, with 'Orphée noir' in 1948.[1] For Fanon, despite the difference in racial stereotypes[2] and the distinctiveness caused by the inescapable visibility of the black man's blackness – as opposed to the Jew who can pass for Gentile (115–16) – the mechanisms of racism are identical in both cases; the identity of the racists is the same ('an anti-Semite is inevitably anti-Negro' (122)), and this creates a necessary solidarity between their victims: 'I joined the Jew, my brother in misery' (122).

This does not of course mean that black and Jewish communities have in reality always co-existed harmoniously, either in France or elsewhere; in particular, the equation of the holocaust with slavery has recently, in the general context of Islamic anti-Zionism, been vehemently rejected by right-wing Jewish writers such as Alain Finkielkraut.[3] But from the Caribbean point of view, the long-standing familiarity with Old Testament narratives of the exile of the Jews – deriving from the massive influence of Christian churches in the islands – formed a natural basis for the appropriation, in the post-war years, of the imagery of the Jewish holocaust as a means of representing the Caribbean diaspora in France. The comparisons with which I am concerned here are thus not strictly speaking between two diasporas – nor, indeed, between Caribbean and Jewish uses of the image of the holocaust – but rather interrogate the way in which the French Caribbean 'imaginaire' turns to the situation of another diasporic people in order to construct a representation of its own situation and, perhaps, to claim recognition of its own suffering through this appeal to the exemplary image of suffering offered by the holocaust. In their ambivalent status as both a gesture of solidarity with the Jews and a possibly rather presumptuous imaginary appropriation of their situation, the texts that I shall be considering do nevertheless illustrate the interconnectedness of different diasporic cultures, and show how these connections are actively put to use in the structuring of individual and collective experience.

The conjunction results in one particular phenomenon, which is the main focus of this article: in certain texts, the French Caribbean experience of living in France is compared to the Jewish experience of the concentration camps; immigration, in other words, becomes a kind of *incarceration*. These texts thus contrast strikingly with more recent and better-known representations of Caribbean migration, which tend rather to emphasize its *mobility*: diaspora is seen as a dispersal of people in a series of centrifugal movements. Edouard Glissant's concept of the 'Tout-monde', for example, envisages a world in which 'the Antilleans scatter themselves everywhere like a powder, without establishing themselves anywhere' – and, in fact, goes on to compare them with the Jewish diaspora: 'nor did we know that these, the Jews, of whom we had no direct or specific knowledge, had multiplied themselves across a wider space than anything we could imagine, in the world' (1993: 385, 386). But in representations of the early period of Caribbean migration to Europe in the 1950s and 1960s, the dominant emphasis is not on movement so much as on an enforced immobility; having reached France (or England – Samuel Selvon's *The Lonely Londoners* (1956) is a classic early example of this) the immigrants gradually realize that they will never be able to save enough money to go home, and life in Europe therefore becomes a kind of exile. So too, the impossibility of returning home, combined often with an unfamiliarity with French society which makes it difficult to move around freely within it, is experienced as a form of imprisonment.

The racist reactions of the French to their presence create a further kind of psychological imprisonment within the self: in *Black Skin, White Masks* Fanon repeatedly describes the refusal of the white French to recognize him as a fellow human being in these terms: 'the other, the white man, who unmercifully imprisoned me' (112); 'Sealed into that crushing objecthood, I turned beseechingly to others' (109); 'I shouted a greeting to the world and the world slashed away my joy. I was told to stay within bounds, to go back where I belonged' ['On me demandait de me *confiner*, de me *rétrécir*'; my italics] (114–15). Another strand of this imagery of imprisonment is linked to the confinement of animals in cages: in Vincent Placoly's *La Vie et la mort de Marcel Gonstran* (1971), for instance, Marcel – living a miserable and isolated life in Paris – is introduced to us as 'this man who lived like a bear in a cage' (11).

There is thus for these Caribbean immigrants to Europe a causal connection between the movement of migration and the resulting enforced immobility or imprisonment of exile. Moreover, this is equally true of the original Jewish diaspora: the movement that brings the 'wandering' Jews to Europe *results*, ultimately, in the confinement of the Jews in ghettoes and then in the Nazi concentration camps. But there are, of course, also many historical and cultural differences in the two peoples' situations. One particularly significant contrast is in their attitude towards the country that they regard as the 'homeland': in an article entitled 'L'identité et le désastre (origine et fondation)', Daniel Maragnes stresses the implications of the Jews' rootedness in tradition and in the sacred texts of Judaism, with their concomitant certainty that Israel is indeed the true homeland of the Jewish people, and goes on:

> There is nothing comparable in the Antilles. Indeed, it is as though exactly the opposite movement occurs, relegating memory to the very margins of existence, as though excluded [...] no symbolic links are established between the individual and the event, no community is assembled around it, no meaning is formed or instituted.
>
> (1998: 276)

With this in mind, I want now to examine two texts by Guadeloupean writers – Gisèle Pineau's *L'Exil selon Julia* (1996), and Simone and André Schwarz-Bart's *Un plat de porc aux bananes vertes* (1967) – in which the theme of exile as incarceration is explicitly linked to the Jewish holocaust, but in which also the Caribbean homeland is evoked in a markedly ambivalent manner.

L'Exil selon Julia is an autobiographical text recounting Gisèle Pineau's childhood and adolescence, but revolving around the figure of her paternal grandmother Julia, familiarly known as Man Ya. Maréchal, Gisèle's father, brings Man Ya from Guadeloupe to live with the family in France in order to rescue her from her violent husband Asdrubal; Man Ya, however, has no desire to leave Guadeloupe and is extremely unhappy at what the text's title makes clear is her enforced 'exile' in France. There are frequent references to her 'melancholy', with which Gisèle gradually comes to empathize – 'So, I can understand Man Ya's melancholy and her fear of dying here better now' (117) – and which she eventually defines as a 'disease of exile' (129).[4] Man Ya spends long periods indoors, while 'her mind travels tirelessly between France and her country Guadeloupe where every day she hopes to return' (16); and she sees the family apartment and the immediate surroundings as a kind of prison: the door always has to be kept locked against dangerous intruders (81) (as opposed to her house in Guadeloupe which is 'open on all four sides [...] Without asking, without knocking, life comes in' (139)); the children have to grow up in 'the jail of these houses' (128); even the trees are 'imprisoned in the concrete of the pavements' (129). Her excursions beyond the immediate neighbourhood are fraught with danger: when she goes to collect the children from school in her son's army greatcoat, she is arrested for illegally wearing French army uniform; when she sets out to walk across Paris to the Sacré Cœur, she has no conception of how far away it is, and gets lost.

But if Man Ya is the most obvious example of the immigrant 'incarcerated' by her depression and her unfamiliarity with Paris, the careful wording of the autobiography's title (not 'L'Exil de Julia', but *'selon Julia'*) alerts us to the possibility that the narrator herself also suffers from being in exile from the Caribbean, despite having spent only a few months of her childhood there. Gisèle's 'exile' is the result of the racism of her teachers and fellow pupils at school in France – and it is in connection with this that the explicit comparison with persecution of the Jews is made. This comparison concerns only a single incident, but takes on added resonance against the background of the determining influence of the Second World War upon the family's life. Maréchal was one of the young 'dissidents' who left Guadeloupe in order to join De Gaulle's Free French forces – at his mother's instigation. She 'pushed' him to join the dissidents only because she wanted him to leave home in order to avoid conflict with his father (18); nevertheless, Maréchal becomes an enthusiastic supporter of De Gaulle – in turn this leads to his decision to emigrate from Guadeloupe with his wife, and to become a professional soldier in the French army.[5] As his daughter explains:

> Who could say that our fates are not linked to that of the General? He is there at the start of daddy's military life. He is the one who gives out honour and congratulations, promotions and war medals. If daddy hadn't gone to join up with him in the Free French, where would we be now? If daddy hadn't worn the uniform of the French army, would my mummy Daisy have agreed to spend her life with him? That's how Antilleans end up being born in France.
>
> (161)

Conversely the French people's rejection of De Gaulle in 1968 precipitates Maréchal into a serious depression and makes him decide to take his family back to the Caribbean: 'The ingratitude of the French is beyond him. No, he definitely cannot stay here. He is preparing his departure' (163).

But if 1968 is traumatic for Maréchal, it also marks the date of the single most traumatic incident of the text – and it is this that draws together the theme of incarceration (now in relation to Gisèle, rather than Man Ya) and the theme of the holocaust. One long chapter consists entirely of letters that Gisèle, aged eleven, sends to Man Ya, who has by then returned home to Guadeloupe. In one of these, she tells her grandmother how she is the only black girl in her class at school, and how one of her teachers persecutes her simply because 'She doesn't like seeing my negro face, my black skin' (152). This teacher gives her punishments for no reason: the most grotesque of these involves making Gisèle crouch on all fours beneath her desk. As Gisèle recounts it:

> So, she punished me by making me go under her desk. Now I go there in practically all her lessons. Like a dog in its kennel. I obey. I breathe in the smell of her feet. I can see the hairs on her fat legs squashed flat under her stockings. I grit my teeth so as not to cry. I can hear the other pupils' voices. I'm ashamed. I'm afraid. Crouching under the desk. No-one protests. No-one defends me.
>
> (152)

The comparison with a dog in its kennel echoes the imagery of imprisoned animals mentioned above; and Gisèle reacts with such a paranoid fear of confinement that she cannot bear to be in a room with a closed door: 'as soon as I am shut into a room, I feel as though I'm suffocating' (152). What is particularly significant, however, is that this description of confinement is followed immediately by a reference to the diary of Anne Frank:

> It'll soon be the Easter holidays. I won't have to see Mme Baron for a fortnight. I'm going to try and write the story of my life, like Anne Frank. Mummy gave me the book. She lived in Holland with her family. Because they were Jews, during the war, they hid in an attic until Hitler's Nazis found them and arrested them in 1944. They were taken to a concentration camp. Her story has made me think. I think that after the holidays, I won't mind going under the desk quite so much. I will think about Anne Frank who stayed huddled in darkness for two years of the war and then died without being able to fulfil her dream of becoming an actress in Hollywood. How can you live in a country that rejects you because of your race, your religion or the colour of your skin? Shut in, always shut in! Wearing a yellow star on your coat. Wearing your black skin morning noon and night under the white people's gaze.
>
> (152–3)

The parallelism between the Jewish and the black situations is emphasized by the parallel syntax of the last two sentences.[6] But the basis for the comparison between Gisèle and Anne Frank is *confinement* ('Shut in, always shut in!') – although Gisèle takes from it also the realization that her own situation is much less serious, which in turn gives her the strength to endure. Above all, perhaps, the fact that she explicitly intends to model her autobiography (that is, the text that we are now reading) on Anne Frank's diary – 'I'm going to try and write the story of my life, like Anne Frank' – is evidence that representations of the holocaust provide a kind of template for representations of the early period of Caribbean exile.

Un plat de porc aux bananes vertes is the story of a Martinican woman called Mariotte who has ended up, alone and penniless, in an old people's home in Paris in 1952; the narrative is written by her, in a series of notebooks that she has to hide from the other residents (not unlike Anne Frank's diary). The novel is striking in the first place for its dual authorship; Simone Schwarz-Bart is Guadeloupean while her husband André was the son, born in France in 1928, of Polish Jewish refugees who were deported from France by the Nazis and died in Auschwitz in 1941; André himself escaped capture and joined the French Resistance. In 1959 he published *Le Dernier des Justes*, a novel, recounting the story of the Jewish people from the middle ages to the holocaust, which was awarded the Prix Goncourt.[7] The Caribbean-Jewish connection is therefore, so to speak, built in to *Un plat de porc*, which makes an extended comparison between the Caribbean subject exiled in France and the Jewish subject incarcerated in the concentration camp. Although in the text itself this is never entirely overt, its double dedication to Aimé Césaire[8] and Elie Wiesel already suggests a parallelism which is stated quite explicitly in the blurb: 'this book [...] bears witness to a collective memory: that of the servitude, the destiny of black peoples – a destiny which, in the eyes of André Schwarz-Bart [...] creates a link between the slaves' descendants and the Jews of the past and present'.[9]

The parallels that are constructed within the novel, however, are not between Jewish persecution and slavery in the Caribbean, but between the world of the camps and the world of the old people's home, in which Mariotte is the only black resident. She, in other words, compares her exile in Paris and her incarceration in the home with the concentration camps. The anti-Semitism expressed by many of the home's inhabitants is paralleled by their racism towards Mariotte. There are some explicit references to the holocaust: for instance, during one of the residents' frequent conversations about death, an old man suggests that the nurses ought to give them all a fatal injection: '"like for the yids: one injection and that's it!"' (76). In particular there is an episode describing

'Biquette', a 'solitary monomaniac' (77) who has been transferred to the home from long-term residence in Charenton psychiatric hospital. The initial emphasis in this passage is on her isolation, which Mariotte describes in terms echoing Fanon's images of 'imprisonment in oneself': 'she would give me a frightened look, without a single word piercing the invisible shell that she surrounded herself with' (77). Her nickname also – a 'biquette' is a young female goat – although it is sarcastically affectionate, evokes (together with her 'crystalline little guinea-pig's eyes' (77)) the metaphors of caged animals that we find elsewhere in the descriptions of Caribbeans exiled in Paris – and Mariotte also refers to herself as an 'old nanny-goat' (26). But Biquette's most striking characteristic is that she claims to be Jewish, although there is no evidence that she really is. She reacts violently to the anti-Semitic remarks of the other residents, hurling herself head first against the walls whenever, as Mariotte puts it, 'the word Jew is pronounced in a way that collides with some memory buried in her dementia, or some fantasy forever imprisoned in her gentle little eyes – the eyes of a melancholy guinea-pig' (78). On one occasion the comment that precipitated this reaction was 'considering the number of Jews still alive: "You'd think that their gas ovens were incubators"'(77) – and in fact Biquette, who has a number written in ink on her forearm, claims that she herself has been in a concentration camp. This, however, is definitely untrue, given the number of years she has been in the Charenton hospital; in fact, it is presumably this psychiatric incarceration that has produced the phantasy of imprisonment in a Nazi camp.[10] Biquette, in other words, although she is white and in all probability Gentile, serves to create a link between Jews and Caribbeans: she is described with the same images that are often used to characterize Caribbean exiles, and she identifies with the Jews, and with their suffering in the holocaust. At the same time, her conviction that she was, or is, in a concentration camp also illustrates the phantasmatic power of the holocaust in the years following the war, showing the extent to which it became an exemplary instance of oppression with which other oppressed groups identified.

Biquette's phantasy equating the old people's home with a concentration camp is just one example of the parallels between the two places. The home, like the camps, is suffused with an atmosphere of imminent death: Mariotte laments 'Isn't death itself enough without us having to die slowly tooth by tooth, limb by limb, even in every organ of the intelligence and the heart?' (71). The similarity to the Nazi death camps is particularly evident in the rumour going round the female ward that, in order to relieve the overcrowding on the male ward, 'the nurses and the hospital nuns had now supposedly been given orders to *dispatch* us as discreetly as possible' (79). Whether this is true or not, the inmates have in any case been left there to die, and oscillate between a determination to survive and the constant temptation of suicide: at the bottom of the main staircase of the home is 'a big worn slab of stone [...] which greets the clumsy and those who are not wholly clumsy – and which, for as far back as we can remember in the history of the home, has had the name: Consolation' (30). The link with Jewish concentration camps here takes the extremely precise form of an intertextual link to *The Last of the Just*, whose description of the camp at Drancy includes a reference to prisoners who 'flung themselves from a seventh-story window on to a certain cement slab which became sadly famous in the camp' (327). The principal reason for the suicidal desires in the old people's home is the level of physical abjection and pain that virtually all of them suffer; 'life' in the home is reduced to a pure question of physical existence that is also reminiscent of accounts of concentration camp prisoners: there is never enough to eat; they have debilitating and humiliating illnesses; and there is a relentless emphasis on urine and bowel movements. Also, Biquette's concentration camp number may be a fake, but it is still the case that all the inmates of the home are, like prisoners, dehumanized by being referred to not by name but by the number of their bed: Sister Marie des Anges, although she is kind to Mariotte, always calls her 'number Fourteen': 'Seriously, number Fourteen, I think it would be good for you' (24). And, as in the camps, this is a world without money; like prisoners, the inmates create their own currency of cigarette ends, which they collect on the rare occasions that they are allowed to go outside, and barter for glasses of wine, extra food or other favours. In Mariotte's case, a sufficient supply of cigarette ends is necessary for her to continue being allowed to borrow the pair of spectacles that her neighbour Madame Bitard owns but does not use herself, except as a means of dominating and tormenting Mariotte (169).

We learn very little of Mariotte's life after leaving Martinique and before entering the old people's home; but towards the end of the novel there are three brief and cryptic references to a Moritz Lévy (149, 180, 205), who appears to have been Mariotte's lover, who died two years previously (the point when she entered the home) and who is possibly the father or grandfather of a little girl who died at the same time. The suggestion that Mariotte has had a Jewish lover forms another kind of parallel between Caribbean and Jewish communities in France and, more specifically, another intertextual link with *The Last of the Just*, in which the main protagonist's brother is called Moritz Lévy.

In these two novels, then, the Jewish holocaust provides a framework within which to situate and represent the Caribbean experience of exile-as-incarceration. But the allusions and parallels that I have described exist alongside a number of equally important differences, which relate in particular to the way in which the lost *homeland* is conceptualized. For Pineau's and the Schwarz-Barts' characters, in other words, the Caribbean plays a more complex and ambiguous role than Zion does for the Jewish diaspora. In the latter case, exile is from the Holy Land: the ancestral home of the Jewish people for thousands of years, sanctioned by biblical authority. When every Passover the Jews repeat 'Next year in Jerusalem' there is – whether or not they literally mean to return – a complete certainty that Israel is indeed their one and only true homeland. The Caribbean diaspora, however, if taken in the sense of the migration from the Caribbean to Europe, is a secondary consequence of the other, original diaspora that was effected by transportation from Africa; and Caribbean literature, especially in the poetry of the Negritude movement, is full of references to the loss of the *original* homeland, which is Africa. Thus while Césaire's famous poem 'Cahier d'un retour au pays natal' (one of the two epigraphs at the beginning of *Un plat de porc aux bananes vertes*) designates Martinique as the land of his birth, much of his other poetry is dedicated to the evocation of Africa as the lost motherland of the Caribbean people.[11] While Caribbean literature of course often celebrates the natural beauty and the culture of the islands, there is no real equivalent to the idealization of Africa that we find in the poetry of Negritude. From this point of view, it is Africa that most closely replicates the status of Zion as the ideal of origin; the Caribbean islands are a *real* home and, for Caribbeans in France, a source of real (and hence often ambivalent) memories rather than the idealized mythical homeland that Israel was for European Jews in the 1940s.[12] The sense of exile and incarceration in Europe that results from their disillusionment, from having to give up their original hopes of a better life, produces a bitterness towards Europe and, certainly, a longing for home – but it is not a simple longing.[13] It often lacks, for instance, the feeling of entitlement that is so strong in Jewish attitudes towards Israel. 'Exile' versus 'home', in other words, is not a straightforward opposition in which 'home' figures as a fully positive term, different in all possible ways from exile in Europe. What we find instead in both novels is a deeply ambiguous evocation of Martinique and Guadeloupe, in which the sense of alienation that blights the characters' lives in Europe also affects their memories of home.

In *L'Exil selon Julia* Man Ya's longing to return to Guadeloupe is entirely wholehearted, and her eventual return is described as a

'Deliverance' (135). But Guadeloupe is inextricably tied up with her husband Asdrubal – had it not been for him and his mistreatment of her, her son would never have forced her to leave her home – and her relationship with him is an overtly ambivalent one in which her hatred of his cruelty and racial contempt for her (he is a mulatto) coexists with the pity she feels for him and her dutiful sense that a wife should remain loyal to the husband whom God has given her. The other characters feel strongly that this attachment to Asdrubal is perverse and destructive; and there is a sense in which Asdrubal functions as a displaced symbol of a suppressed love-hate relation to the island itself. Thus Man Ya's attachment to Guadeloupe is presented as entirely visceral and, literally, *unreasonable* – almost as though she is deluding herself:

> She wants only one thing, to go back to her land of Guadeloupe...
> even if it is true that this cursed land bewitches, ties down people's
> fates. She doesn't philosophize on the how and why of this attach-
> ment to her land. Reason collapses in the face of the heart's impulses.
> There are no words, only the lack which blinds and stuns you. There
> are no grand theories, only naive memories that memory itself trav-
> esties, annoying trifles, an ecstatic pantomime.
>
> (137)

All the other adult Guadeloupeans in France, as Gisèle notices, express contradictory, consciously ambivalent attitudes towards the island:

> To tell the truth, the grownups constantly wavered between the
> intoxication that blossomed on each return home and the renais-
> sance which was said to accompany each period of exile. They talked
> about their Country with love, nostalgia, and bitter disillusionment...
> they loved it, yes, but in an equivocal way, like a youthful love affair
> that one can never forget even if it never bore any fruit.
>
> (29)

Gisèle herself has only lived in Guadeloupe for a few months when she was very young; nevertheless she too regards it as her homeland, wishes that her parents had never emigrated (28) and, particularly after Man Ya's departure, dreams of going to live there permanently (140). Yet when the family do finally leave France and return to the Caribbean, the experience for Gisèle and her brothers and sisters is not exactly that of a homecoming. The fact that Maréchal is first posted not to Guadeloupe but to the sister island of Martinique can in itself be read as indicating a slight disjunction: that this is a return to somewhere that is nearly, but not quite, home. Fort-de-France greets them on their arrival with a disconcerting mixture of the familiar and the strange, of recognition and misrecognition, so that 'To realize that we have finally arrived at our destination, to understand that our feet are really treading this ground that we have dreamed of for so long, is a painful and violent mental exercise' (175). The day after their arrival, Gisèle and two of her brothers decide to walk to the sea that, from the windows of their house, appears to be close at hand (176). They set off confidently, sure that they will not get lost in this place that miraculously combines novelty and familiarity: 'We walk without ever losing sight of the sea. The places are not strange to us. Everything here is unknown and yet recognized' (177). At first, they experience a euphoric sense of belonging that they never attained in France: 'Each step brings us closer to ourselves. The poverty that surrounds us speaks to us, comforts us, says to us: "This is where you come from!"'(178). But the closeness of the sea turns out to be deceptive, and as they gradually discover that almost the whole of Fort-de-France lies between them and the ocean, their surroundings cease to appear welcoming and reassuring: an old man of whom they ask the way to the sea merely laughs at them (179); they realize that they are completely lost; and their euphoria turns to fear: 'Suddenly, fear takes hold of us. We've come too far [...] Too many expressions on these faces. We're not used to it' (180). The busyness of the streets around them creates a kind of sensory overload in which faces, bodies, voices, bright colours and loud noises become so overwhelming that they begin to appear not only unfamiliar but actively hostile. Most strikingly, these three black children find themselves – in terms resembling the stereotypical reaction of the white visitor to the colonies – seized with panic at being surrounded by black people: 'No, we are not acclimatized to this excess, these eloquent faces, this fever inhabiting the street. And then there are all these black people around us. So many black people, or more or less black' (181). They wish they had never left the security of the fort – in other words, the French army – and realize that 'We know nothing about this place' (182).

Thus a journey which had started as a euphoric expression of self-realization ('Each step brings us closer to ourselves') through the realization of an almost spiritual homecoming, ends as a panic-stricken admission that they do not belong here: Fort-de-France is in no sense their home. But while this emphasizes the cultural and emotional distance between France and the Antilles, the journey is given a further significance that paradoxically brings the two places together – but with equally negative connotations. In the course of this section of the narrative, the children's attempt to walk to the sea that they have seen from their house is explicitly paralleled (177, 179, 182) with Man Ya's attempt, recounted much earlier in the novel, to walk with Gisèle's brother Elie to the Sacré Cœur. In both cases, the journey's destination recedes as they walk towards it and initial confidence gives way to confusion and fear, as well as the realization that they are in danger of succumbing to a hostile environment. Man Ya, of course, did in fact eventually reach the Sacré Cœur and return triumphantly to the family's apartment, and the comparison between the two events is invoked to encourage them to persevere: 'Elie leads our procession, singing out the best bits of his journey across Paris hand in hand with Man Ya. Let's keep walking! Right to our destination, just like Man Ya who didn't know the Paris streets but still got there' (177). Nevertheless, her long walk across Paris was a desperate attempt to alleviate her misery at living there, and merely served to emphasize her isolation and the hostility of her environment: there was no sense of recognition or of homecoming involved. As a result, bringing these two incidents together in the text inevitably minimizes the joyful elements of the children's journey. Moreover, it also suggests, even more ominously, that Fort-de-France may pose the same kinds of problems for them as Paris did for Man Ya – problems perhaps symbolized by the cockroaches, mosquitoes and other pests that constitute the 'five plagues of the return to the non-native land', as one of the chapters is tellingly entitled (193).

This disillusionment does not mean that the novel has an unhappy ending. But Gisèle's successful adaptation to life in the Caribbean is made possible precisely by her realization that it is not home but a new place with strange ways of behaving that she will have to learn. With patience, she tells herself, the mysteries of Fort-de-France will be revealed to her and eventually 'you will wake up one morning and find that you too are inhabited by the very spirit of the new world' (184). Her mother expresses the ambiguity of the children's position, but also their determination to make a new life here: 'They are from here without really belonging here, but they try to belong, every day, passionately, with the determination of people from the city embarking on a return to the land' (210–11).

Man Ya's return to Guadeloupe, on the other hand, is entirely unproblematic: Asdrubal no longer beats her, she is delighted to be back in her old house and garden, and even more delighted when she is eventually rejoined by Maréchal's family. All of this contributes to the happy ending of *L'exil selon Julia* – which thus contrasts markedly with *Un plat de porc aux bananes vertes.* Unlike Man Ya's, Mariotte's old age continues in unrelieved despair until her death in the old people's home – she never returns to Martinique. But the two novels do nevertheless share a very similar questioning of the ideal of the homeland. For instance, *Un plat de porc* also creates parallels as well as contrasts between the past in Martinique and the present in Paris: Mariotte's memories start from and frequently return to her dying grandmother, who is described in similar terms to the old women in the home; and a key remembered scene takes place in a prison cell, echoing the theme of incarceration that dominates the representation of the home.

But a more pervasive undermining of the ideal of the homeland in this novel occurs through its exploration of the disjunction between memory and phantasy. Since Simone Schwarz-Bart is a native of Guadeloupe, and the couple lived there, one might have expected them to choose Guadeloupe as the homeland of their heroine. Indeed, in the notes at the end of the novel, Simone apologizes to her Martinican friends for using Guadeloupean rather than Martinican creole phrases in the text (213). The reason for the choice of Martinique, I think, lies in the circumstances of Mariotte's departure from the island: she left in 1902, just after the eruption of the Mont Pelé volcano which destroyed the town of St Pierre, killed her mother and obliterated her village. In other words, it would seem to be important to the novel as a whole that Mariotte migrates from a place that has been destroyed: in the narrow sense, she has no home to return to. She is longing for something which is not only spatially out of reach, but also belongs to the distant past; in one of the imaginary conversations she has with her grandmother, she says: 'I whispered to Man Louise how much I regretted leaving Martinique...even though all my family was buried under the ashes of Mont Pelé' (52).

Although she knows this, she still longs to return to Martinique as it was before the eruption. This creates a tension between her memory of what happened and the phantasy of return that depends upon repressing the memory – a tension that is perceptible in the way in which the text moves from a sudden involuntary memory of seeing the island for the last time to an idyllic image of St Pierre as she *wishes* to remember it:

> Suddenly it appeared to me, as on that last time, as the boat which carried towards Guyana its load of refugees from St Pierre [...] gained the open sea: a small piece of green land surrounded by multicoloured water with, on the summit of Mont Pelé, the gaping mouth of the crater still adorned with the plume of blueish ash that had smothered my life, a few hundred metres lower down.[...]

But the St Pierre of my imagination did not present the spectacle of the end of the world.

(84)

– and this leads into a detailed description of peaceful boats in the harbour, churches, the theatre, hills which are not covered in lava but still green and fertile, and the evocation of her village and her mother's house (84). The break between the two paragraphs signals the transition from an actual memory to the 'imagination' of wish-fulfilment – although it is noticeable that even this second idyllic description contains an allusion to the disaster of 1902: the houses 'exhaled the faint sound of memory eternally defying death' (84).

Mariotte's evocation of Martinique is mainly devoted to much earlier memories, which centre on a short period in her childhood during which her grandmother Man Louise dies and her mother visits her lover, Raymoninque (who may or may not be Mariotte's father) in prison, accompanied by Mariotte, and brings him the 'dish of pork with green bananas' that gives the novel its title. But the same subtle ironic disjunction between her longing to go home, and her actual memories of home, is evident throughout; other aspects of the memories also point to this hiatus between what actually happened in the past and what Martinique represents for Mariotte on an emotional level.[14] For instance, her principal reason for wanting to go home has to do with *recognition* – the opposite, in other words, of Fanon's figuration of exile as 'imprisonment in oneself'. She imagines what her old age would have been like had she stayed in Martinique and remained part of the community, known to and accepted by everyone: she would have told stories to the children, the neighbours would have kept her up to date with the local gossip, and after her death someone would have tended her grave and kept the memory of her alive (132–3). One cannot help noticing, however, that in her real memories her grandmother constantly rejects her; and in one key scene in which Raymoninque refuses to acknowledge her presence as he is being arrested, the emphasis is on her distress at this *lack* of recognition: 'So why, if he cared for me a little, did he ignore me, why did he not speak a single word to me, or even look at me as I was trotting along beside him? [...] why didn't he turn round even once in my direction [...] Oh, why?' (114–15).

The central image of the 'dish of pork with green bananas' provides another powerful example of this complex relationship between memory and longing, which problematizes the evocation of home as a straightforward opposition to exile. Mariotte and her mother take the dish to give to Raymoninque in his prison cell; Mariotte, of course, is not allowed to eat any of it; it smells so wonderful that she can hardly stop herself from crying (117), she watches Raymoninque eat it, licks the banana leaves it has been wrapped up in (120), and, on returning home, eats a handful of earth in the cemetery to 'calm her stomach' (129). This is the image that gradually comes to sum up for her all her memories of Martinique; everything else fades away:

> Suddenly everything disappeared, Martinique, the home, everything vanished into thin air and all that remained before my dazzled eyes [...] all that was left was the portion of pork that I held out to Raymoninque, in the last century, with regret ... because I knew it was the last piece and that there was no more left at home: none at all!'
>
> (131)

That is, the whole novel is structured around Mariotte's longing for Martinique: but the whole of Martinique itself is concentrated in the memory of this dish of pork *that she was not allowed to eat.* Her symbol of Martinique is not one of fulfilment, but of desire and lack.

It is thus entirely appropriate that the end of the novel replays the scene in the same register of non-fulfilment. Mariotte decides that she wants to eat Caribbean food one more time before she dies, and manages, with great difficulty, to walk out of the home to the famous Creole restaurant in the Rue Gît-le-Cœur that she used to frequent. Standing outside its door, she imagines a scene in which she is recognized and welcomed by its owner and sits down to eat a 'dish of pork with green bananas'. This imaginary vision is evoked in vivid and lengthy detail (201–9); but then she realizes that she cannot face entering the restaurant because she would not be able to stop herself from crying (as she had done in Raymoninque's prison cell). So she turns round, sets off back to the old people's home, but suffers a stroke on the way home and is brought back by ambulance. She writes her notebooks in the two weeks that follow this incident, and, since the text ends abruptly in mid-sentence, we assume that she dies at that point.

Thus the *object* of the exile's longing is itself a longing for something precious that was always out of reach. This double structure – a longing for a longing – echoes the double structure of diaspora in the Caribbean in which migration to Europe is superimposed on the original African diaspora, with the result that the Caribbean home always figures as a less than ideal homeland, and can never wholly fulfil the phantasy of return from exile. For Gisèle Pineau and her brothers, Guadeloupe is not, ultimately, 'home' but a new country; for Mariotte, Martinique is a lost home that in reality never fulfilled her desires. Thus whereas the Jewish holocaust acts as a powerful image and reference point for these evocations of the French Caribbean situation in post-war Europe, the Caribbean experience of diaspora in these years is also more emotionally ambivalent – not in its relation to France, but in its complicated attitude towards a 'home' that is itself characterized by lack and longing.

Notes

1. Translations are mine throughout, except where reference is made to a published English translation. Daniel-Henri Pageaux comments: 'Jean-Paul Sartre's work is traversed by Jews and Negroes. They appear in his literary works in diverse forms: types, motifs, themes. But the Jewish condition and the black condition, the Jewish "situation" and the black "situation", to use one of the keywords of Sartre's thought, are problematized in these two seminal works. Published one immediately after the other in the period after the war, *Réflexions sur la question juive* and *Orphée noir* [...] are still today a dual lesson in lucidity and courage' (1998: 229).
2. 'When it is a question of the Jew, the problem is clear: he is suspect because he wants to own the wealth or take over the positions of power. But the Negro is fixated at the genital; or at any rate he has been fixated there. Two realms: the intellectual and the sexual' (1986: 165).
3. Finkielkraut's notorious interview with the Israeli newspaper Ha'aretz (November 2005), although mainly directed at Muslim Africans, contains the claim that: 'If you want to put the Holocaust and slavery on the same plane, then you have to lie. Because [slavery] was not a Holocaust' (http://questionscritiques.free.fr/edito/haaretz/finkielkraut_171105.htm).

   See also Jean-Yves Camus (2006) for an interesting account of the extent to which the campaign during the 1990s to get the French government to publicly recognize the role France played in the slave trade, modelled itself on the Jewish community's campaign for recognition of French responsibility for the holocaust.
4. See Sam Haigh (2006) for an analysis of the 'racial melancholia' suffered by both Maréchal and Man Ya.
5. See Haigh (2006) for a detailed analysis of Maréchal's ambivalent melancholic/euphoric attitude to migration to France.
6. Although Pineau also seems to echo Fanon quite closely here, in the distinction he makes between the Jew whose appearance does not necessarily declare his race, and the black person who is always immediately recognizable as such (Fanon 1986: 115).
7. All references will be to the English translation of this text.
8. Césaire's *Discours sur le colonialisme* (1955) makes a large-scale comparison between Nazism and colonialism, seeing Hitler's Germany not as an aberration, but as the logical culmination of colonialism and hence, he argues, of Western civilization.
9. Kathleen Gyssels elaborates on André Schwarz-Bart's identification with Caribbean culture in these terms: 'Schwarz-Bart is fascinated by the Other, the Antillean in whom he recognizes himself as a Jew, the descendant of a

     people reduced to slavery. [...] After *Le Dernier des Justes*, the Jewish author developed an insatiable curiosity for the Antillean universe and its history' (1997: 96).

10. Myriam Warner-Vieyra's *Le Quimboiseur l'avait dit* (1980), whose protagonist is a young Guadeloupean girl forcibly interned in a mental hospital in France, is a slightly later example of the theme of exile as psychiatric incarceration.

11. See Martin Munro (2000) for an analysis of the image of Africa in Césaire's poetry and plays.

12. See, for instance, *The Last of the Just*, in which the hero Ernie Levy comforts the children being transported to Auschwitz with a vision of 'the Kingdom of Israel': where 'children can find their parents, and everybody is happy. Because the country we're going to, that's our kingdom, you know. There, the sun never sets, and you may eat anything you can think of. There, an eternal joy will crown your heads; cheerfulness and gaiety will come and greet you, and all the pains and all the moans will run away' (339). As well as providing a source of references in the later *Un plat de porc*, *The Last of the Just* also contains its own allusions to the parallels between Jewish victims and Caribbean slaves: in the final scene in the crematorium, Ernie reflects that the Jews 'for two thousand years never bore arms and never had either missionary empires or coloured slaves' (348).

13. Selvon's *The Lonely Londoners* expresses a rather similar ambivalence towards the prospect of returning home to the Caribbean; in the novel's closing pages the central character, Moses, reflects on his constant postponement of the decision to return home and starts to wonder whether he really wants to leave London: 'Every year he vowing to go back to Trinidad, but after the winter gone and birds sing [...] and then the old sun shining, is as if life start all over again, as if it still have time, as if it still have another chance [...] but it reach a stage, and he know it reach that stage, where he get so accustom to the pattern that he can't do anything about it [...] Why you don't go back to Trinidad. What happening man, what happening' (140–1).

14. Kathleen Gyssels emphasizes the 'traumatic' nature of Mariotte's actual memories of Martinique (1997: 190).

Bibliography

Camus, J. (2006) 'The Commemoration of Slavery in France and the Emergence of a Black Political Consciousness', *The European Legacy*, 11.6, 647–55.

Césaire, A. (1955) *Discours sur le colonialisme* (Paris: Présence Africaine).

Fanon, F. (1986 [1952]) *Black Skin, White Masks* (London: Pluto Press). [First published as *Peau noire, masques blancs*.]

Glissant, E. (1993) *Tout-monde* (Paris: Gallimard).

Gyssels, K. (1997) *Filles de Solitude: essai sur l'identité antillaise dans les (auto-) biographies fictives de Simone et André Schwarz-Bart* (Paris: L'Harmattan).

Haigh, S. (2006) 'Migration and Melancholia: from Kristeva's "dépression nationale" to Pineau's "maladie de l'exil"', *French Studies*, 60.2, 232–50.

Maragnes, D. (1998) 'L'identité et le désastre (origine et fondation)', *Portulan*, 2, 273–80.

Munro, M. (2000) *Shaping and Reshaping the Caribbean: The Work of Aimé Césaire and René Depestre* (Leeds: Modern Humanities Research Association, Texts and Dissertations, 52).

Pageaux, D. (1998) 'Sartre, les Juifs, les Noirs...et les autres', *Portulan*, 2, 229–46.

Pineau, G. (1996) *L'Exil selon Julia* (Paris: Editions Stock).

Placoly, V. (1971) *La Vie et la mort de Marcel Gonstran* (Paris: Editions Denoël).

Sartre, J. (1947) *Réflexions sur la question juive* (Paris: Gallimard).

Sartre, J. (1948) 'L'Orphée noir', preface to Léopold Sédar Senghor (ed.) *Anthologie de la nouvelle poésie nègre et malgache de langue française* (Paris: Presses Universitaires de France).

Schwarz-Bart, A. (1961 [1959]) *The Last of the Just* (London: Secker and Warburg). [First published as *Le Dernier des Justes*.]

Schwarz-Bart, S. and A. Schwarz-Bart (1967) *Un plat de porc aux bananes vertes* (Paris: Editions du Seuil).

Selvon, S. (1956) *The Lonely Londoners* (London: Alan Wingate).

Toumson, R. (1998) 'Deux figures du destin', *Portulan*, 2, 9–18.

Warner-Vieyra, M. (1980) *Le Quimboiseur l'avait dit* (Paris: Présence Africaine).

8
Vijay Singh's Indo-Fijian Work Ethic: The Politics of Diasporic Definitions

Mohit Prasad

> The indenture they signed was for five years' slavery in the cane fields of his Britannic Majesty's Crown Colony of Fiji – to them it was *girimit* [*sic*], an agreement – and it contained some of the most pernicious clauses thought up by man. There were such things expressed and inferred as "a fixed immigration ratio of four men to one woman," no choice of place or method of employment; women to work in the fields for at least the first seven months of their pregnancy; housing conditions worse if anything than those from which they had escaped; working hours unlimited. And all for a few pence a day.
>
> (Walter Gill, *Turn North-East at the Tombstone* (1970), p. 38)

Introduction

This essay offers an analysis of the Indo-Fijian diaspora in two distinct phases, from the original group of indentured labourers who came to Fiji from India in the late nineteenth and early twentieth centuries, to the second-wave diasporic communities of expatriate Indo-Fijians that formed in the wake of the Fiji military coups of 1987 and 2000. In exploring the latter it focuses in particular on the Indo-Fijian diasporic community in the suburb of Liverpool in Sydney, Australia, investigating the way in which the international success of Indo-Fijian golfer Vijay Singh has been celebrated among local and expatriate Indo-Fijians alike as a product of the much-vaunted Indo-Fijian 'work ethic' putatively forged on the colonial plantations. As the essay will demonstrate, celebrations of Singh as exemplar of the Indo-Fijian 'work ethic' points towards a wider cultural phenomenon in which the myth of a composite Indo-Fijian diaspora is invoked at times of celebration or crisis. Such valorizations of the Indo-Fijian work ethic have served, for example, to counterbalance the traumatic legacy of indenture and, more recently, to bolster a sense of communal solidarity in the wake of increasing ethnic fundamentalism and anti-Indian legislation follow-ing the coups. The idealized performative value ascribed to work ethics perpetuates the process of mythologization that began with the affirma-tion of the work ethic as a central component of the Indo-Fijian cultural ethos during indenture. It has become central to the identity politics of the Indo-Fijian diaspora, remaining a constant in the changing worlds Indo-Fijians inhabit in Fiji and in the countries of destination for the second-wave diasporic communities.

Migration, indenture and work ethics: The origins of the Indo-Fijian diaspora

The first Indian immigrants arrived in Fiji on 14th May 1879, some five years after Fiji became a British colony. The ship *Leonidas*, captained by Captain McLachlan, sailed from Calcutta on March 3rd and arrived off Levuka (the former capital of Fiji) on Wednesday May 14th. The *Leonidas* was cordoned off and quarantined due to reports of '11 deaths due to cholera and six of dysentery [...] Communication with the vessel under these circumstances is of course slow, but from what we learn there are 373 male and 149 female coolies, independent of children, all whom are under the charge of Dr Welsh' (*The Fiji Times*, 17 May 1879, 3).

The report marks the beginning of just over forty years of servitude and solitude for the Indo-Fijian diaspora. From 1879 to 1916 (shortly before indenture was abolished in 1920), over 60,000 indentured Indian labourers were transported to Fiji's sugar, banana and coconut estates.

Indenture was formalized with the signing of an agreement (approx-imated as 'girmit' by the labourers or 'girmitiyas') that listed the conditions of work, pay, accommodation and provision of basic facili-ties (Lal 2004: 6; Keown 2007: 118). The indenture period normally lasted five years, after which labourers could work for five more years in order to earn their passage back to India (Campbell 1989: 175–6; Keown 2007: 118). The system did contain some benefits: for many girmitiyas, living conditions were better than they had been in India, and caste divisions became less entrenched as people from different backgrounds were forced to work and live at close quarters (V. Mishra

1977: 396; Lal 2004: 12; Keown 2007: 118). However, working conditions were tough and wages – based on the amount of work an individual completed – were often very low, making the return journey to India impossible for many (Lal 2004: 13; Keown 2007: 118).

Almost 70 per cent of the emigrants were between the ages of 20–30 and almost 20 per cent were aged between 10–20 years, with only 0.2 per cent of the population aged over 40 (Gillion 1962: 209). These figures point to a relatively young new migrant society in Fiji: only a small proportion of community leaders were drawn from the elder sectors of the population, thereby overturning the community dynamics of the Indian homeland, which was firmly rooted in the caste system, with councils of elders leading cultural and religious activities. The crossing of waters, the shared traumas of sea journeys, removal from the social strictures of India and subsequent hardships as indentured labourers, led to the erosion of the caste system and the development of a more egalitarian cultural dynamic which entailed an appreciation of the qualities of resilience, resistance, protest and the capacity for hard, often menial, work. However, it is important to recognize that in spite of the development of this communitarian ethos, the Indo-Fijian diasporic community was – and remains – culturally and religiously diverse. Of the original immigrants, the Sanatani, Arya Samaj and Muslim sectarian/religious groups remain the most influential in Fiji, with Christian Indo-Fijians as a significant minority. Gujarati and South Indian free migrants who arrived in the late nineteenth and early twentieth centuries came from various Hindu denominations, while Sikh free migrants added another facet to Fiji's religious diversity.

During and beyond the indenture period, free migrants, ex-indentured labourers and their descendants established a living from agriculture, various trades and commerce (Lal 2004: 22–3; Keown 2007: 118), but although Indo-Fijians have played (and continue to play) a significant role in Fiji's business community, their socioeconomic advancement has been hampered by land tenure laws established in colonial Fiji. Aware of the damage that indigenous land alienation had caused in other British colonies, Fiji's colonial administrators decided to protect indigenous Fijian landholdings, and even today, over 80 per cent of Fijian land remains in indigenous ownership, leaving Indo-Fijians largely dependent upon the granting of leases (Nandan 2000: 22; Keown 2007: 118–19). The protectionist policies of the British administrators led to the segregation of Indians and indigenous Fijians, and since that period the two cultures have had very little contact, maintaining separate educational, religious and other amenities to this day (Lal 2004: 24; Campbell 1989: 175–6; Keown 2007: 119).

Significantly, the development of the much-vaunted Indo-Fijian work ethic took place towards the end of indenture, when the Colonial Sugar Refining Company (CSR) of Australia, which had dominated sugar production in Fiji, introduced the tenant farmer system for its former labourers from 1912 onwards (Gillion 1973: 171). The Indo-Fijian 'work ethic', one could argue, was driven largely by the aspiration to break free of the legacy of indenture through education and eventual economic self-sufficiency. Within a colonial system in which most Indo-Fijians could not own land, the notion of work ethics was linked to claims of belonging to the land in Fiji through labour, and, in the case of Hindu Indo-Fijians, with their *'karma'* – the rewards of life and salvation based on a life devoted to work, prayer, worship, family and community. In his introduction to *The Indo-Fijian Experience* – a collection of essays and creative works celebrating 100 years of indenture in Fiji – Subramani summarizes the aspirations of Indo-Fijians wishing to escape the legacy of indenture as follows:

> It was more important to fight poverty and illiteracy, and generally survive in the new environment. Henceforth they pursued some of the worst aspects of the colonialist's monetary culture which resulted in further disintegration of spiritual values and helped complete the transformation of the feudal Indian into an individual.
>
> (Subramani 1979: x)

In recognizing the Indo-Fijian 'work ethic' as a predominantly post-indenture phenomenon, it is worth, at this point, exploring the problems attendant upon popular valorizations of the work ethic as a product of the indenture period itself. Under indenture, work was carried out under a system of tasking under the watchful eyes of overseers or *coolumbers* (the Indo-Fijian term for field supervisors or overseers, anglicized from the system of 'call numbers' used to identify and task the workers), enforced usually with a bullwhip from horseback. A coterie of *sirdars* (local assistants to the overseers, from the Hindi 'Sardar' or leader) or handpicked henchmen ensured total conformity. It was not a system that promoted the ideals of the idle time theory of late capitalism, which itself carries connotations of a Western middle-class existence, with neat divisions of labour and leisure time. Fiji has its own theories and semantics on idle time to be found in the phrases *Moku Siga* (Fijian) and *Deen Maaro* (Fiji Hindi), both of which literally translate as 'killing time'.

Alongside the *Moku Siga* ethos in the islands are the practices of talanoa (informal conversation) and the consumption of *yagona* or *kava* (a mildly narcotic drink made from the roots and stem of the Piper methysticum plant) where one invariably accompanies the other. The practice of *Moku Siga* or *Din Maaro* is part of a particular Indo-Fijian ethos that works against the doctrine of a work ethic bound to the mythic constructs of the *girmit* period. In this respect, the valorization of work ethics becomes performative. Indo-Fijians invoke the mythological nexus of indenture, hard work and success in order to celebrate achievements that are variously personal, communal, and – in the case of Vijay Singh – iconic. On the other hand, Indo-Fijians in Fiji and those among the second-wave diasporic communities also celebrate the *lack* of a work ethic in their enjoyment of the simple pleasures of *Moku Siga* and *Din Maaro*. In most instances this phenomenon is linked with the invocation of an Oceanic or Pacific Island identity that is romanticized as the basis of a free-spirited individuality, contrasted with those who seek material gain.

In his book *Turn North-East at the Tombstone* (1970), Walter Gill offers an ultimately brave and sad account of indenture from his experience as an overseer for the CSR during the final years of indenture. The book, which makes plain the mechanics and logistics of work under the indenture system, is in parts a novel, autobiography, life story, history, an anthropological treatise, and a sociological study of Fiji between 1919 and 1934.

The book becomes a unique index of the use of labour examined from the position of the overseer rather than that of the 'detached' academic observer. A large part of the text's appeal and empathy with local conditions comes from Gill's familiarity with local vernaculars, especially Hindi and Fijian. Gill, as he outlines in his preface, chooses to translate this in the text rather then venture 'to copy Kipling, the master of Hindustani/English' (n.p.). His account is that of a shared life with those on the bottom rungs of the colonial ladder: among them indentured labourers, freed Indian workers/farmers, indigenous Fijians and blackbirded labourers (those recruited by Europeans but commonly under conditions of coercion and exploitation). Gill quickly realized that like his charges, he was also harnessed to the colonial corporate machine, where only the corporate bottom line – profits – mattered.

The strategies employed by overseers, who exerted an often brutal form of control over a sometimes wilful labour force, were built upon a set of alliances made between the CSR overseers, managers and their local sirdars. Gill details various instances of the brutal treatment of workers and concludes:

And now I have some explaining to do. If we, the overseers and sird-ars caught up in the rotten system of indenture servitude fathered by Big Business on that most fecund of whores, cheap Asiatic labour, had managed to survive in the tooth-and-claw jungle of the cane game, it was only by out-animalizing the horde of near human apes in our charge. And I mean apes, because a percentage of the men and women, regardless of what they were when they left India, had been changed by the terrors and conditions of the sea journey, and their years of servitude, into something like simian humans. It was also typical of the era that we white men had no inkling of wrong-doing, and when it came to coolie eating coolie, the sirdar system left the whites, as sadistic bullies, in the infant class. So if 'to excuse is to accuse,' then I have done just that.

(Gill 1970: 65)

Gill's observations refigure the indenture experience, exposing its vio-lence and brutality that, in his social Darwinist view, produced a form of recidivism among the labourers. Although his rhetoric is tainted by colonial stereotypes, it nevertheless exposes the fact that the indenture experience involved relentless and punishing work in order to achieve '*taas*' (the allotted task), and in this context the romanticized concept of a voluntary 'work ethic' among Indo-Fijians is clearly spurious.

In the decades following the abolition of indenture, references to the *girmit* period have often been made in times of crisis or trauma, and have also featured prominently in Indo-Fijian political propaganda – from the late 1920s (when the British colonial administration first granted Indo-Fijians a limited voice in the Fiji Legislative Council) to 1987, when Fiji's first multi-ethnic government was elected to power (Lal 1992: 87).

The indenture period, and its associated traumas, has also featured prominently in a wide range of Indo-Fijian literary works. One of the most sustained explorations of indenture appears in Subramani's short-story collection *The Fantasy Eaters* (1988), which features a number of dispossessed and disillusioned characters suffering from what Vijay Mishra calls the 'girmit ideology'. This ideological construct, Mishra argues, posits the experience of indenture as akin to a 'failed millennial quest', in which the harsh realities of life on the Fijian plantations (and in the coolie lines) shattered labourers' 'dreams' of a 'promised land' in which they would 'escape from the degrading realities of Indian life' (1977: 395; Keown 2007: 120).

The coups (discussed later in this essay) have added a further layer of complexity to explorations of indenture and diaspora in more recent Indo-Fijian literature: in his play 'Ferringhi' (2001), for example, Sudesh Mishra posits the playing of a popular Bollywood song on the theme of building a home as an allusion to the settling of Fiji by the Indo-Fijian diaspora. The song *'tinka tinka chun kar tum ne / Nagari ek basayi'* (Bits of soil you chose / To build a settlement) is a rejoinder to an earlier song calling on people to take flight after a coup *'Chal urdh ja re panchi / ke abh desh huwa begana'* (Time to take flight little bird / this land has now become foreign) (344). These emotive references to space, history and flight are given a further context in the play by Aslam – one of the five central characters who explore their personal and collective traumas, histories and memories during the course of the play. Responding in telling fashion to a call for subservience to an indigenous Fijian land-owner, Aslam reflects: 'This jus like second girmit' (352). While these kinds of references reflect a common attitude to indenture as trauma in the individual and collective consciousness of Indo-Fijians, later sections of this essay focus more closely on celebratory representations of the *girmit* heritage as a foundation for the legendary Indo-Fijian 'work ethic', exploring the ways in which the success of international golfer Vijay Singh has been traced back to the hardships and resulting resilience of the Indo-Fijian indentured labourers and their descendants.

The coups and the second phase of Indo-Fijian migration

As stated above, the military coups that took place in the closing decades of the twentieth century triggered a second phase in the migratory history of Indo-Fijians, as thousands of skilled workers left the country in the wake of increasing ethnic fundamentalism and anti-Indian legislation.

After Fiji gained its independence from Britain in 1970, the first few years saw a period of comparative stability under the governance of the Alliance Party (led by indigenous Fijian and powerful traditional chief, Ratu Sir Kamisese Mara), which protected the interests of Fiji's 'ruling class' of chiefs as well as Europeans and wealthy Indians. In 1987, however, the indigenous Fijian-dominated leadership was superseded by a multi-ethnic coalition led by Dr Timoci Bavadra, an indigenous Fijian with the support of the Indo-Fijian community. Bavadra's government included roughly equal numbers of Indians and indigenous Fijians, but within a month of being elected to power, Bavadra was ousted during a military coup led by Lieutenant Colonel Sitiveni Rabuka, who claimed to be acting on behalf of indigenous Fijians who were worried about potential racial discrimination under the new government. Following a series of unsuccessful negotiations, a second coup took place in September 1987, after which Fiji was declared a republic, and Governor-General Ratu Sir Penaia Ganilau (an indigenous Fijian) was appointed President with Ratu Sir Kamisese Mara as Prime Minister. A new constitution (implemented in 1990) severely disadvantaged Indo-Fijians, reserving most political offices, employment opportunities, educational and training scholarships, government loans, grants and funding for indigenous Fijians. After several years of further negotiation, the 1997 constitution reopened the role of Prime Minister to citizens of all ethnicities, but inter-ethnic tensions intensified again in May 1999, when a multi-racial coalition led by Mahendra Chaudhry – Fiji's first Indian Prime Minister – came to power. In 2000, Fijian nationalist George Speight (of mixed Fijian and European descent) led another military coup that removed Chaudhry from power. Although Speight was eventually arrested and the suspended constitution restored, when democratic elections took place once again in 2002, the interim Prime Minister Laisenia Qarase defeated Chaudhry, thereby securing the continuing dominance of indigenous Fijians in the most powerful offices of government (Keown 2007: 119).

The exodus of Indo-Fijians that took place during the post-coup period was accompanied by renewed references to the traumatic history of the Indo-Fijian diaspora, but it is perhaps revealing that the general Indo-Fijian response to the 2006 Fijian coup saw fewer references to the *girmit* experience as trauma. The general perception among Indo-Fijians was that the 2006 coup was a reaction against the racist policies of the Qarase-led government that was re-elected in 2006. The policies of the Qarase government had further marginalized Indo-Fijians from the land, from fishing rights, education, employment in the civil service and statutory bodies – effectively denying them equal citizenship in Fiji.

This turbulent period of Fijian history has led to the formation of new 'second-wave' diasporic communities of Indo-Fijians in a diverse range of countries within and beyond the Pacific, from southern hemisphere countries such as New Zealand and Australia, to Canada and the United States in the north. Later sections of this essay take, as a case study, the Indo-Fijian diasporic community in Liverpool, a local government area in South-Western Sydney (Australia). Comprising a main city centre and a cluster of neighbouring suburbs, Liverpool hosts one of the highest concentrations of diasporic Indo-Fijians in the post-coup era. In discussing the vicissitudes of the second-wave Indo-Fijian diaspora more generally, however, it is important to recognize the triangular dynamic between the new countries of habitation, the natal 'homeland' of Fiji and the ancestral 'homeland' of India.

In elaborating his concept of the 'girmit ideology' (outlined earlier in this essay), Vijay Mishra has discussed the role of this triangular dynamic in the development of a putatively communal Indo-Fijian ideology and consciousness. His most recent reassessment of this phenomenon appears in the chapter entitled 'The *girmit* ideology', published in his 2007 monograph *The Literature of the Indian Diaspora: Theorizing the Diasporic Imaginary*. Here, Mishra outlines two significant transitional stages in the development of the Indo-Fijian diaspora. The first he links to the 'excitement' of the 'first 40 years of indenture', during which there was 'a constant process of assimilating later migrants into a socially inclusive community' that was 'marked by a highly imaginative and egalitarian sense of social cohesion and purpose' (2007: 26). The second is described as the 'ideology of the "fossil", which meant also the triumph of myth over history': this is interpreted as a more static, diachronic ideology that overtook the 'excitement of reconstitution' of the first stage (26). It is in this second stage, Mishra argues, that India is 'realised' through mythic interpolations of place, space and time in creating the 'diasporic imaginary' of both the ideal motherland and that of an 'ethnic enclave in a nation state that defines itself, consciously, unconsciously or through self-evident or implied political coercion, as a group that lives in displacement' (14). While Mishra's arguments have proved highly influential, critics such as John O'Carroll, Sudesh Mishra and Mohit Prasad have critiqued and revised Mishra's theories, which are considered problematic in that they do not take sufficient account of internal differences and divisions within the Indo-Fijian community (O'Carroll 2002; S. Mishra 2002; Prasad 1999: 74–93).

Notwithstanding these differences, it is legitimate to argue that India, as the mythological 'motherland' of the Indo-Fijian diaspora, is frequently romanticized in popular and folk songs, among Indo-Fijian literary texts in Hindi and in English as well as in various religious and social rituals. India remains a constant point of reference for Indo-Fijians, through food, religion, Bollywood films, music and stage shows, satellite television and the Internet. However, while these connections create a clear sense of an Indian 'imagined community' within Fiji, it is important to recognize that there are differences in the way in which different sectors of the Indo-Fijian community interpret their relationship to the ancestral homeland. The majority of the free migrants who arrived in Fiji towards and beyond the end of indenture, for example, retained tangible geographical and familial links with India, while the early indentured labourers and their descendants have experienced a much more tenuous link to the Indian 'homeland': for the majority of Indo-Fijians, India is remote in both space and time, and rendered even more distant through the seismic historical shifts which took place during and beyond independence and Partition.

Further, in legal and political terms, it is clear that the Indo-Fijian diaspora cannot define itself as Indian, even if others choose to do so. Indo-Fijians are Fijian nationals in Fiji, while members of the second-wave diasporic communities take up nationality as per citizenship in their new countries of residence. For India itself, the Indo-Fijian diaspora remains an alien entity, requiring visas to travel in and out, and not eligible for citizenship on the basis of place of origin. The offer of dual citizenship by India, formalized under the Overseas Citizenship of India (OCI) Act in 2005, was not extended to Fiji, nor to most of the other Indian diasporic communities whose origins lay in the labour migrations under indenture. It is significant that in spite of widespread knowledge of this discriminatory legislation among Fiji's Indians, there was little public outcry about the ruling – underscoring the relative lack of material contact between Fiji and the Indian homeland. Nevertheless, this development serves to further underscore the continuing conditions of exile that bear upon the Indo-Fijian community: barred from their mythic and celebrated homeland, even in their 'new' homeland of Fiji, the vast majority of Indo-Fijians maintain an unstable existence on leased land, or land under threat of reversion to original indigenous Fijian ownership.

In spite of these uncertainties, for those Indo-Fijians who left Fiji following the coups, Fiji (unlike the mythical homeland of India) is retrievable in specific and immediate ways. There is family to write back to, send remittances to, visit or sponsor in efforts to obtain visas for loved ones, either as visitors or as migrants. And, as I will argue below, the success and global rise to prominence of golfer Vijay Singh has furnished diasporic Indo-Fijians with a new focus for valorizations of the Indo-Fijian 'work ethic' as an enduring cornerstone of Indo-Fijian cultural identity, that is traceable back to Fiji.

Golf and the work ethic: Vijay Singh as Indo-Fijian figurehead

Since the colonial period, the game of golf has formed an important facet of Indo-Fijian cultural identity, and Vijay Singh's rise to fame has further enhanced the status of the game among Indo-Fijians. Even before Singh's entry onto the global golf circuit, references to golf abounded within Indo-Fijian popular and literary culture. A short survey of literary and autobiographical texts by Indo-Fijians, for example, reveals a surprisingly high number of references to the centrality of golf in Indo-Fijian culture.

Subramani holds the course record among Indo-Fijian writers for the most references to golf. Many of his relatives (the Goundar and Reddy families from his birthplace in Batnikama, Labasa) are well known golfers who continue a family tradition in the game. This familial connection to golf no doubt accounts for his recollections of golf and Labasa in various autobiographical pieces in the collection *Altering Imagination* (1995), including the following:

> The hills, the barracks, the sugarcane fields, the river lined with mangroves, where night comes suddenly; the silent, empty golf course, the mysterious bungalows; and midway between the house and the New Lines, an ancient banyan tree with intricate roots and overhanging branches are full of ghosts at noonday casting deep shadows at night over the mud path – the landscape of my childhood memories.
>
> (68)

These allusions to golf in Labasa within the family circle are later extended in Subramani's Fiji-Hindi novel *Dauka Puraan* (2001). The image recalled by Subramani is typical of the landscape around the former Colonial Sugar Refinery mills and plantations. This description of Labasa around the main township that grew around the CSR mill on Vanua Levu, the second of Fiji's two large islands, could be repeated with reference to Penang in Rakiraki, Rarawai in Ba and Lautoka on the main island of Viti Levu – right down to the obligatory banyan tree. The Indo-Fijian connection to golf is firmly rooted in the plantation golf courses where Indo-Fijians were welcome only as caddies and, until the 1960s, were not allowed to play on these courses, many of which had been built upon the labour of their forefathers.

In *Altering Imagination*, Subramani alludes to this heritage in a more detailed account of the neo-colonial associations of golf in Fiji:

> The golf course is something else the CSR has left behind. In spite of the drought, the greens are still lush and well-kept [...]
>
> The golfers are homegrown kids: mill labourers, mechanics, farmers. Some of them had been caddies before. Apart from the golf course, the Europeans have left something else behind: the familiar

golf course names. The golfers call each other Tony and Robert, and one or two of them have even cultivated the mannerisms of their favourite Sahebs.

Golf is not simply a recreation. It is a passion. Many a husband has squandered his pay packet here. It also is a source of family feuds and rivalries.

(1995: 60–1)

In this passage, Subramani invests golf with significance beyond mere recreation in the lives of the descendants of indentured labourers and mill workers. He hints at the neo-colonialist aspects of the game, given the aspiration of many Indo-Fijians to play the game of the 'sahebs' and to excel at it – at least at the local level. The fact that descendants of the indentured labourers have inherited the golf course from the former CSR colonial masters is ironic given the general history of exclusion and division in sports under colonialism. Some of these inter-ethnic sporting divisions lasted into the late 1960s. For example, among Indo-Fijians, football or soccer is the main sport, formalized through the founding of the Fiji Indian Football Association in 1938. The Association's constitution included an exclusionary clause that restricted the game to 'Asiatics and Europeans'; the Fiji Indian FA remained the national association for the sport until 1961, when the clause was withdrawn and indigenous Fijians were finally allowed to participate in the sport. The withdrawal of the clause enabled the formation of the Fiji Football Association (FFA) in 1962 and paved the way for affiliation with the Fédération Internationale de Football Association (FIFA) in 1963 (Prasad 1997: 47–73).

Soccer remains the main sport played and followed among Indo-Fijians both in Fiji and in the second-wave diasporic communities. Fans identify primarily with district teams that play in the various divisions in national competitions and tournaments in Fiji – there is little evidence of a nationwide fraternity of fans to complement this parochial support for the district teams. The increasingly exclusionary nature of race and politics in Fiji to some extent explains the lack of national football pride: a prominent example of this was witnessed when the Indian soccer team toured Fiji in 2005, and the national Fiji soccer captain Esala Masi ended up pleading for fan support among the mainly Indo-Fijian crowd who, he claimed, were cheering for the visitors (*The Fiji Times*, 11 August 2005, 38). However, pride in the district soccer team from one's own area of origin remains the primary motivation for soccer supporters both in Fiji and within the second-wave diasporic communities.

In this context, and as I will argue further below, one could argue that Vijay Singh transcends such localized parochialism, in that he has become an iconic sporting hero whose achievements and work ethics are valorized as a source of inspiration for all Indo-Fijians.

The relationship between sport, colonialism and inter-ethnic rivalry in Fiji approximates similar dynamics in other parts of the former British Empire such as the Caribbean and the Indian subcontinent, whose formerly colonized peoples have excelled in sports such as cricket. In his classic text on cricket, *Beyond a Boundary* (1963), the Afro-Trinidadian intellectual C. L. R. James has analysed the game in terms similar to those discussed in this essay, discussing its socio-political and cultural significance in the former British colonies of the Caribbean. In her discussion of cricket and colonialism in the Caribbean, Belinda Edmondson points out that the West Indian cricket team – world champions for most of the 1980s and 1990s – became the 'most potent sign of Caribbean political and social unity' and 'cricket, with its attendant "European" ideology, has given access to a common West Indianness across national and cultural lines' (1994: 113).

I would argue that since Vijay Singh's rise to international fame, golf has occupied a similar role in Fiji: Singh has become a national icon not just for Indo-Fijians, but also for indigenous Fijians, and his success has earned him a form of honorary indigenization in the Fijian and international media, in which he has been described as the 'big Fijian'. This is significant in a country in which ethnic labels have proved contentious: although the term 'Indo-Fijian' is widely used to refer to Fiji's Indian community, members of this community are far from agreed on its exigency, while many indigenous Fijians prefer the Fijian vernacular term *'Kaindia'* or *'from / belonging to India.'* Official forms in Fiji categorize the diasporic community as 'Indians', although nationality in passport and travel documents is entered as Fijian/Fiji National. Singh's designation as 'Fijian' therefore appears, however superficially, to transcend Fiji's inter-ethnic divisions.

As discussed above, a number of Indo-Fijian writers have referenced the socio-political significance of golf in their work. Where Subramani has emphasized the colonial associations of golf in Fiji, other Indo-Fijian writers such as Sudesh Mishra have explored the way in which the golf course has functioned as a micro-political arena for Fiji's elitist postcolonial leadership. Popular urban myths and anecdotes in Fiji, some of which may be apocryphal, place at least two coup plots being hatched on the fairways of the Fiji Golf Club at Vatuwaqa, or at the Pacific Harbour Golf Club. Mishra makes reference to the central role assigned to political dealings on the golf course in popular discourse in Fiji in his play 'Ferringhi':

> Voice 3: (offstage) I am the Director of Mnemonic Prosecution. You are under arrest for infringing the Deletion Act.

> Voice 1: (offstage) Which I, Turaga, His Excellency, the President of Bakwas, decreed at the 14th hole. A rare birdie it was too.

> (2001: 372)

The satirical tone of this extract plays on both the golf course as a private space for politicians and business interests and the elitist nature of the game. In spite of the elitist and colonialist associations of the game of golf in Fiji, Vijay Singh's success in the game is traced to his 'humble' beginnings. Singh came from an off-plantation background and recounts growing up in a one-roomed tin shack outside Lautoka, close to the CSR Lautoka Golf Course, and sleeping top-and-tail with his siblings. Singh began his career in 1980 by winning a local golf tournament on his home course at the Nadi Open; as a teenager he had already chalked up an impressive resumé on the Fiji circuit.

On the PGA tour, regarded as among the toughest of all sports competitions, Vijay Singh's achievements are extraordinary given that he worked his way up from Nadi, to the jungles of Borneo as a club professional, to doing what was predicted as the impossible in golf: dethroning Tiger Woods from his number one spot. This goal was achieved in 2004, when Vijay Singh won nine tournaments and over US$10 million in prize money, overtaking Tiger Woods.

Indeed, the success of figures such as Vijay Singh and Tiger Woods has helped to erode conceptions of golf as a primarily white, Western pursuit, even though the game remains exclusivist in various ways (given that the cost of equipment and membership of clubs tends to further entrench an elitist hierarchy that stretches from Florida to Fiji). Further, Singh's success has, within Indo-Fijian popular culture, been linked with the celebrated work ethic discussed earlier in this essay: although golf is a leisure pursuit, the hard work associated with becoming a professional golfer – particularly one as successful as Singh – has invited comparisons, however spurious, with the toughened labourers of the indenture period. Singh's rise from humble beginnings has functioned as a source of pride for fellow Indo-Fijians such as writer and former Member of Parliament Satendra Nandan, who mentions Singh in his memoir *Requiem for a Rainbow* (2001): 'We'd curse the cows in Hindi and wipe our false tears. Then begin playing *gullidanda*, an early version, I suspect, of golf. Vijay Singh chased chickens on my father's farm' (138). For those Indo-Fijians who left Fiji in the wake of the coups, the legend of Singh has formed a focus for a diaspora that continually seeks new mythologies to sustain a sense of a shared past. Although the game of golf, and Singh himself, are undeniably associated with a predominantly male, educated, middle-class version of Indo-Fijian culture (and one of which I am acutely aware in writing this essay), Singh's media presence has rendered him accessible to a wide spectrum of Indo-Fijians regardless of gender, class and religious divisions. This accessibility, and the celebration of Singh's 'work ethic' among Indo-Fijians, has helped to sustain the myth of a shared communal identity that has gained new associations in the period of out-migration and ontological uncertainty following the coups.

Diasporic dynamics among Indo-Fijians in Liverpool, Australia

Situated in South-Western Sydney, Australia, the local government area of Liverpool contains one of the largest communities of diasporic Indo-Fijians that has formed in the post-coup era. This community was formed through an extended period of migration that began in the 1960s: most of these early migrants were skilled workers whose numbers were later augmented by family sponsored arrivals through to the 1980s. The beginnings of a second-wave Indo-Fijian diasporic community in Liverpool and further afield can be linked to the demand among Indo-Fijians for overseas tertiary education, with Australia and New Zealand as particularly popular destinations. Many of these graduates, who entered legal, medical, teaching and other professions, either remained in or migrated back to the countries in which they obtained their qualifications following an initial return to Fiji. The gradual relaxing of immigration requirements for Australia and New Zealand, and the recognition of professional degrees from the University of the South Pacific as well as some vocational qualifications from Fiji, has led to further migration. Prior to 1987, most of this migration was motivated primarily by economic and familial considerations. After 1987, however, migration to overseas locations, including Liverpool, accelerated due to the coups, with mainly family-sponsored new migrants gravitating towards settlements established by earlier migrants. Cheaper land, housing and access to work in factories and industries around the Liverpool area were additional factors in attracting large numbers of Indo-Fijians to the district. The suburb has become, in many ways, a microcosmic version of Fiji, with large tracts of the older parts of the central business district taken over by Indo-Fijian businesses and professionals.

Some of the earliest Indo-Fijian businesses established in Sydney included small retail outlets that became known by the generic label of the 'Fiji Shop'. From isolated businesses established in areas such as Newtown (an inner-city suburb) in the 1970s, the number of 'Fiji Shops' expanded exponentially in the post-coup area, as large numbers of new migrants settled in Liverpool and in the western suburb of Blacktown. The main product lines in these shops include Indian spices, 'pooja samagri' (a generic mix of goods that are an integral part of Hindu religious ceremonies) and copies of Bollywood movies, but these core commodities are supplemented with distinctly 'island' produce – including root crops, coconuts, dried fish, curry leaves, island seafood, coconuts, tinned fish, corned mutton and various other products sourced from Fiji. With the influx of Indo-Fijians since 1987, many Liverpool streets are now 'colonized' by the Indo-Fijian diaspora, which maintains a wide range of businesses from the expanded spice, DVD and produce shops, to ice-cream parlours, restaurants, butcheries and even 'adults only' shops. The patois among these shop owners is Fiji Hindi, with cricket, rugby union and league, Vijay Singh and the exploits of the Fiji national rugby team or the various district soccer teams back home among the topics of discussion. In his autobiography *Mr. Tulsi's Store: A Memoir* (2001), Indo-Fijian emigré Brij Lal provides the following apt summary of the lives of Indo-Fijians in Liverpool:

> It is a mini-Fiji, with its temples, mosques, churches and its spice and grocery shops, video outlets, fashion houses selling sari and salwar kamiz, restaurants and takeaway joints. A variety of social and cultural organizations competing with each other for membership and funds, serves the community. Cultural evenings of song, music and dance, the celebration of festivals such as Holi, Diwali and Eid, are regular fare there. Newspapers proliferate, disseminating news about forthcoming events, soliciting contributions for this cause or that, announcing news of death, births and marriages. Pettiness and bickering, the bane of our community, are alive and well there, causing fissures and frictions which enliven the mindless suburban life.

(196)

Liverpool City Council statistics provide a useful index of demographic trends within the local Indo-Fijian community. Second only to the Australian-born members of the community, migrants whose place of birth is recorded as Fiji made up the largest single community in Liverpool by 2001 (see Table 8.2 below). The non-recording of place of origin for the Australian-born children of these migrants makes the total number of Indo-Fijians difficult to quantify, but even in the absence of these statistics, it is clear that Liverpool now hosts one of the world's largest communities of diasporic Indo-Fijians outside Fiji itself. The high number of family sponsored migrants, who make up 48.5 per cent of total arrivals between 1996 and 2004 (see Table 8.1 below), follows the general trend of migrants in this category to settle near sponsors and contribute to the social and welfare networks among families in the area. The concentration of people from Fiji in Liverpool mirrors in many ways the familiar pattern of family migration among diasporic communities of Italians, Chinese, Indians and other groups around the globe.

According to Table 8.2, 4509 people born in Fiji resided in Liverpool in 2001. Included in these numbers would be ethnic Fijians and people of other races from Fiji. Excluded from these figures are Australian-born Indo-Fijians, the newest hyphenated sub-group among diasporic Indians in this area. Various estimates, based on figures released by the Fiji Bureau of Statistics and the Australian Bureau of Statistics (ABS), suggest that between 1970 and 2001, 150,000 Indo-Fijians left Fiji. Fiji Bureau of Statistics figures reveal that a further 12,057 people migrated between 2002–3. It is estimated that in 2008, 80,000 Indo-Fijians live in Australia, and that Liverpool has some 30,000 or more, making it the largest single overseas community of Indo-Fijians (http://www.statsfiji. gov.fj/Tourism/residents.htm).

Table 8.1 Top 5 Countries by Migration Stream for Local Government Area: Liverpool (C)

Settlers Arriving from 1 July 1996 to 30 June 2004

Country of Birth	Humanitarian	Family	Skill	Special/Other	Total
Croatia	1075	4	32	0	1111
Iraq	914	9	179	0	1102
Fiji	0	514	485	1	1000
Former Yugoslavia	860	6	74	2	942
India	0	506	238	0	744

Source: Liverpool City Council.Com: Top 5 Countries by Migration Stream for Local Government Area: Liverpool, 2 March 2004, accessed 4 January 2005.
http://www.liverpool.nsw.gov.au/scripts/viewoverview_contact.asp?NID=11293

Table 8.2　Liverpool's Culture: Birthplaces and Ancestry

	2001 number	2001 %	1996 number	% change 96–01
Australia	85,484	55.5	73,525	16
Fiji	4509	2.9	2303	96
Vietnam	4195	2.7	2855	47
United Kingdom	3871	2.5	4331	–11
Italy	3299	2.1	3355	–2

Source: *Liverpool City Council.Com*: Liverpool's Culture: Birthplaces and Ancestry, 2 March 2004, accessed 4 January 2005.
http://www.liverpool.nsw.gov.au/scripts/viewoverview_contact.asp?NID=11293

In an academic study of the Liverpool community that I conducted at the dawn of the new millennium, I analysed the position that golf – and the success of Vijay Singh – occupied in the Indo-Fijian diasporic imaginary. 109 completed questionnaires were collected from a total of 400 that were distributed in the Liverpool area between July 2002 and March 2003. In 35 out of the 53 interviews that were conducted for the study, golf featured as a prominent topic of interest among the Indo-Fijian diaspora in Liverpool, alongside familiar subjects such as food, entertainment, fashion and team sports like soccer. Respondents expressed a strong sense of communal Indo-Fijian identity when it came to the topic of golf, reflecting Vijay Singh's position as among the top golfers in the world during the period in which these surveys took place.

Respondents showed an immediate grasp of the jargon of golf. The key facts and figures on Vijay Singh's achievements were invariably rattled off with remarks on the enormous amounts of money earned and his high profile among international sporting stars. Vijay Singh was also the focus for discussions of the legendary Indo-Fijian work ethic; the general consensus was that Singh's success was not surprising given the 'nature' of Indo-Fijians and their capacity for hard work. The mythologization of Vijay Singh centred on his humble beginnings and his rise to fame as a product of the work ethic.

As indicated earlier in this essay the much-vaunted 'Indo-Fijian work ethic' has two contrasting facets, allowing members of the diaspora to enact the role of the 'victor' or the 'victim' depending on the context. Within the Liverpool community, Vijay Singh's success was translated into a mythic greatness that enacted a celebratory model of the labouring heritage of Indo-Fijians.

Among golf players there was a particular sense of achievement and celebration as Vijay Singh continued to accumulate international victories.

In Liverpool, significant numbers of Indo-Fijians play golf, most having started in Fiji, but some inspired by Singh to take to the fairways. Among these players, at least one respondent indicated that he had spent a substantial amount of money grooming his son for a career as a professional golfer. During the survey he outlined plans for his son to break into the professional tour with the 2003 Fiji Golf Open as a starting point. Vijay Singh was an obvious role model and his achievements, putatively based on his exemplary work ethic, were taken as indicative of the possibilities for other Indo-Fijians to follow suit and take up golf as a vocation. Given the iconic status of Vijay Singh among golfers from Fiji, and particularly among Indo-Fijians, it is not surprising that his achievements and work ethic are posited as the template for success in golf as well as in other aspects of life. The identitarian utility of work ethics and the iconic status of Vijay Singh transcends various social divides, notably the sectarian basis of the Indo-Fijian diaspora that is faithfully transported and rigorously adhered to in second-wave diasporic communities.

The assertion of this community identity based on wider definition of 'Indianness' also spreads across the rather tense lines between 'India Indians' and 'Fiji Indians' in Liverpool. The assertions of individual and collective identities between the two groups have resulted in highly publicized and divisive debates on origins and identities. While relations between 'India Indians' and 'Fiji Indians' in Australia have not been the subject of any detailed study, anecdotal evidence, and some coverage in locally distributed newspapers (such as *The Fiji Times* and *The Indian Sub-continent Times*), have highlighted tensions between the two diasporic Indian groups that stemmed largely from attitudes expressed to each other on identitarian issues. Among these issues is the subject of India as a place of origin. Among Indo-Fijians there is a perception that 'India Indians' tend to dismiss them as a mongrelized group and downplay their rights of direct claim to Indian heritage and culture. This perception is significant given the special attention given to the place of India by theorists like Vijay Mishra in shaping the Indo-Fijian 'ideology and consciousness'.

Within this context of a divided notion of identity and links to India, it is significant that the Indian Tourism Board in Australia hosted a special function to mark Singh's achievements, capped by his rise to the status of top-ranked player in the world during 2004. The Indian media were quick to pick up on Vijay Singh's Indian heritage and he was celebrated as one of their own among the sporting fraternity in the place of origin of his ancestors. Singh was invited to (and played in) a skins tournament in India in 2005, and in 2008, for the first time, he played in the Indian Open. Such achievements have again been interpreted as a product of the celebrated 'work ethic' by Indo-Fijians within and beyond Fiji. It is a source of great pride for Indo-Fijians that someone from Fiji, of Indo-Fijian background, became the world's number one player in the most competitive of sports. Indo-Fijian taxi drivers in Lautoka in Fiji as well as Liverpool in Sydney are quick to pounce on the idea of the work ethic and elevate it to the mythic proportions of *girmit* as part of the Indo-Fijian work ethos and value system.

Conclusion

The other famous Indo-Fijian Vijay – Vijay Mishra – has argued that 'How to free oneself from the weight of departure and the dreams of apocalypse constitutes one of the key elements of the diasporic imaginary' (2007: 50). One aspect of this process, and one that seems to dictate life for many Indo-Fijians, is the myth of the work ethic: it began as the means to make the transition from *girmitiya* to being free. From being free – but on the shifting ground of leased land – came the impetus to acquire education. Once the coups began, education was the main route to emigration, leading to the exponential growth of the second-wave Indo-Fijian diaspora. For individuals such as Vijay Singh, playing (or 'working at') a specialty sport has offered another escape route.

The Indo-Fijian diaspora is as much a product of history as it is a performance of the narrative acts of inscribing place, people, event, incident, accident, coincidence, causality and the 'official record'. For the Indo-Fijian diaspora, the real and performative aspects of work ethics come together in the figure of Vijay Singh. His achievements are seen to embody a glorious rise from the hardship and trauma of indenture, *girmit* and coups, to international eminence – and all of this on the back of an unflinching striving for progress and achievement as a member of the 'hardworking' Indo-Fijian diaspora. The international media makes the Vijay Singh persona immediately accessible to the Indo-Fijian diaspora even as he is domiciled in Florida, not Fiji, reified as the epitome of the ethos of hard work. For Hindu Indo-Fijians, he is the exemplar of *karma*, the achievement of salvation or *moksha* through an exemplary work ethic in the personal, professional, social, cultural and religious spheres. And he plays golf.

Bibliography

Campbell, I. C. (1989) *A History of the Pacific Islands* (Christchurch: Canterbury University Press).
Edmondson, B. (1994) 'Race, Tradition, and the Construction of the Caribbean Aesthetic', *New Literary History,* 25.1, 109–20.
Gill, W. (1970) *Turn North-East at the Tombstone* (Adelaide: Rigby).

Gillion, K. L. (1973 [1962]) *Fiji's Indian Migrants: A History to the End of Indenture in 1920* (Melbourne: Oxford University Press).

James, C. L. R. (1963) *Beyond a Boundary* (London: Hutchinson).

Keown, M. (2007) *Pacific Islands Writing: The Postcolonial Literatures of Aotearoa/ New Zealand and Oceania* (Oxford: Oxford University Press).

Lal, B. (1992) *Broken Waves: A History of the Fiji Islands in the Twentieth Century* (Honolulu: University of Hawai'i Press).

Lal, B. (2001) *Mr. Tulsi's Store: A Fijian Journey* (Canberra: Pandanus).

Lal, B. (2004) '*Girmit*, History, Memory' in B. Lal (ed.) *Bittersweet: The Indo-Fijian Experience* (Canberra: Pandanus), pp. 1–29.

Mishra, S. (2001) 'Ferringhi' in I. Gaskell (ed.) *Beyond Ceremony: An Anthology of Drama from Fiji* (Suva: Institute of Pacific Studies and Pacific Writing Forum), pp. 332–91.

Mishra, S. (2002) 'The Time is Out of Joint', *SPAN*, 52, 136–45.

Mishra, V. (1977) 'Indo-Fijian Fiction: Towards an Interpretation', *World Literature Written in English*, 16.2, 395–408.

Mishra, V. (2007) *The Literature of the Indian Diaspora: Theorizing the Diasporic Imaginary* (London: Routledge).

Nandan, S. (2000) *Fiji: Paradise in Pieces*, ed. Anthony Mason (Adelaide: CRNLE).

Nandan, S. (2001) *Requiem for a Rainbow* (Canberra: Pacific Indian Publications).

O'Carroll, J. (2002) 'Envisioning the Real: Two Mishras on a Girmit World', *SPAN*, 52, 101–26.

Prasad, M. (1997) *Sixty Years of Football in Fiji* (Suva: Fiji Football Association).

Prasad, M. (1999) 'Subaltern Laughter *a la* John Mohammed', *Dreadlocks Indentured*, 2, 74–93.

Subramani (ed.) (1979) *The Indo-Fijian Experience* (St Lucia: University of Queensland Press).

Subramani (1988) *The Fantasy Eaters* (Washington, DC: Three Continents Press).

Subramani (1995) *Altering Imagination* (Suva: Fiji Writers' Association).

Subramani (2001) *Dauka Puraan* (Delhi: Star Publications).

9
French Atlantic Diasporas

Bill Marshall

At first sight, the notion of a French diaspora or diasporas seems counter-intuitive amidst dominant readings of French history and the resulting versions of national identity. The received wisdom is of France as the centralized nation-state par excellence since 1789 and even before; as a country of immigration rather than emigration, distributing colonial officials or elites around the world, but producing no significant settler populations except in Algeria; and as a European nation that industrialized later and more unevenly than was the case in Britain and Germany, even retaining half its working population on the land well into the 1930s. In fact, the Atlantic space in particular has seen massive movements – voluntary but also involuntary – of French-speaking populations. The occlusion of these French diasporas from the French national narrative is all too familiar:

> as long as the field of historiography was dominated by a powerful tradition melding republicanism, nationalism, and often colonialism, the destinies of migrants who, by leaving France, had broken the implicit social contract linking them to the destiny of the nation, was neglected.[1]

(Weil 2005: 5)

Moreover, the diverse social, economic and cultural realities that these diasporas contained and generated inform the ambivalences of all identity production, including the term 'diasporic' itself.

Recent theoretical writing on diasporas has indeed emphasized movement, displacement, dislocation and relocation, nomadism, the problematization of national categories, the creation of multiple identities

189

and hybridities. Jana Evans Braziel and Anita Mannur warn, however, against too easy an appropriation of the term:

> It is often used as a catch-all phrase to speak of and for all movements, however privileged, and for all dislocations, even symbolic ones. [...] [W]e caution, therefore, against the uncritical, unreflexive use of the term 'diaspora' to any and all contexts of global displacement and movement; some forms of travel are tourism, and every attempt to mark movements as necessarily disenfranchising become imperialist gestures.
>
> (Evans Braziel and Mannur 2003: 3)

However, this laudable attempt to disentangle 'movement' from automatic association and identification with the subaltern nonetheless continues to endow the 'diasporic' with a culturally and politically progressive charge. The writers' admonition of attend to 'specific geopolitical circumstances' is limited to the latter's role in *precipitating* 'the movement of people and communities' (Evans Braziel and Mannur 2003: 3) rather than in the *making* and *unmaking* of identities, or in the modes of relation between these two terms (when do 'people' belong to, or see themselves as, 'communities' or otherwise?) as human populations form relationships with new social, cultural and physical environments.

The Atlantic is a set of specific geographies and histories within which these processes can be traced. Paul Gilroy's project on *The Black Atlantic* is thus enormously influential for its emphasis on hybridity and its challenge to African (-American) and other nationalisms. The ship is his central organizing symbol – seen as 'a living, micro-cultural, micro-political system in motion', a new chronotope in the Bakhtinian sense of a certain historical mapping of time and space:

> It should be emphasised that ships were the living means by which the points within that Atlantic world were joined. They were mobile elements that stood for the shifting spaces in between the fixed places that they connected. Accordingly they need to be thought of as cultural and political units rather than abstract embodiments of the triangular trade. They were something more – a means to conduct political dissent and possibly a distinct mode of cultural production. The ship provides a chance to explore the articulations between the discontinuous histories of England's ports, its interfaces with the wider world.
>
> (Gilroy 1993: 16–17)

The Middle Passage is thus one of a circulation of ideas, of key cultural and political artefacts – be they for example jazz, or W. E. B. du Bois's take on European nationalism and romanticism. To the realities of mobility and circulation may be added the processes of cultural transformation which then pertain: 'There are large questions raised about the direction and character of [...] culture and art if we take the powerful effects of even temporary experiences of exile, relocation, and displacement into account' (Gilroy 1993: 18). For some figures begin as African-Americans or Caribbean people:

> and are then changed into something else which evades those specific labels and with them all fixed notions of nationality and national identity. Whether their experience of exile is enforced or chosen, temporary or permanent, these intellectuals and activists, writers, speakers, poets and artists repeatedly articulate a desire to escape the restrictive bonds of ethnicity, national identification, and sometimes even 'race' itself.
>
> (Gilroy 1993: 18)

For example, substitute 'France' for 'England'; 'French, Breton or Norman' for 'African-Americans and Caribbean people', and it is immediately obvious that the category of the Atlantic is immensely suggestive for a de-centred, non-hierarchical reconceptualization of France and its constituent and connected spaces and territories as well as of French culture(s) in general. However, it would be clearly naive simply to trace the French on to the Black Atlantic, as if those mobile, diasporic historical experiences were equivalent or commensurate. The mapping of the Atlantic that I propose in this essay is as a space of tensions: between movement and identity, hybridity and assimilation, flight and community, boundlessness and boundedness, deterritorialization (processes of decoding or unfixing) and reterritorialization (codes of grounding and of checking flows of meaning) – *ex-tension* and *in-tension* therefore, marked by forces that are not only both centrifugal and centripetal, but also undergirded by powerful material circumstances and urgencies. In addition, the other major contribution of Gilroy's work to this debate is the constant, inescapable, and therefore healthy reminder that the Atlantic, far from being a utopian space of free and easy hybridities, is always also *sub-tended* by wrenching disjunctures and displacements, by relations of domination – especially the slave trade and its racialized terror, along with its aftermath and memory – and that the French avatar is constantly shadowed by this reality.

What are these French Atlantic diasporas? First and foremost, there occurred the largest movement of population in European history after the expulsion of Jews and Moors from fifteenth- and sixteenth-century Spain, namely the exile of the Huguenots – which may have involved up to 200,000 individuals – following the Revocation of the Edict of Nantes in 1685. Scholars now tend to emphasize an Atlantic versus a continental spatial division of this diaspora – overcoming the division between Europe and its colonies – in which the 'Atlantic' means the British Isles, the coast of the Netherlands, continental and Caribbean North American colonies as well as the Cape of Good Hope (Denis 2003). La Rochelle Protestants formed a high proportion of emigrants here, in that Huguenots seeking refuge in that Atlantic space tended to favour routes and networks known to them (for example La Rochelle to Boston via London) from colonial and North Atlantic trade and finance. Indeed, it has been said that the Revocation of the Edict of Nantes 'strengthened Huguenot economic power by dispersing Huguenot merchants among the leading trading centers of Europe' (Nash 2003: 217). Migration to the Americas tended to be 'second-stage', via England – approximately 2000 out of 50,000. Their arrival in British North America, fortunately for them, was well timed. Not only did they enjoy property and franchise rights unrestricted on religious grounds, they arrived at a time of massive expansion of the English (British after 1707) colonies, when cheap land was readily available. They became slave owners and not just in the southern colonies: Auguste Grasset, who had emigrated to New York from La Rochelle via London, was killed in a slave rebellion in the city in 1712 (Goodfriend 2003: 246, 253). They settled especially in New York (at 11 per cent forming the third largest ethnic group in the city in 1695, after the Dutch and English at 50 per cent and 26 per cent respectively), Massachusetts and South Carolina. By 1700, Huguenots (of which a third hailed from La Rochelle where there was a high proportion of merchants) formed 10 per cent of the white population of South Carolina, which had only been founded in 1670, but whose growing importance had drawn the attention of Huguenot merchants in London. French Protestants went on to form 30 per cent of the first generation of South Carolinian merchants, and their success lay in the exploitation of their transatlantic mercantile connections. Today, one of the main tourist attractions of the city of Charleston is the Manigault House, built in 1803 as an emanation of a dynasty founded by two Protestant Rochelais merchants, Pierre and Joseph Manigault, who emigrated there in 1690 and became the wealthiest men in the thirteen British colonies, owning nearly 300 slaves (Van Ruymbeke 2004a).

As elsewhere in the colonies, Huguenots quickly assimilated to the host Anglophone culture, with high rates of intermarriage, while ethnic or national belonging to 'France' was rendered superfluous by the overriding importance attached to the religious question. The last French institution in Charleston, the French church, closed in 1719. Neither expecting nor desiring a return to France, the Huguenots transferred their allegiance to South Carolina and thence to the United States; not surprisingly a greater proportion of them supported the American Revolution than settlers of British descent. (In Massachusetts, Paul Revere was the son of a Huguenot silversmith, Apollos Rivoire, from Wallonia; that other icon of the American national narrative, Davy Crockett – or Crocketaigne – was from similar lineage.)

The best-known emanation of La Rochelle's Huguenot diaspora was of course the foundation of the agricultural community of New Rochelle in Westchester County near New York in 1688–9. In 1709, the community split over whether to conform to Anglican doctrine, which was accepted by the majority. The community remained poor for most of the eighteenth century, although it owned slaves in significant numbers: they formed 18 per cent of the population. Here the role of historical memory and the insertion of the Huguenot narrative into national American narratives are significant. Huguenot-Americans laboured to create narrative homologies between themselves and the nation's Puritan founders. In 1911 the town of New Rochelle presented to La Rochelle a stone – supposedly where its Huguenot founders disembarked – in a direct reference to the famous Plymouth Rock in Massachusetts. This identification of a rock near the foundation site of a community was a not infrequent practice by settlers and immigrants in the late nineteenth and early twentieth centuries (Van Ruymbeke 2004b). In the same year, a delegation from New Rochelle attended the inauguration in the place de l'hôtel de ville in La Rochelle of a statue – which the American town had also partly funded – to Jean Guitton, the Protestant mayor who had defied Cardinal Richelieu during the siege of 1627–8.

The large number of slaves in New Rochelle was partly due to the West Indian origins of some of the settlers. Indeed the consistory – founded in 1692 – was headed by David de Bonrepos, who had been a minister on St Christopher, where since its foundation in 1629 the majority of colonists had been Protestant. The prevalence of Protestantism was because of the La Rochelle connection, as Colbert in the 1660s had chosen it as the supply base for France's West Indian colonies, while its financiers had supplied the capital for the Compagnie des Indes Occidentales – even though its charter prohibited the participation of Protestants,

although the stipulation was generally ignored. The Protestant population of the islands was strengthened by the arrival in 1654 of Dutch and
Walloons expelled from Brazil, where they had perfected the technique
of sugar cane cultivation and once settled in their new home, set about
contributing to the economic take-off of the French Antilles. After
1685, Protestants on the islands – who controlled between a third and
a quarter of sugar production on Guadeloupe and Martinique – had to
choose between abjuring their religion and escaping, usually to North
America (Lafleur and Abénon 2003). (The Code Noir, promulgated the
same year as the Revocation of the Edict of Nantes, is careful to insist
on the Catholicization of slaves, and article eight even prohibits marriage outside the Catholic faith; offspring of Protestant marriages were
considered therefore to be illegitimate.)

Within the framework of French Atlantic diasporas, the second great
displacement in chronological terms – involving fewer numbers in total
than the Huguenots but more specific to the boundaries posed by the
Atlantic –, is that of the dispersal of the Acadians in and after 1755.
'Acadie' had been formed as a French colony in 1604 in present-day
Maine, moving the following year to the Annapolis basin in present-day
Nova Scotia. Despite internally and externally generated instabilities,
a distinctive egalitarian, endogamous, pioneering, relatively isolated
and insulated agricultural identity developed in the periods after the
colony's return to French rule in 1632 and again after the 1713 Treaty
of Utrecht, which saw the definitive takeover by the British. In 1755,
however, in the context of the outbreak of the Seven Years' War – which
was to seal the destiny of French North America – what is referred to as
le grand dérangement saw the exile and dispersal of up to 13,000 of these
'French Neutrals', following the Acadians' refusal to swear an uncondi-
tional oath of allegiance to the British Crown. Some Acadian families
were shipped to British jurisdictions such as Maryland and Philadelphia,
while others made for Quebec and more remote parts of the Gulf of
St Lawrence region, including the Madeleine islands and Miquelon, while
up to 3000 eked out a dependent existence in France itself. Reluctant to
integrate with the feudal structures of rural society and attached to
'Acadie' rather than to France itself, many resettled in Nantes after
abandoning a new agricultural community near Poitiers-Châtellerault.

Two distinct Francophone communities resulted from this upheaval.
The resettlement of Acadians north and east of their original territory,
primarily in what is now the 'Acadian coast' of New Brunswick, eventually produced a cultural renaissance in the late nineteenth century,
as new educational elites, emerging from the Collège Saint-Joseph

(the Francophone higher education institution founded in 1854), established new identity claims in the face of English Canadian hegemony. Today, the Acadians form a third (250,000) of the population of New Brunswick – the only officially bilingual Canadian province. The other group ended up in Louisiana, 1000 via the British North American colonies and the West Indies, along with up to 2000 via France. Indeed, in 1785 seven ships left Nantes taking 1600 Acadians (disgruntled by their existence in France, as we have seen) to a new life in Louisiana in a voyage paid for by the Spanish Crown, the new sovereign power in the territory.[2] They first settled in rural areas, on frontages on the Mississippi and bayous west of New Orleans as well as on pastures west of the Atchafalaya basin.

The transformation of Acadians into Cajuns is eloquent testimony to the play of French Atlantic forces and tensions described above, as the new communities composed with the new natural and social environment. Relations with native groups in Acadie itself had been complex – characterized by close cooperation with the Micmacs, particularly in fur-trading – but then turned ambivalent when the latter remained close allies of the French while the Acadians had become, nominally, at least, British subjects. Acadians in the more eastern zones of settlement in Louisiana faced conflict with native tribes agitated by intercolonial rivalry, since their territory was now located in a border zone between Spanish and British jurisdictions. Relations with French-born and Creole populations were often tense, since the latter groups wished to perpetuate themselves as a colonial aristocracy and to establish a feudal system in the Mississippi valley – consequently casting the egalitarian and less pretentious Acadians in the role of peasants. But the latter's blend of cultural conservatism – on choosing to leave Nova Scotia they had rejected what Carl Brasseaux terms 'the insidious death of assimilation' (Brasseaux 1996: 34) – and adaptability is no better illustrated than in their eventual adoption of slavery. The first recorded Acadian slave purchases date from 1765, but numbers increased as families understood that the labour required for the development of a *habitation* went far beyond the capacity of the pool of relatives. As social and economic differentiation, indeed stratification, developed between poorer and more prosperous (and ambitious) Acadian settlers – with 40 per cent in the river districts owning slaves by 1785, the year of a slave rebellion – attitudes polarized even further. By the time of the Louisiana Purchase in 1803, a large majority of the river settlers owned slaves, and had come to identify, tacitly or not, with the doctrine of white superiority. Between 1790 and 1810, therefore, the Acadian exiles became increasingly fragmented among an upwardly mobile group that aspired to the Creole planter caste (and to bourgeois professions), those who sought to perpetuate traditional lifestyles in farming that produced only small surpluses, and those caught between, including artisans and crafts-men. Indeed, as the wealthier prospered in the antebellum period – particularly in the production of cash crops, notably sugar – they tended to assimilate culturally first to the Creole aristocracy and then to the Anglo-Americans (70 per cent of Louisiana's population in 1860, com-pared to 25 per cent when it entered the Union in 1812). The combina-tion of these class and regional differentiations between Acadians, the catastrophic economic collapse during and after the American Civil War followed by a long downturn in Louisiana's fortunes (which lasted until the 1920s if not the Second World War) and the violent racial polarizations of postbellum society, led to the increasing cultural iso-lation of those 'Cajuns' who refused, or were unable, to assimilate to American social, economic and linguistic norms – just as Acadian and Creole elites rushed to do so. Negative representations contributed to the entrapment in poverty of much of that population, so that 'Cajun' came to depict a new cultural identity, or set of identities, united by whiteness and by poverty: 'The term *Cajun* thus became a socioeco-nomic classification for the multicultural amalgam of several culturally and linguistically distinct groups' (Brasseaux 1992: 105). In areas where English-speakers were not in the majority, Creole and 'Foreign French' (that is, French-born) populations, along with those of Acadian ances-try and poor Anglo-Americans, were assimilated through exogamy into this new amalgam, with the linguistic hybrid of Cajun French emerg-ing as the lingua franca of the lower classes. The assimilated elites were in the vanguard of restrictions on the use of French in educational institutions during the First World War and 1920s; it was not until the 1960s that a 'Cajun renaissance' in music and poetry was accompanied by new, official moves to promote the French language in Louisiana. Charles J. Stivale has explored, in Deleuzean terms, the tensions in the field of Cajun music between territorialization and deterritorialization, tradition/authenticity and becoming or *errance*: for example in the complex domain of relations with black Creole cultural forms, which can be traced along axes of exclusion/racism and hybridity – notably of course in *zydeco*, which mixes Cajun music with rhythm and blues (Stivale 2003).

The third major French Atlantic diasporic displacement is that of refu-gees from Saint-Domingue, principally, if not exclusively, to New Orleans. The process began in the 1790s: for example, Louis Guillaume du Bourg, born in Cap Français, was the founder of the city's first newspaper, *Le Moniteur de la Louisiane* in 1794; the first mayor in the American period, James (Jacques François) Pitot, settled in New Orleans in 1796, via Philadelphia from Saint-Domingue, where he had been in the sugar business. This displacement of refugees culminated in 1809–10, when Joseph Bonaparte's usurping of the throne of Spain led to war and the expulsion of exiles from Cuba (a large Francophone community had settled in Santiago de Cuba, birthplace of, among others, the Parnassian poet José Maria de Heredia and the political radical Paul Lafargue); 10,000 of whom pitched up in New Orleans (in roughly equal numbers of whites, free people of colour and their slaves), adding themselves to the 5000–10,000 that had arrived since 1791. This doubled the French-speaking population of the city. These arrivals swelled the ranks of the Francophone merchant and professional classes, and contributed much to the cultural dynamism of the following decades, since the educational attainment and even basic literacy among the white Creoles were low, despite the *ancien régime* pretentions of the upper classes.

This influx from Saint-Domingue also significantly increased the presence of free people of colour. Often but not always lighter-skinned, they contributed to the unique character of New Orleans, with its three-tiered Caribbean-type society at odds with the polarizations of American racism. They represented 29 per cent of the free population in 1810 (the majority of the city's population were slaves until 1840), although as the city boomed and its population grew this figure had fallen to 6 per cent by 1860. Moreover, if most were artisans, many others were property-owners (constituting 60 per cent of all the property in the United States owned by African-Americans, and forming by far the wealthiest such group), while 5 per cent – a large figure for the time – were professionals. Some were also slave-owners. Their presence – itself a testimony to the relative racial fluidity of the French colonial period – had increased dramatically during Spanish rule, due largely to the greater ease of manumission (slaves could buy their freedom, a provision not available in French colonial jurisdictions until the reign of Louis-Philippe) and their contribution to the defence of the city with their own militia. As American rule meant an institutionalization of racial exclusions – not least a denial of voting rights, a ban on inter-racial marriage in 1808 and segregation in theatres in 1816 – they often looked to the traditions of the Enlightenment and republican France for inspiration and support, particularly when slavery was definitively abolished and suffrage extended to black males throughout the French empire in 1848. Their literacy rate of 80 per cent in 1850 was higher than for Louisiana whites, and the assertion of their cultural capital counted for much in an increasingly hostile social environment.

Saint-Domingue, particularly in the latter half of the eighteenth century, had possessed a vibrant cultural and intellectual life, despite its largely rural population distribution: eight towns had theatres; there was a branch of the Académie française, and scientific and other Enlightenment societies such as the Cercle des Philadelphes. Throughout the French colonial period and beyond, the colonies had close links: Saint-Domingue was the base for exploration – d'Iberville had set out there for Louisiana in 1698; ships often sailed on to Louisiana from the Caribbean territory. From the presence of French 'buccaneers' on the island of Tortuga off Hispaniola in the early seventeenth century, through the first French administration in the west of the latter island in 1651 and continuing after the formalisation of the Treaty of Ryswick in Spain in 1697, Saint-Domingue became the richest colony in the world and possibly the richest that has ever existed. Its population breakdown by 1789 was 31,000 whites, 25,000 free people of colour and 434,000 slaves; it was the world's largest producer of sugar and coffee. That enormous slave population was the result of a continuously increasing importation of captives from Africa, peaking at 39,000 for the year 1790, a result not only of huge demand for slave labour but also of the harsh conditions on the plantations, with a 6–10 per cent annual mortality rate. This constant renewal meant that a living African culture was always present among the slaves. A minority of the whites were *grands blancs* (wealthy owners of large plantations), a majority were *petits blancs*, but both groups were concerned not only to preserve the institution of slavery, they were also willing to press for autonomy from royal and then revolutionary power in France to protect their interests: their vision being of an autonomous or semi-autonomous slave-owning American polity as in the United States. The free people of colour made up nearly half the free population and several hundred of them were wealthy plantation owners. Their existence is due to articles 9 and 55 of the 1685 Code Noir (which said that any slave married to a free person was automatically free, and that masters could free their slaves at will) and also of course to widespread sexual activity between white men and black women, which often included paternal recognition of the offspring.

At first, social differentiation in Saint-Domingue was based on class rather than colour, with fluid use at census time of categories such as *blanc*, *nègre* and *mulâtre*. However, as John Garrigus (2006) has argued, the aftermath of defeat in the Seven Years' War and of the 1763 Treaty of

Paris saw an increasing racial codification of life in the colony. To an extent, there was an inevitability to this, in that the existence of a large free black or coloured population contradicted the racist premises on which slavery was based. But this disciplining also arose from the anxieties of both the French government and the white colonists over external threats, and the envy of recent white immigrants over the visibly increasing wealth of the coloured population – a result to some extent of their greater presence in the cultivation of the now booming commodity of coffee (on hillside sites not suited to sugar plantations) and also of indigo traded illegally, outside the French *exclusif*, with the British and Dutch (Garrigus 1993). With this convenient common cause, the authorities excluded free people of colour from certain professions and civic roles, segregated them in theatres, and restricted their dress and mode of transport. During the early phase of the French Revolution, the free people of colour of Saint-Domingue were determined to make the demand for (restored) civic equality the most important issue associated with the colonies. To an extent then, the French Atlantic phenomenon of the *gens de couleur libres* is to be associated as much with racial codification as with racial fluidity; there exists not so much a question of why there were so many people of that category, but why, and how, the category came to exist at all.

The historical narrative that followed is well known. The slave revolt of August 1791 and the resulting sacking of the political capital and thriving cultural centre Cap Français (now Cap Haïtien) did not come out of the blue: despite experiencing fewer slave revolts than elsewhere in the Caribbean in the eighteenth century, *marronnage*, or runaway slaves forming outcast communities, had been rife in the difficult and mountainous terrain; in 1758 their leader François Mackandal had been executed for organizing a mass revolt that sought to poison planters en masse. The revolts were a combination of factors such as the large proportion of African-born slaves, and of the revolutionary events in France propelling the free people of colour into the role of catalysts for questioning the whole legitimacy of the racist slave system. The upheaval of the 1790s, and the desire of republicans in France to counter British and Spanish ambitions, led to the abolition of slavery first in Saint-Domingue in August 1793 and in all the French colonies in February 1794. Toussaint L'Ouverture's manoeuvring of this complex political situation ended with his capture by Napoleon's forces and death in a Jura prison in 1803, but by the end of that year Napoleon's attempt to reconquer Saint-Domingue and reinstate slavery had been defeated, and the independent republic of Haiti was proclaimed on 1 January 1804.

For New Orleans, then, the Saint-Domingue connection was crucial for the prolongation of Francophone culture there:

> Several historians even contend that the resistance to Americanisation and the maintenance of French cultural domination in New Orleans, and more generally in the territory of Louisiana, were possible only thanks to the presence of the foreign French [...] and of the refugees from Saint-Domingue.
>
> (Dessens 2005: 255–6)

There were also the profound political repercussions of the Haitian Revolution for both blacks/coloureds and whites, with its racial violence acting as a scarecrow for the latter (the biggest slave revolt in Louisiana history took place in 1811 on the 'German Coast' upriver from New Orleans, and was led by former *saint-dominguais*) and its emancipation as a beacon for the former (Hunt 1988). Indeed, a coda to this story is that of the 'return' of New Orleanians to Haiti in the oppressive years leading up to the American Civil War; 681 free people of colour, many of them second or third-generation immigrants from Saint-Domingue, did so in the late 1850s:

> Exiles in their own country, Louisiana's free creoles of colour retraced the path that first brought them across the gulf separating them from their Caribbean cousins in Haiti, a path that had been nurtured and defended over the years and had grown to be an important part of the collective *gens de couleur* identity.
>
> (Duplantier 2007: 69)

In 1862, a poet among these, Joseph Colastin Rousseau – who had married the granddaughter of Colonel Joseph Savary, a former soldier in Haiti who had commanded one of the coloured battalions in the Battle of New Orleans against the British in 1812 – published an article in the Port-au-Prince newspaper *L'Opinion nationale*. 'Souvenirs de la Louisiane' attempts to promote a proto-Caribbean identity while recognizing the differences between Haiti and New Orleans, differences that in fact led many migrants to return with the Union victory.

The influx of Francophones had held off but could not postpone indefinitely the inevitable majority status of the English language and Anglo-American political control, not least as waves of immigration – New Orleans was second only to New York in this respect – brought in tens of thousands of Irish and Germans, so that by 1850 almost half of the population had been born outside the Americas. But important legacies of the Saint-Domingue connection can be found in nineteenth-century Louisiana's Francophone literary output (for example the mixed race Victor Séjour, 1817–74, who enjoyed success as a playwright and whose violent anti-slavery short story *Le Mulâtre* of 1837 – and set in Haiti – is the first by an African-American), as well as the culture of voodoo and in the Louisiana Creole language. Even jazz is marked by the contribution the Saint-Domingue exiles (as well as French slave-holding practices enshrined in the Code Noir that gave slaves Sundays off) made to the musical 'gumbo' of New Orleans: Caribbean Creole folk songs as well as a classical musical – including piano – tradition among the free people of colour (the parents of the Paris Conservatoire-trained composer Edmond Dédé were from Saint-Domingue).

As well as the three examples of forced exile as a result of civil conflict, war and revolution outlined in the above, it is also possible to speak of more straightforward economic migrations, as occurred elsewhere. In fact, the most massive example is 'intra-New World': the emigration in the last three decades of the nineteenth century of 900,000 Québécois to work in the mills and factories of New England and elsewhere in the industrial United States – a result of a high birth rate and rural exodus, which spawned, among other figures, Jack Kerouac, born in Lowell, Massachusetts in 1922, to whom we shall return. It is true that earlier French settlement of Canada and Louisiana was much more limited than English, then British, emigration to the New World. It is estimated that 70,000 to 75,000 people travelled from France to Canada during French rule (1608–1763), with 13,000 to 14,000 people settling there for good or at least for a long period. The founding migration for the approximately 70,000 people living there at the time of the British Conquest (compared with 1.3 million in the British American colonies) – and for most of the seven million Franco-Québécois of the early twenty-first century – consists of 8500 to 9000 people who stayed in Canada and produced children. In its early years – New Orleans was founded in 1718 – Louisiana was almost a penal colony, its first 7000 settlers a motley crew of artisans and urbanites, as well as criminals and prostitutes. However, French settlement in the Americas did not end there. Emigrants from metropolitan France came for economic reasons (indeed, certain areas of France, notably the south-west, easily attain the European average for transatlantic migration in this period, prompting the question, in any historical discussion, of 'which France?') and also fled the political upheavals of the nineteenth century as well as the loss of Alsace-Lorraine. In Louisiana, the 'foreign French' were migrants from metropolitan France, particularly the south and west, from 3000 to 7000 people a year from the 1830s, with New Orleans a haven for political exiles: royalists in the 1790s, anti-bonapartists after 1799, bonapartists after 1815 (Blaubarb 2005) and republicans after 1851. In 1851, 20,000 French immigrants arrived in the United States for example, and there were French-language newspapers in New York, Philadelphia, Charleston and also San Francisco, where the 1849 Gold Rush attracted thousands of French citizens; there was even an entirely French company of Union troops, the Lafayette guards, during the Civil War. In total, it is estimated that 353,000 French people emigrated to America between 1820 and 1900; 751,000 between 1820 and 1978. In the United States census of 2000, 1.6 million respondents declared that they spoke French at home, the third highest figure for a language other than English, after Spanish and Chinese. More than 13 million Americans are believed to be of French descent.

There were also important migrations to Latin America. In the seven-year period 1835–42, for example, Montevideo received nearly 33,000 immigrants, of whom over half – nearly 18,000 – were French, more than the next largest groups (Spanish at just over 8000 and nearly 8000 Italians) combined. In 1843 the French therefore represented over half the foreign population, and a quarter of Montevideo's as a whole. A large majority – 80 per cent – came from the western Pyrenees: that is the French Basque country, Béarn (the area south of Pau) and Bigorre (south-east of Lourdes). These mountainous, isolated areas, with the Spanish frontier to the south and the underdeveloped expanse of the Landes to the north, were largely untouched by the nascent tourism of the coast and by many aspects of French republican centralization. Impoverished, strongly Catholic and with a high birth rate, the inheritance system of their over-whelmingly agricultural and fragile economy exclusively favouring the eldest son, their populations were ready to respond to the voluntarist immigrant recruitment policies of successive Uruguayan governments, as a result of which the population tripled in a generation. The drive that followed independence gave immigrants a grant of 10,000 pesos, property guarantees, dispensation from military service and sometimes land grants. It is estimated that by 1860 more than a third of Uruguay's population, or their parents, had been born in France, and the figures were higher for Montevideo. They contributed to the development of Uruguay's charac-teristically large urban middle-class, as well as spawning the three *poetas franceses*: Jules Laforgue, Lautréamont and Jules Supervielle.

French Atlantic diasporas are thus characterized by extreme diversity, and by the impossibility of situating them chronologically in relation to French national narratives centred on the founding event of 1789, or ideologically, in that the sub-tension of slavery and the slave trade provokes a rethink of the limits and contradictions of French republicanism and universalism, alongside their belated fulfilment in the general emancipation of 1848. Unlike the Anglophone, Hispanophone or Lusophone Atlantic worlds, Francophone communities found themselves, crucially, overwhelmingly in minority situations, often as a result of defeat in war. That diversity of origins meant that for long periods of time, Francophone communities in the Americas lived unconnected with each other in dramatically different social, cultural, political and natural environments – like scattered islets of an archipelago. Indeed, a 1983 collection of essays by Dean Louder and Eric Waddell, recently reprinted, *Du continent perdu à l'archipel retrouvé*, is precisely an account of those 'îlots' of French language and culture in North America – in Quebec, Acadie, Ontario, Manitoba, New England and southern Louisiana – which have lived alternately through isolation and connection. In 1955 commemorations finally brought together *Acadiens* and Cajuns, even 're-uniting' families split two hundred years before.

'Archipelago' is of course a key term in the writings of Edouard Glissant, according to whom, in the new 'world totality' there is no longer any '*organic* authority' and 'everything is an archipelago' (Glissant 1996: 22). He thus calls for '*archipelagian* thought, in other words thought that is non-systematic, inductive, exploring the world-totality and granting writing to orality and orality to writing. Today I witness the *archipelagization* of continents' (Glissant 1996: 43–4). Typically, he takes the Caribbean as the model, the archipelago corresponding to a scattering of islands – units of human communities – that are both separate and interlinked, whose identity production is always already bound up with the non-totalizable, self-differentiating reality Glissant calls 'Relation'. (The original Ancient Greek of course initially referred to the Aegean, the 'chief sea' of that civilization, characterized by a large number of scattered islands.) The 'archipelagization' of continents in the contemporary world would thus mean an overcoming of the centripetal tendencies of thought and culture associated with the latter kind of land mass. Crucially, then, the archipelago is distinct from the isolated island (or isolated island group: the inhabitants of Saint-Pierre et Miquelon, for example, refer to their territory as the 'archipel', in a very self-enclosed way). However, if continents can become archipelagos, then the latter can be sought elsewhere than in literal island chains. The notion of the French Atlantic thus enlarges Glissant's notion of the original archipelago out of the Caribbean and also historically, as he often underestimates the processes – indeed the rapidity of processes – of creolization that pertained in the early modern, compared to the modern and post-modern worlds. The French Atlantic points to a vast cultural space which, including France and North America, is always already 'archipelagized' in a way that contradicts the monolingual and often mono-cultural biases of those territories' national narratives.

Indeed, Glissant is often uncertain as to whether the term 'Creolization' might apply, for example, to the cultural interchanges wrought by French diasporas in North America in addition to the Caribbean. The urban Montreal dialect, *joual*, is praised for its undermining of the 'unicité' of French (Glissant 1996: 55), but he is unwilling to give it the status of an example of 'creolization', even though it certainly fits his working definition (as opposed to that officially used in the discipline of Linguistics) of the bringing together in unpredictable fashion of heterogeneous cultural or linguistic elements.

One figure who has no such doubts is the geographer Jean Morisset, who has dedicated his life to the conceptualization, and study, of *l'Amérique canadienne*: that cultural world created by the diaspora of seventeenth, eighteenth and even nineteenth-century *Canadiens* who gave birth to new languages and ethnicities in the north and west of the continent (Morisset 1985: 44). These *Canadiens* were the *coureurs de bois*, young men who left the settled life of the townships and farms of New France for a nomadic existence trapping and trading furs with Amerindian populations in the *pays d'en haut*, 'going native' or establishing sexual and procreative relationships with Amerindian women. They were crucial intermediaries between European and Amerindian culture; this also helped open up the North American continent for European exploration – one of the reasons that French place names persist as far west as, for example, Idaho (Boise, 'boisé) and even beyond. There also arose the new ethnic group of Metis – approximately 100,000 strong in contemporary North America (mainly Manitoba and North Dakota) – who are Catholic, of mixed race and speak French or 'Metchif/Michif': a creole of French and Cree. They too experienced diasporas, were displaced by American expansion westwards and eventually settled in the Red River area of contemporary Manitoba – but the encroachment of Canadian sovereignty led to rebellions in 1869–70 and 1885, and the execution of their leader, Louis Riel.

Morisset's *L'Identité usurpée* (1985) breaks with any 'territorialization' or 're-territorialization' associated with the national, bounded entity of post-Quiet Revolution Quebec and the hegemony of a sovereignty project that for him looks more to France and to ethnic purity than to the *Canadiens'* distinctly North American, *métissé* identity. He has little truck with the adjective 'French' in 'French-Canadian', for 'Canadian' is a term that has been 'usurped' by English Canada, which he refers to as 'BNA', 'British North America'. Tellingly, he lambasts metropolitan French culture for its myth-making about (Anglophone) 'America', or its invention of a *Latin* America without French that resolutely excludes its own creolized, *canadien* offshoot: 'in the eyes of France, real America could not exist in French, precisely for fear of its dream of America turning into an indecipherable nightmare speaking joual or creole' (Morisset and Waddell 2000: 271). Invoking Jack Kerouac – in and through whom the French-Canadian *coureur de bois* becomes a *coureur de routes* – Morisset opts for 'la Franco-Amérique': 'The epithet "franco" is eaten up by the substantive "America", so the inevitable outcome of the use of the term is the triumphant proclamation of our origin in and belonging to this continent' (Morisset 2001: 288). Indeed, Eric Waddell speculates: 'What if Jack's work marked the decline of the Franco-American universe (since it seemed to recount a world slipping away from everyone, including himself) and the impossibility of it being integrated into the great Anglo-American whole?' (Morisset and Waddell 2000: 195).

French Atlantic diasporas therefore run the gamut of different positions on the diagram of forces noted earlier: they may reterritorialize on specific boundaries, identities and group memories (Quebec, Acadia, but decidedly not 'France'), or radically deterritorialize (the Kerouac-Morisset take on the *Canadien*); they all 'become-other' and engage in processes of hybridization, although one logical outcome can be assimilation. The latter is a case where diasporic identities cease to be defined as movement without conquest, and the examples of slaveholding Acadians or free people of colour emphasize the way in which the category always needs to be articulated with class as well as ethnicity or race.

This is why the Deleuzean vocabulary (which of course inspired the later Glissant) of particles and flows seems so useful. The French Atlantic can be seen as a field of forces and tensions, with a line of flight of minimal particles – molecules – of Frenchness moving across the ocean and into the Americas, ceaselessly extending and folding, even as they sometimes form molar structures – 'arborescences' rather than decentred, non-hierarchical rhizomes – of identity and territory. Deleuze and Guattari conceive the 'minor' not in terms of numbers, but in terms of the relationship between becoming and the territorialization/deterritorialization process. They take among other examples

Quebec artists of the 1960s, who were conscious that their language was 'minor' in relation not only to the vast North American and Canadian Anglophone majority, but was peripheral and relatively deterritorialized faced with the 'major' language that is standard metropolitan French. The point is not to talk about Quebec French as a particular dialect, but to realize that *'minor' and 'major' attitudes can be adopted towards this – or indeed any – language and culture*. One solution is to fall back on to a new territorialization – 'the Canadian singer can also bring about the most reactionary, the most Oedipal of reterritorializations, oh mama, oh my native land, my cabin, olé, olé' (Deleuze and Guattari 1986: 24) – while another is to follow the logic of the 'minor' status – its capacity for proliferation and innovation (becoming), its antithesis therefore to the rank of master and its undermining of the 'major' culture's pretensions to the natural, normal and universal: 'It is a question not of reterritorializing oneself on a dialect or patois but of deterritorializing the major language' (Deleuze and Guattari 1988: 104). Minorities have their own territorialities, but must also be considered as 'seeds, crystals of becoming whose value is to trigger uncontrollable movements and deterritorializations of the mean or majority' (Deleuze and Guattari 1988: 134). The potentially (but not automatically) progressive cultural-political force of diasporas is their capacity – in their association of movement, the hybrid and the 'minor' – for the undermining of positions of mastery and for the proliferation of the new.

Notes

1. Translations are mine throughout, except where reference is made to a published English translation.
2. The Acadian presence in Nantes is commemorated by a mural by the American artist Robert Dafford in the rue des Acadiens on the butte Sainte-Anne. For more on the Acadians in Nantes, see Braud (1994).

Bibliography

Augeron, M. and Guillemet, D. (eds) *Champlain ou les portes du nouveau monde: cinq siècles d'échanges entre le Centre-Ouest français et l'Amérique du Nord* (La Crèche: Geste Editions).

Blaubarb, R. (2005) *Bonapartists in the Borderlands: French Exiles and Refugees on the Gulf Coast, 1815–1835* (Tuscaloosa: University of Alabama Press).

Brasseaux, C. A. (1992) *Acadian to Cajun: Transformation of a People, 1803–1877* (Jackson: University of Mississippi Press).

Brasseaux, C. A. (1996) *The Founding of New Acadia: The Beginnings of Acadian Life in Louisiana 1765–1803* (Baton Rouge: Louisiana State University Press).

Braud, G-M. (1994) *De Nantes à la Louisiane* (Cholet: Ouest Editions).

Deleuze, G. and Guattari, F. (1986) *Kafka: Toward a Minor Literature*, translated by D. Polan (Minneapolis: University of Minnesota Press).

Deleuze, G. and Guattari, F. (1988) *A Thousand Plateaus: Capitalism and Schizophrenia*, translated by B. Massumi (London: Athlone Press).

Denis, P. (2003) 'Huguenots and their Legacy in Apartheid South Africa' in van Ruymbeke and Sparks (eds) *Memory and Identity*, pp. 285–309.

Dessens, N. (2005) 'From Saint-Domingue to Louisiana: West Indian Refugees in the Lower Mississippi Region' in B. Bond (ed.) *French Colonial Louisiana and the Atlantic World* (Baton Rouge: Louisiana State University Press), pp. 244–62.

Duplantier, J-M. A. (2007) 'Creole Louisiana's Haitian Exile(s)', *Southern Quarterly*, 44.3, 68–84.

Evans Braziel, J. and Mannur, A. (2003), 'Nation, Migration, Globalization: Points of Contention in Diaspora Studies' in Evans Braziel and Mannur (eds) *Theorizing Diaspora* (Oxford: Blackwell), pp. 1–22.

Garrigus, J. (1993) 'Blue and Brown: Contraband of Indigo and the Rise of a Free Coloured Planter Class in French Saint-Domingue', *The Americas*, 50, 233–363.

Garrigus, J. (2006) *Before Haiti: Race and Citizenship in French Saint-Domingue* (London: Palgrave Macmillan).

Gilroy, P. (1993) *The Black Atlantic: Modernity and Double Consciousness* (London: Verso).

Glissant, E. (1996) *Introduction à une poétique du divers* (Paris: Gallimard).

Goodfriend, J. D. (2003) 'The Huguenots of Colonial New York City: A Demographic Profile' in van Ruymbeke and Sparks (eds) *Memory and Identity*, pp. 241–54.

Hunt, A. N. (1988) *Haiti's Influence on Antebellum America: Slumbering Volcano in the Caribbean* (Baton Rouge: Louisiana State University Press).

Lafleur, G. and Abénon, L. (2003) 'The Protestants and the Colonization of the French West Indies' in van Ruymbeke and Sparks (eds) *Memory and Identity*, pp. 267–84.

Louder, D. and Waddell, E. (2007) *Du continent perdu à l'archipel retrouvé: le Québec et l'Amérique française* (Sainte-Foy: Presses de l'Université Laval).

Morisset, J. (1985) *L'Identité usurpée: l'Amérique écartée* (Montreal: Nouvelle optique).

Morisset, J. (2001) 'Une vie en translation, ou le vertige et la gloire d'être Franco' in D. Louder, J. Morisset and E. Waddell (eds) *Vision et visages de la Franco-Amérique* (Quebec City: Septentrion), pp. 285–313.

Morisset, J. and Waddell, E. (2000) *Amériques: deux parcours au départ de la Grande Rivière du Canada* (Montreal: l'Hexagone).

Nash, R. C. (2003) 'Huguenot Merchants and the Development of South Carolina's Slave-Plantation and Atlantic Trading Economy, 1680–1775' in van Ruymbeke and Sparks (eds) *Memory and Identity*, pp. 208–40.

Séjour, V. (1837) *Le Mulâtre*, www.centenary.edu/french/textes/mulatre.html, accessed 1 May 2008.

Stivale, C. J. (2003) *Disenchanting Les Bons Temps: Identity and Authenticity in Cajun Music and Dance* (Durham, NC: Duke University Press).

van Ruymbeke, B. (2004a) 'La Manigault House de Charleston: musée et lieu de mémoire huguenot aux Etats-Unis' in Augeron and Guillemet (eds) *Champlain ou les portes du nouveau monde*, p. 143.

van Ruymbeke, B. (2004b) 'New Rochelle Rock: symbolisme et mémoire autour d'un bout du rocher du Nouveau Monde' in Augeron and Guillemet (eds) *Champlain ou les portes du nouveau monde*, p. 141.

van Ruymbeke, B. and Sparks, R. J. (eds) (2003) *Memory and Identity: The Huguenots in France and the Atlantic Diaspora* (Columbia: University of South Carolina Press).

Weil, F. (2005), 'Les Migrations de France aux Amériques: histoire et mémoire' *Migrance*, 26, 5–8.

Postscript

10
Postcolonial Transplants: Cinema, Diaspora and the Body Politic

Elizabeth Ezra and Terry Rowden

A major consequence of the diasporic movement of people across national borders – albeit one that has not received the analytical attention it deserves – has been the compromising of ethical and legal systems, which had previously been naturalized as modes of national self-recognition and corporeal integrity. The body politic can only function politically, that is, it can only foster a shared sense of community and responsibility when the lines between acceptable and unacceptable behaviour are clear and accepted by all 'good' citizens.[1] The focus on political subjectivity as citizenship can, however, lessen our recognition of the corporeal reality of subaltern bodies whose availability for exploitation is enabled precisely by their often structurally agonistic relation to the category of 'good citizen'. Because of this agonistic potential, the body politic often rejects those intrusive agents that are deemed to threaten its survival and integrity. The transnational seepage and viral or even metastatic potential of bodies coded as alien (in ethnic and/or gendered terms) is perceived to compromise the ability of political bodies – be they nation states or other types of federal unions – to function in terms of boundary maintenance and cultural reproduction.

From the perspective of the official organs of the body politic as such, the subaltern or alien body is perceived as fundamentally dangerous and unappealing when acting in the service of its own particularized objectives, but as salubrious and life-giving when servicing the agendas or fitness of the whole, whose needs are usually synecdochically reduced to those of the most privileged class. It is the fact that their boundaries and allegiances are unclear and that they are variously appropriable by narratives of use and uselessness that gives contemporary diasporic communities and individuals, in their subalternity, their particular positioning as viral or virile, vampiric or lifegiving. The boundary blurring of both the transplant – in all its literal and metaphorical guises – and transgender identity compromises traditional notions of corporeal integrity just as diasporic movement compromises notions of national and cultural integrity. This is especially true as the ability of diasporized individuals and communities to maintain contact with their communities of origin lessens their general investment in assimilation as their unquestioned *terminus a quem*.

In this essay we will argue that recent filmic depictions of transplanted and transgendered bodies are emblematic of anxiety about the loss of cultural identity in much contemporary European – particularly French and British – film. Contemporary collective identities must incorporate transnational and transcultural adaptability as the movement from here to there becomes easier physically (and, concomitantly, as the movement of information has been rendered instantaneous and, for all practical purposes, borderless). Just as the airline terminals and train stations that have made the European Union a living reality are designed to be as unthreateningly generic and immediately readable as possible, other workspaces are becoming similarly interchangeable. Ultimately, the very blandness of these spaces facilitates the disparate lifestyles of those at both ends of the economic spectrum for whom transnational movement is a way of life. For the contemporary migrant the first action that is performed when stepping into a new place is no longer to try to get his or her bearings, but to go to work. Place has not given way to placelessness, but to the omni-placeness and cultural disorientation of what we have termed the *transplantation*. By this we mean one of the sites where the actual grunt work of difference and inequality takes place by enabling the production of the things that make leisure and privilege possible for people who would not (or would only) be caught dead in those places. In other words, these are the kinds of places that citizens in good standing and in pursuit of good health or good times visit but leave, places where dirty and not-so-pretty things (as in the film by Stephen Frears, which we will examine below) are left behind and then cleaned up by 'the people you do not see'. One does not see these people because the very fact that they have been relegated to such places is indicative of their lack of good standing, of the fact that they are not 'connected'.

Transplantations are sites such as hotels, sweatshops, farms, factories, hospitals, brothels and battlefields where underpaid work, increasingly performed by immigrants both legal and otherwise, not only takes place but is essential to the site's existence as a productive or money-making enterprise. Not only are these sites made recognizable by the particular types of low-paid labour that takes place in them, but also by the discourses that are committed to reforming them and in one way or another liberating their denizens. The result of globalization is that these once localized sites are no longer invisibly local enough for those who benefit from them to carry on with business as usual. For the disenfranchized, this delocalization has catalysed a new culture of transnational activism and political self-awareness.

This essay will focus in particular on the representation of immigrants as transplants in recent French and British cinema. Postcolonial immigrants are represented in various ways as perpetual interlopers in the metropolitan centres of the two largest former colonial empires. Comparison between French and British films that depict immigrants from the former colonies shows very different relations between postcolonial subjects and their families. The British films tend to show postcolonial immigrants in familial or quasi-familial settings, with the younger characters struggling to break free of the constraints of tradition in order to integrate more fully into mainstream British culture. The French films repeatedly construct models of intrusion, in the form of male subalternity as a threat to French family life. The single males shown in these films without strong family bonds conform to the stereotype of the lawless troublemaker who threatens to destabilize French domestic and legal institutions by his very presence. In relatively recent mainstream UK hits such as *East is East* (Damien O'Donnell, 1999) and *Bend it Like Beckham* (Gurinder Chadha, 2002), as well as the earlier *Bhaji on the Beach* (Gurinder Chadha, 1993) and *My Beautiful Laundrette* (Stephen Frears, 1985), young second-generation immigrants must define themselves in relation (even if this relation is an oppositional one) to their parents and their national 'homeland', eventually coming to an uneasy truce. French films, on the other hand, tend to depict unattached males separated from their families and doomed not to integrate fully into French mainstream culture in part because they do not fit into the idealized structure of the nuclear family.

Many French films from the mid-1990s to the mid-2000s focus on young male characters of North African origin (Beurs) cast adrift from their families and the 'old country'. Hamid Naficy has written of the Beurs' 'bitter realization that they are French but not quite, that they are North African but not quite, and that they have no home to which they can return' (Naficy 2001: 98). As if to demonstrate this sense of homelessness, Beur characters are most often depicted as single (usually male) figures, outside of nuclear family structures and often wandering aimlessly through the urban landscape. The absence of the nuclear family in these French films better emphasizes the central characters' status as 'transplants', as foreign bodies, viruses in an alien 'host'.[2] Both French and British films consistently use corporeal metaphors to represent the transplantation of immigrants into the body politic and to belie conventional notions of French and British colonial history, which assume that the French empire worked by means of assimilation or cultural integration, whereas the British empire allowed a much greater degree of cultural autonomy. Strikingly, however, both French and British films also go beyond metaphor in using corporeality as a dramatic element of their narrative structure. In other words, specific body parts are given a literal rather than figurative function in the unfolding of the film as both story and visual spectacle.[3]

Transplantations

Throughout history, diasporic movement has been catalysed not only by the dreams and nightmares of alienated subjects seeking better lives 'over there', but just as strongly by the various types of commodification by means of which, as corporeal objects, they have been interpellated or into which they have been dragooned. The atomized bodies of immigrants and the poor are subjected to dehumanizing forms of commodification and atomization as they are drawn into the webs of transnational exploitation that, in its dystopian dimension, characterizes economic globalization. This denaturalizing dynamic can be most starkly figured as the movement of one person's body part into the body of another person in an organ transplant, but this dynamic also has a non-metaphorical dimension. Laura Marks terms 'transnational objects' those objects 'created in cultural translation or transcultural movement' (Marks 2000: 78). Increasingly, as biotechnological advances outstrip the availability of 'raw materials' to sustain them, body parts themselves are becoming depersonalized transnational objects. In the hierarchy of global citizenship, bio-objects like organs and stem cells have become valued components in the supplementation and survival of the bodies that matter by the body parts of those that do not. Both the metaphor and the reality of the transplant – of the human being reduced to parts that can then be commodified and assigned a 'street value' – are the logical conclusions of the process of globalization.

In Stephen Frears's *Dirty Pretty Things* we find the most explicit representations of both the dangerous transplant as a socially destabilizing force and the subaltern body as an exploitable resource. For many,

Frears established the cinematic vocabulary for representing multiethnic London in his breakthrough films *My Beautiful Laundrette* (1985), to which we will return, and *Sammy and Rosie Get Laid* (1988). A generation later in *Dirty Pretty Things*, we see not only the continuation of Frears's 'attraction to the working and underclasses' (Barber 1993: 224), but also the complete collapse of the social hopefulness of his early films. The black-market kidneys that drive the film's plot are stark emblems of economic despair. As Nancy Scheper-Hughes has noted: 'The kidney as a commodity has emerged as the gold standard in the new body trade, representing the poor person's ultimate collateral against hunger, debt, and penury' (2003: 1645).

If slavery is the ultimate form of reification, it can be imagined as a form of transplantation *in toto* to the extent that in enslavement, one person's entire biological apparatus becomes both the prosthetic supplement to the master's will and the productive engine of his privilege. Correlatively, when the human body is viewed as a collection of transplantable organs, the subaltern body is reduced to the potential of being literally 'farmed'. As Scheper-Hughes observes: 'In general, the circulation of kidneys follows established routes of capital from South to North, from East to West, from poorer to more affluent bodies, from black and brown bodies to white ones, and from female to male or from poor low status men to more affluent men' (2003: 1645). It is no coincidence that we speak of organs as being 'harvested', thereby transferring the idea of labour from the underclass body to the 'surgeon' who performs the act of harvesting and ultimately to the masters who enjoy the harvest. These images of the harvesting of organs, of storage, and, even more troubling, of stockpiling suggest just how far outside its conventional ethical parameters the selling of organs takes physicians and other health care professionals as healers. As Thomas H. Murray has pointed out: 'The very words used to describe what physicians do – they "take care of patients" – come from the language of personal, moral, nonmarket relationships' (1997: 356). In an era of globalization, the plantation as the site of slave labour (and thus the epitome of reification) has been given new life in the image of the transplant (as both the body in motion and the body literally in pieces and available for purchase).

The fact that in addition to the significantly named 'Baltic' hotel, the action of *Dirty Pretty Things* takes place mostly in a morgue and a sweatshop makes it clear that the hands-on dynamics of exploitation and privilege involve both mobility and access. Instead of functioning primarily as a place for either temporary accommodation or illicit sexual affairs, The Baltic, like these other locations, functions as a 'transplantation'.

Transplantations like The Baltic are the places of employment for immigrants working in the hotels of advanced capitalist countries, as well as the sweat-shop workers in Nike factories in Nepal and the well-educated, middle-class Indians working long hours in the call centres of multinational corporations in India. The 'trans' in 'transplantation' signifies the crossing of the border between more and less industrialized countries. In transplantations, the border traffic tends to be one-way: citizens of less-industrialized countries work in sites owned by companies originating in the more industrialized countries. This is why it is currently inconceivable to imagine British, American, French or German citizens working in a Nepalese-owned sweatshop in Chicago or London.

In *Dirty Pretty Things* the characters occupy what seems to be almost a post-national version of London in which difference has become feral and created a dystopian world where white Britishness is so thoroughly marginalized from the city's urban reality that it can only swoop in vampirically at the end in order to retrieve the foreign but vital body parts without which, the film suggests, the ailing body of white Britain itself cannot survive. It is the futility of his efforts to function as a good citizen in both London and Nigeria that has led to the expatriate protagonist Okwe's global deracination and downward mobility. The cautionary image of the doctor who scrubs toilets is one of the new stereotypes enlivened by the globalization of diaspora as a phenomenon that has lost much of its class-based specificity. Similarly, the image of a human heart in a toilet starkly literalizes the disposability of the subaltern body. Significantly, even Okwe's 'good' black body, which contains his 'good' (and 'black') heart, is never allowed to compromise – not even by way of a kiss – that of the Turkish woman who, while not British, is still white and European in ways that he can never be. The fact that Senay, the immigrant who finds herself struggling for survival in London, is Turkish, indicates ambivalence about the ability of an 'alien' (read 'Muslim') state like Turkey, to be successfully transplanted into the European body politic (despite the fact that the role of Senay is played by the cinematic figurehead of European adorableness, Audrey Tautou). Senay can only free herself from the force of her Turkish difference by first becoming 'Italian' and then, like Okwe, by leaving Europe altogether, suggesting that despite its bid for inclusion, Turkishness as such is finally, like Okwe's African heart which beats only for Africa, something that must be rejected.

In Claire Denis's *L'Intrus* (*The Intruder*, 2004), the ethical problematics of the reliance of the wealthy on the healthy bodies of the poor for survival are even more bluntly revealed. In Denis's film the physically declining European subject facing death becomes an amoral entity committed to using his resources to achieve what the film makes clear will be an undeserved supplement to a corrupt life; as Louis Trébor, a loner who ignores his loving adult son and young grandchildren, pays for his black-market heart transplant with money earned by presumably dubious means. This corruption is made even more unsettling by the fact that, unlike the claustrophobically urban *mise-en-scène* of *Dirty Pretty Things,* much of *L'Intrus* takes place in surroundings of stereotypically unspoiled nature on the Swiss-French border. Correspondingly, *L'Intrus* itself – whose story is presented out of sequence and whose coherence is not immediately apparent – is 'corrupted' as a narrative presumably as a means of preventing the viewer from easily identifying with a character whose 'bad heart' must so clearly be rejected. The film's fragmentary aesthetic, as a series of parts to be assembled, evokes the motif of the transplant, of disparate parts amalgamated into a 'whole'. Trébor rejects his own flesh and blood (in a metaphorical sense) as his own flesh and blood (in a literal sense) have rejected him. After he murders an 'intruder' who has been attempting to cross the border illegally into France, we learn that Trébor himself is a migrant: a fluent Russian speaker with a Russian passport. Trébor is or has been an immigrant, but, having made his fortune, he becomes a cosmopolitan traveller, capable of crossing borders with ease, and of gaining a kind of access to the cultures he frequents by paying people for their services. He travels to Tahiti to search for a son he believes he fathered with a Polynesian woman many years earlier. Unable to find him, he bids the villagers to find his son, and they, realizing that such a person may never have existed in the first place, literally audition young local men to play the role. Too late, it turns out, Trébor desperately attempts to find replacements for things beyond repair: someone else's heart, someone else's son. In what demands on a narrative level to be read as a dream sequence, Trébor observes the body of his neglected son Sidney being wheeled out of a morgue, to reveal a long scar on his chest that suggests he has had his heart removed. Sidney, emblem of fatherly solicitude toward his own small children, haunts Trébor as the victim of his own paternal heartlessness. (A Russian woman who has witnessed the murder Trébor committed haunts him more assiduously, following him on his world travels. She is likely a phantom from his past, representing the ghostly intrusion of his own conscience.)

According to Jean-Luc Nancy, in his book *L'Intrus*, on which Denis's film is based: 'Once [the immigrant] is there, as long as he remains a foreigner, instead of simply becoming "naturalized", he keeps coming; he continues to arrive, and this arrival does not cease to be, on some level, an intrusion' (Nancy 2000: 11; our translation). The past, too, is an intruder of sorts, an idea reflected not only in the non-linear sequence of the scenes in *L'Intrus*, but also in the use of footage from another, unreleased film, *Le Reflux* (directed by Paul Gegauff), shot in 1962 in Polynesia, and featuring a much-younger Michel Subor, who plays Louis Trébor in Denis's film. The only temporal cue that *L'Intrus* provides is the presence or absence of the long scar running down Trébor's chest and abdomen, which indicates whether a given scene takes place before or after his transplant operation. Martine Beugnet has argued that:

> In *L'Intrus*, the deep scar that runs across the body of the main character finds its visual equivalent in the duplication of man-made borders that deny the openness of even the wildest of landscapes and in the frames that similarly limit and fragment the film's images: frontiers and customs, walls, blinds, doors, windows; scars (as incongruous and rectilinear as the human borders that divide the surface of the earth). The film speaks of a world of violent and paranoid ownership, fixated on the delimitation and defence of a territory where the foreign body is always the intruder, always reducible to a threat, to be hunted, driven away or destroyed.
>
> (Beugnet 2007: 144–5)

The scar is a trace that signals prior violence. Tellingly, in *L'Intrus* Trébor's daughter-in-law is a customs officer who uses attack dogs, at the ready to wound and maim, to keep illegal cargo from crossing the border into France. She is therefore one of the figures charged directly with protecting the integrity of the European Union against dangerous contaminants.

In Denis's earlier film *J'ai pas sommeil* (*I Can't Sleep*, 1994), the intrusive 'foreign body' as crosser of boundaries is just as starkly and disturbingly literalized. The fact that the victims of this intrusion are elderly French women murdered in their own homes, often for little more than small change, reinforces the notion of the absolute vulnerability of the old guard in relation to the onslaught of menacingly queer foreign bodies. In this film, the transgendered Caribbean serial killer Camille, — based on Thierry Paulin, the notorious 'Monster of Montmartre' who may have murdered more than twenty elderly French women – moves through a world in which there is no place for him other than as an exotic or entertaining object; unlike the Lithuanian actor (played by Katerina Golubeva, who portrays the enigmatic Russian woman haunting

Trébor in *L'Intrus*) who comes to France and, it is implied, will use the cash she steals to begin the process of assimilating into a 'good' European subject. It is this assimilation that the film suggests is impossible for the black or alien subject who must either leave (like Senay and Okwe in *Dirty Pretty Things*) or die. The only other option is the loss of true subjectivity – the living death, that is represented by the life of underclass labour that brought the subaltern subject (or his or her ancestors) to the metropolis – or the castigation to which many people who sell organs are subjected in their home communities when their 'scar of shame' is revealed.[4] If prostitutes are people who 'sell' themselves (or, as is very often the case, are sold), thus compromising their humanity in an act of objectification, organ sellers' self-reduction to flesh for sale makes them literally beyond recognition.

Transsexualities

The dynamics of transplantation and assimilation are intensified when the borders to be crossed are not only national and cultural, but sexual or gendered as well. The etymology of 'sex' (illustrated so memorably in Plato's *Symposium*) refers to the reunion of two halves that once formed a whole. When individuals' sexual or gender identity, by virtue of its self-sufficiency, complicates this model of incompleteness – that is, when they desire not the 'other' but the 'same', or when they are not 'one' or the 'other' but both – their integration into the larger body politic is compromised because they fall outside the reproductive economy of the traditional nuclear family. In a transcultural context, however, this self-sufficiency can be perceived as a virtue from the perspective of both 'transplant' and 'host', leading (for individuals) to escape from the strictures of patriarchal oppression, or (for institutions) to the exploitation and objectification of otherwise threatening cultural differences.

In *East is East*, the Khan family's integration into white British culture is complicated by the fact that the family is composed of an interracial couple (a Pakistani father and white British mother) and bi-racial children. Like that of the transgendered person, it is their in-betweeness – their corporeal interconnection across lines of ethnic difference – that gives their situation its particular poignancy. In the context of the culturally hegemonic racialist discourse of 'purity' and 'contamination', their white Britishness is always in a sense under erasure. Their very existence challenges the notion that 'east is east' just as the existence of the transgendered challenges the idea that 'male is (always) male' and 'female is (always) female'. The Khan family's in-betweeness is replicated by the form and narrative arc of the film: a strange hybrid of teen comedy and tense drama, it effectively plays like an episode of *The Brady Bunch* with domestic violence. As in *My Beautiful Laundrette*, although more fleetingly, it is homosexuality that functions as a means of escape from the complicated dynamics of ethnic particularity or the lack thereof. *East is East* is, however, particularly provocative in presenting the world of the gay couple – figured by the hat shop in which the oldest son works with his lover after bolting from the arranged marriage that his father has contracted for him – as one completely devoid of any distinguishing characteristics other than an empty slavishness to fashion.

The film *Kinky Boots* – with its portrayal of teleological investment in fashion as a life-affirming cultural site – suggests that the best way for dying European industries to survive is to refashion themselves as purveyors of the unnatural accoutrements of deviant lifestyles and experiences. The 'drag queen' is particularly useful as an image of both viral contagion and succour for the body in decline, because the transgendered body has routinely been positioned as that of little more than a special kind of prostitute. This is a result of the fact that few societies have offered the transgendered any means of supporting themselves other than through the display and sexual purveying of their 'exotic' bodies or, more specifically, the exoticizing presentation and supplementation of their 'normal' bodies. It is this dynamic of presentation and supplementation that grounds the plot and 'humour' of *Kinky Boots*. It is interesting and perhaps not coincidental that the actor Chiwetel Ejiofor plays both the provocative but assimilable Lola/Simon in *Kinky Boots* and the essentially neutered but somehow unassimilable Okwe in *Dirty Pretty Things*. In *Dirty Pretty Things* Okwe's anti-capitalist resistance to the notion that the people who can afford things should, for that reason alone, have unfettered access to them, positions him as the kind of alien who should obviously, in the classic expression of xenophobia, just 'go back to where he came from'. Unlike the genuinely transgendered Jaye Davidson – whose peek-a-boo penis earned him short-lived fame and an Academy Award nomination for *The Crying Game* and then did 'go back to where he came from' by returning to the fashion world – Ejiofor has become one of the most internationally recognized black British actors working today.

The relationship between Davidson's character Dil and the IRA operative Fergus in *The Crying Game* and the idea that homosexuality, or at least bisexuality, is contagious underscores the idea of shifting and unstable boundaries that is at the heart of national anxieties about immigration and the effects of certain types of unsanctioned and, implicitly, 'unnatural' contact. One of the reasons why terrorism has achieved its prominence in global and transnational discourses is because the terrorist can be imagined as someone who can without warning subject privileged bodies to the type of atomizing dismemberment to which less privileged bodies have throughout history been routinely subjected. It is not a coincidence that the terrorist mode of delegitimation to which the French aristocracy was subjected during the French Revolution was decapitation: a literalization of the body in pieces and of the figurative rejection of the 'head of state' (although, as is often overlooked in contemporary discourse, the French 'terror' was a form of 'state' rather than 'anti-state' terror). IRA terrorism has lost much of its cinematic appeal in the light of terrorists whose alien status does not have to be established by expository back narratives given the self-evidence of corporeal difference (that is, what airline security personnel are told to identify as 'a Middle-Eastern look') as a potential marker of ideological difference.

In *The Crying Game*, which depicts a world driven by anxiety about territorial boundaries and threatened by bodies deemed foreign, transgression occurs along (and across) both national and gendered lines. Okwe says of organ sellers in *Dirty Pretty Things* that 'they swapped their insides for a passport', and these words could just as easily be used to refer to the corporeal border crossing (or criss-crossing) between one gender category and another. If most transgendered people do not surgically reassign their bodies, such reassignment nevertheless functions as the potential endpoint for transgendered subjectivity; in narratives of radical change and new possibility, surgery is often the utopian transformative gesture for the transgendered that organ selling is for the hopelessly subaltern. Although in terms of will and agency the transgendered individual might seem to fall into a completely different category from organ sellers or transplant recipients, the appeal of representations of transsexuals or 'drag queens' for straight audiences as a component of diasporic and immigrant communities is that they literalize the image of the person who seems to be one thing, but is in fact something else. Becoming a resident of another country, like becoming another gender, begs the question of what can be retained and what must be left behind. In the extremes of organ transplant and actual sexual reassignment surgery, what is gained and what is lost when the other is literally incorporated into one's self?

Like immigration, alternative sexualities and gender identities represent a threat to the integrity – in other words, the threat of dismemberment – of the body politic, just as the transgendered and homosexual characters represent a supposed threat to the reproductive economy valorized in models of the nation-state. In three high-profile French films of the last decade that feature Maghrebi characters – *Wild Side* (Sébastien Lifshitz, 2004), *Chouchou* (Merzak Allouache, 2002) and *Drôle de Félix/The Adventures of Felix* (Olivier Ducastel and Jacques Martineau, 2000) – the central characters are gay or transgendered. *Wild Side* focuses on a three-way relationship between a transgendered French sex worker by the name of Stéphanie; a second- or third-generation Maghrebi man named Djamel, who is also a sex worker; and a Russian immigrant named Mikhail. Nick Rees-Roberts's observation about *Wild Side*, which, he suggests, attempts to find some common ground between 'gay assimilation' and 'precarious immigration' (Rees-Roberts 2007: 154), could be applied to all three films. The perceived threat to the nuclear family and by extension to the body politic is acknowledged in these films' attempts to construct alternative family structures. The explicit establishment of surrogate families in these films (whose culmination is the gay, transgendered wedding ceremony in *Chouchou*) serves to offset such a threat – it is notable that all three films emphasize the construction of alternative family units based on elective affinities rather than biology. In *Wild Side*, Mikhail, who speaks almost no French, indicates that he misses his family in Russia, and Djamel points to himself and Stéphanie in order to convey the idea that they are his family. *Drôle de Félix* – about a gay man's road trip from Dieppe to Marseille to find his father, whom he has never met – is punctuated by on-screen titles assigning familial roles to people Félix befriends along the way ('mon petit frère', 'ma grand-mère', 'mon cousin'). The final title, 'Mon père', refers not to Félix's biological father, whom he ultimately decides not to meet, but to a kindly older man (played by Maurice Bénichou) whom Félix encounters shortly before arriving in Marseille.

Sometimes, as in Stephen Frears's landmark film *My Beautiful Laundrette* (1985), spurning the traditional nuclear family is equated with spurning the traditions of the 'old country'. Frears's film itself is something of a transplant in that it was originally made for television before gaining a theatrical release. *My Beautiful Laundrette* unfolds primarily from the perspective of the gay Pakistani Omar, who is torn between the desire to love Britain – as represented by his relationship with his white British schoolmate Johnny – and his commitment to maintaining his standing in his Pakistani family. The fact that some in the Pakistani family have used their move to Britain to bolster their status as members of the financially stable bourgeoisie is complicated by the fact that this status is made possible primarily by their ready recourse to criminality. The oxymoronic idea of a beautiful laundrette parodies the notion of capitalism as a beautifying agent that one finds in many discourses that promote globalization. However, as an old-school image of capitalist villainy, Omar's cousin Salim does everything but twirl his mustachios. In his investment in both his own ethnicity and in unfettered moneymaking, Salim, unlike his father, is a robber who has no desire to be a baron. Omar's father, on the other hand, prefers the assimilationist path that leads through the fetishized site of 'university'. Finally, the working-class entrepreneurship that Omar embraces is, according to his father, nothing more than 'cleaning dirty underpants'. It is the proximity of Omar's enterprise to the life of the body and not that of the mind that his intellectually accomplished father finds most disreputable. The film's ending suggests that the impossibly complicated dynamics of relating to one's ethnic compeers can be transcended by the assumption of life as a queer couple. It is notable that the interracial gay relationship succeeds while the interracial heterosexual one is revealed to be untenable, suggesting that, although ostensibly threatening to the reproductive values of the nation-state, homosexuality is actually a reassuring alternative that does not in fact threaten the 'white' metropolitan nuclear family in the same way that the single male postcolonial subject or the heterosexually reproductive immigrant family is represented as doing.

Similarly, in the French context, Carrie Tarr has suggested that audiences may find the portrayal of homosexual or transgendered Maghrebi men less threatening than that of heterosexual Maghrebis, whose sexuality is perceived as intimidating to white Frenchmen (Tarr 2007: 17). As early as *La Haine* (Mathieu Kassovitz, 1995), the critically acclaimed box-office success that was the first film to bring the social unrest of life in the French *banlieue* to the attention of a large international audience, immigrants from former African colonies (especially those of the Maghreb) have largely been depicted in French films as young men separated from (or simply shown outside the context of) their families. As Jill Forbes has described the film's three protagonists: 'Though they reject the cultures associated with their families [...], they have not been accepted into the national community in a way that community accepts' (Forbes 2000: 172). There are no major female characters in *La Haine*, and only the briefest glimpses of the family life of the three central male characters. The single male characters in these films confirm viewers' preconceived notions of patterns of postcolonial immigration, namely the invitation to Maghrebi males to work in France in the 1950s and 1960s. The majority of these workers ended up settling in France, eventually bringing their families over to join them. In the mid-1990s, when *La Haine* was made, second- and even third-generation Beur men would be historically somewhat removed from their immigrant forefathers, yet the emphasis on single males is a ghostly evocation of the past, in Jean-Luc Nancy's sense of the perpetual 'intruder', which enables him to speak of: 'a general law of intrusion: there is never a single intrusion; as soon as an intrusion takes place, it multiplies, and manifests itself in its ever-forming internal differences' (Nancy 2000: 31–2; our translation).

The flipside of this representation of young immigrant males as alienated loose cannons is that of the hyper-fertile Maghrebi woman, whose capacity, like that of the alien mother in the classic science fiction *Alien* quadrilogy, to create seemingly endless numbers of unassimilable subjects threatens to swell the ranks of 'unwashed immigrants' into a flood that will sweep away all of the things that make 'us' human. If it is the dangerous activity of the male that represents social threat, it is the generativity itself of the female body that positions alien women as disruptive forces. These opposing and yet complementary figures revive tired stereotypes from the colonial era, whose potency is still apparent in their continued application to women in developing countries. The dearth of Maghrebi women in French films is all the more remarkable considering that, since the late 1980s, issues of postcolonial immigration in France have revolved around recurring incidences of what has come to be known as 'the headscarf affair', in which girls of Maghrebi background have been forbidden to wear the traditional Muslim headscarf to school on the grounds that the expression of religious affiliation is a violation of France's integrationist model of secular republicanism. (This ban was voted into law in March 2004, after decades of fudging the issue.) In the French republican context, the wearing of the headscarf would transgress the taboo of making private faith a public issue, through the exhibition of individual religious belief in an institutional public setting. Similarly, in the tradition of the Muslim hijab, a woman's bare head could (on a structural level) be analogous to a sexual organ, as a body part that is an intimate representation of femininity; like the sexual organs, the woman's hair or entire head is covered, to be exposed only to her husband. To bare the head in public in this context is in some respects tantamount to pornography, the moral equivalent of the exhibition of the genitals in a public forum. Both instances of exposure – the literally and the metaphorically pornographic – are antithetical to the preservation of the nuclear family. (This dynamic of exposure is emblematized in *East is East* when one of the sons, an art student, makes a graphically realistic rubber cast of female genitalia, the exhibition of which ultimately prompts the break-down of relations between his family and another immigrant Pakistani family with whom the father is trying to organize an arranged marriage.) In the fundamentalist Islamic context, sex outside of marriage threatens the Muslim family and thus the very fabric of Muslim society, whereas, conversely, from the French republican perspective, the proliferation of the Muslim nuclear family is itself perceived as destabilizing.

It thus comes as little surprise that an exception to the virtual absence of female Maghrebi characters in French films is, again, the figure of the prostitute. In Coline Serreau's *Chaos* (2002), the central character is Noémie, a French-Algerian woman who runs away from her father when he is about to force her into an arranged marriage back in Algeria. She is abducted by a pimp, coerced into taking heroin until she becomes addicted and then forced into prostitution. One evening, she is beaten and left for dead by the men who run the prostitution ring, and the attack is witnessed by a bourgeois couple on their way to a dinner party, who do not stop to help. The woman, Hélène, overcome with guilt, tracks down Noémie in hospital and visits her assiduously until she slowly returns to health. Hélène and Noémie then plot to escape together, and to avenge their physical abuse and emotional neglect, respectively.

Noémie is escaping from a repressive patriarchal society, but so is Hélène. Both women reject their families, who do not have their best interests at heart, and form a community of women, a surrogate family, composed of Hélène, her long-suffering mother-in-law (neglected by Hélène's estranged husband Paul), as well as Noémie and her younger sister (whose father attempts literally to sell them into marital servi-tude). Noémie breaks free from the constraints of patriarchal tradition, but so do Hélène and her mother-in-law.

Although it is possible to read the film's representation of Islam as a negative caricature of fundamentalism, the fact that all the women in the film – regardless of their nationality, age, marital status or religion – are oppressed in some way by men, suggests more continuity than dis-tance between Islamic Maghrebi culture and secular French culture. Hélène and Paul's son Fabrice, a womanizer whose callousness resem-bles that of his father, gets his own comeuppance when two of his girlfriends join forces and take over his flat. Although Noémie's Algerian father cruelly sacrifices his daughters' hopes of happiness for the sake of tradition, it is significant that Noémie's most violent tormentors are the French pimps and kingpins of the prostitution ring into which she is abducted. Noémie's escape from prostitution thus coincides with the dissolution of Hélène and Paul's marriage. Hélène and Noémie can join forces so effectively, the film suggests, because their situations are somehow analogous: both are objectified within the patriarchal order, Hélène within the nuclear family structure, and Noémie both within (she is oppressed by her father) and outside (in her job as a sex worker) of this structure. But their situations are not only analogous, they are also linked: the marginalized sexuality that Serreau depicts in the form of prostitution ostensibly threatens but ultimately reinforces the French republican patriarchal order.

Similarly, in both French and British films depicting immigrant communities, homosexual or transgendered relationships are often presented as viable, indeed in many ways preferable, alternatives to hegemonic domestic structures. These alternatives have a dual nature – at once utopian and instrumental – in that they do not threaten the forms and functions of the nuclear family and the attendant forces of reproduction. Single heterosexual Maghrebi males in French narratives of immigration, isolated from their immediate families and roaming the streets in search of potential conjugal partners, pose a far greater threat to French family life than do homosexual or transgendered subjects. Emblematically, the commodification of bodies in prostitution – a form of labour to which the transgendered and immigrant women are often driven – is a particularly destructive form of the reification of both human subjectivity and corporeality in the exploitation of labour.

Postcolonial transplants in both British and French films tend to be imperfectly assimilated, achieving an uneasy status as resident 'intruders', admitted into the body politic only to be perpetually marginalized. As transplants, they are detached from their cultural, political and, in the case of the transgendered, even biological histories, and then grafted on to sites of illicit or semi-licit employment far from the legitimating eye of mainstream visibility. What all of these films reflect is the degree to which narratives of cultural and sexual difference, regardless of how disinterested they may seem in the physical reality of the body, are inevitably grounded in corporeal difference and exploitability or commodification. The 'body politic' is not just a metaphorical body, but a physically heterogeneous one as well. Recent filmic depictions of immigrants in European metropolitan centres, particularly those of Britain and France, underscore an instrumentalization of different groups and individuals analogous to that of the various limbs and organs of the biological body. Similarly, representations of the postcolonial transplant as the object of globalization, and of the 'transplantation' as the site of this objectification, can help us understand the dynamics of acceptance and rejection in which assimilation on the one hand and the maintenance of cultural distinctiveness on the other are the agonistic poles of globalization as a lived experience.

Notes

1. In this essay we will be using the term 'body politic' in its most basic sense as 'the people of a politically organized nation or state considered as a group'. For instance, the 'French body politic' consists of those people who, in terms of national and international recognition, can legally refer to themselves as French and for whom being 'French' is their primary form of civil self-recognition.
2. See the debates surrounding concepts such as 'host' country and 'guest worker' in Rosello (2001).
3. For instance, in Julian Jarrold's *Kinky Boots* (2005) the 'kinky boots' themselves are necessary because drag queens are physically male, exert heavier force when donning pencil-thin stilettos and naturally men tend to have bigger feet than women.
4. For an extensive consideration of the physical, psychological and social consequences of organ selling from the perspective of the 'donors' see Scheper-Hughes.

Bibliography

Barber, S. T. (1993) 'Insurmountable Difficulties and Moments of Ecstasy: Crossing Class, Ethnic, and Sexual Barriers in the Films of Stephen Frears', in L. Friedman (ed.) *Fires Were Started: British Cinema and Thatcherism* (Minneapolis: University of Minnesota Press), pp. 221–36.

Beugnet, M. (2007) *Cinema and Sensation: French Film and the Art of Transgression* (Edinburgh: Edinburgh University Press).

Forbes, J. (2000) 'La Haine' in J. Forbes and S. Street (eds) *European Cinema: An Introduction* (Basingstoke: Palgrave Macmillan), pp. 171–80.

Marks, L. U. (2000) *The Skin of the Film* (Durham, NC: Duke University Press).

Murray, T. H. (1997) 'Gifts of the Body and the Needs of Strangers', in C. Levine (ed.) *Taking Sides: Clashing Views on Controversial Bioethical Issues*, 7th edn (Guildford, CT: Dushkin/McGraw Hill), pp. 350–8.

Naficy, H. (2001) *An Accented Cinema: Exilic and Diasporic Filmmaking* (Princeton: Princeton University Press).

Nancy, J-L. (2000) *L'Intrus* (Paris: Galilée).

Rees-Roberts, N. (2007) 'Down and Out: Immigrant Poverty and Queer Sexuality in Sébastien Lifshitz's *Wild Side* (2004)', *Studies in French Cinema*, 7.2, 143–55.

Rosello, M. (2001) *Postcolonial Hospitality: The Immigrant as Guest* (Stanford: Stanford University Press).

Scheper-Hughes, N. (2003) 'Keeping an eye on the global traffic in human organs', *The Lancet*, 361 (10 May), 1645–8.

Tarr, C. (2007) 'The Porosity of the Hexagon: Border Crossings in Contemporary French Cinema', *Studies in European Cinema*, 4.1, 7–20.

Index